BALLOU LIBRARY
BUENA VISTA UNIVERSITY
610 WEST FOURTH STREET
STORM LAKE, IA 50588-1798

Creating Another Self

CREATING ANOTHER SELF

Voice in Modern American Personal Poetry

Samuel
Maio

THOMAS JEFFERSON UNIVERSITY PRESS
Kirksville, Missouri
1995

Copyright © 1995 by Thomas Jefferson University Press
at Truman State University
Kirksville, Missouri, 63501-4221 USA

Distributed by arrangement with
University Publishing Associates, Inc.
4720 Boston Way, Lanham, Maryland 20706

3 Henrietta Street, London WC2E 8LU England

British Cataloging in Publication information available.

Maio, Samuel, 1955–
        Creating another self : voice in modern American personal poetry / Samuel Maio.
            p.   cm.
        Includes bibliographical references and index.
        ISBN 0-943549-33-7 (cloth : alk. paper) ISBN 0-943549-38-8 (paperback)
        1. American poetry—20th century—History and criticism. 2. Persona
(Literature). 3. Self in literature.   I. Title.
PS310.S34M35   1995
811' .509353—dc20   95-6311
                                                                                        CIP

All rights reserved. No part of this work may be reproduced or transmitted in any format by any
means, electronic or mechanical, including photocopying and recording, or by any information stor-
age or retrieval system, without permission in writing from the publisher. Printed in the United States
of America.

∞ The paper used in this publication meets the minimum requirements of the American National
Standard for Permanence of Paper for Printed Library Materials ANSI Z39.48, 1984.

Contents

ACKNOWLEDGMENTS VII

One   THE POET'S VOICE AS PERSONA 1

Two   THE CONFESSIONAL MODE 29
        Robert Lowell 30
        James Wright 54
        Anne Sexton 71

Three   THE PERSONA MODE 93
        John Berryman 94
        Weldon Kees 122
        Galway Kinnell 138

Four   THE SELF-EFFACING MODE 163
        Mark Strand 165
        Charles Simic 191
        David Ignatow 207

Five   PERSONAL POETRY IN THE 1990S 225
        Bruce Weigl 229
        Garrett Hongo 231
        Jim Barnes 236
        Frank Graziano 243

WORKS CITED 265

INDEX 273

Acknowledgments

The author gratefully acknowledges the following periodicals which first published a portion of chapter 2 and much of chapter 5 as articles or essay-reviews,
sometimes in different form:

The Bloomsbury Review, vol. 12, no. 2 (March 1992) "Above the River: The Complete Poems
  of James Wright"
The Bloomsbury Review, vol. 8, no. 6 (Nov./Dec. 1988) "The Poetic Voices of James Wright"
Cimarron Review, no. 105 (Oct. 1993) "Jim Barnes's *The Sawdust War*"
Concerning Poetry, vol. 20 (1987) "Bruce Weigl's *The Monkey Wars* and Galway Kinnell's
  The Past"
The Midnight Lamp, no. 1 (Spring 1989) "'Out of the Horror, A Musical Ache': On Bruce
  Weigl's *Song of Napalm*"
Paintbrush, vol. 19, no. 38 (Autumn 1992) "Memoirs of the Sawdust War Generation"
Quarterly West, no. 20 (Spring/Summer 1985) "The Collected Poems of George Garrett"
Quarterly West, no. 18 (Spring/Summer 1984) "Garrett Hongo's *Yellow Light*"
Vortex: A Critical Review, vol. 3 (Autumn 1988) "Murder as Post-Modern Pastiche: On the
  Poetry of Frank Graziano"

One

∾

The Poet's Voice As Persona

THE TITLE OF THIS STUDY is an adaptation of a remark made by the poet Richard Hugo, who said about poetic voice: "Voice is usually something that grows out of stance. It has to do with how strong a person's urge is to reject the self and to create another self in its place." Voice, as T. S. Eliot defined it in his essay "The Three Voices of Poetry," is the method by which the poet speaks. The voice is the speaker of the poem, not necessarily the poet—as often wrongly assumed, especially with reference to the personal poetry such as I here address. As he continued with his interview with David Dillon, Hugo argued that a type of self-rejection was "necessary to write the poem . . . apparently it is up to a point," and that many theories regarding poetic composition, such as "Keats's informing and filling another body, Eliot's idea of escaping the personality, Valéry's idea of creating a superior self, Yeats's notion of the mask, Auden's idea of becoming someone else for the duration of the poem," have as their basis "an assumption that the self as found, as given, is inadequate and has to be rejected" (111). So too, I submit, did the generation of poets writing personal poetry in the wake of this mostly modernist aesthetic. As Hugo implied in terms of his own practice, each rejects the self in favor of a persona, the speaker of a poem. Both "personal poetry" and "persona" need clarifying in context of my application of them.

Personal poetry acts to reveal the poet's self as it is defined by the experience depicted in the poem. Alan Williamson has termed as "personal" that contemporary poetry which is principally informed by "images of the self—or of the nature and quality of subjective experience" (1). Although "subjective experience" serves as a useful phrase (in that it is sufficiently broad) to describe the representation of the poet's self in poetry, my thesis is that the poet creates a persona—one called "I" or by a proper noun—to act as the personal poet's speaker, and it is this speaker's self which is defined by the poem's "images of the self," and only to the extent they are depicted in the poem. Therefore the personal poet, consciously or not, substitutes for his or her literal, historical self a *literary* self as voice of the poem, one that is sincere but not altogether authentic.

Lionel Trilling delineated the "sincere" self of a poet, or that which is believable in presenting (as speaker) a subjective experience of the poet's life with veracity, from the "authentic" self, or that which resembles more accurately the literal self overthrown—regardless of a poet's intentions to the contrary—in the poem's composition. His thesis of *Sincerity and Authenticity* is, succinctly stated, that the poet revealing his or her private (literal) self publicly—by presenting this self in the poem—is authentic; the poet presenting a self that differs, however slightly, from the private self—which self John Berryman referred to as the one with a social security number—is sincere, but nonetheless only partially veracious in some instances.

The poet may want only to be authentic, as Ezra Pound desired of his *Personae* (1909) about which he said he tried to eliminate the "complete masks of the self in each poem." But the very nature of a poet's craft, having to select which aspect of one's authentic self could best conform to the dictates of art—symbolism, rhymes, "images of the self"—while functioning as poetic voice, precludes that aspiration. As Pound learned, at best "one gropes, one finds seeming verity," he admitted in his well-known "Vorticism" essay. That Pound settled on calling his book *Personae* indicates finally his understanding that a literal rendering of one's self without masks is restrained by the finite, linguistic system of a poem; no single poem or gathering of poems could represent all of his authentic self. Instead, each poem defines yet another mask of the poet: a persona necessarily adopted as voice. The most that a poetic groping at authenticity can achieve is a poet's finding "seeming verity," having discarded all other aspects of the literal self as irrelevant to the poem at hand. Remaining is a literary self, at once sincere even though a persona. Further, the concept of "representing" one's authentic self by the images presented in the poem would undermine Pound's intention. One only can recreate the authentic self by use of images—likenesses or similitudes, that is—of that self. The Italian word *imago*, which Pound would have known, means something close to our "icon," a persona of self when used in the context of personal poetry.

The personal poet intending a sincere voice, conversely, discovers a part of his or her authentic self revealed by the creative process. R. P. Blackmur's defining persona in his "The Language of Silence" as "a translation of what we did not know that we knew ourselves: what we partly are" appropriately describes the sincere-intending poet's discovery. That the poet consciously chooses "I" in his or her aesthetic decision of a persona proposed to represent the sincere (public) self does not separate fully that poet's authentic self from the poem. The use of the persona "translates," unknowingly to the poet, the sincere into the partially authentic. Trilling's definition of sincerity encompasses the personal poet's betraying his or her authenticity when in fact using a sincere self as voice in that, he writes, sincerity is "a congruence between avowal and actual feeling" (2). The act of declaring one's autobiography through the medium of poetry and a persona-speaker necessitates our referring to a personal poet's voice as sincere, or public in Trilling's terms. But it is this act which also blends the poet's private and public selves. That an "I" persona is sincere does not exclude the revealing of authentic elements—facts, emotions—in the poem regardless of the poet's intentions to mask them by a deliberate use of persona. Therefore any personal poet ultimately engages a persona of the self, whether called "I" in a poem mostly based on autobiography as is Robert Lowell's in his "Life Studies" sequence, or called "Henry" as is Berryman's. That persona is the poem's voice.

The authentic self of the poet—the private self devoid of his or her conscious or unconscious literary persona—is of course a compilation of selves, as Pound learned and as Robert C. Elliott wrote in his book *The Literary Persona* while reviewing critics' difficulties in distinguishing poet from speaker:

> In the first person grammatical category there are depths and perplexities of an endlessly alluring kind. How extraordinary it is that "I" somehow encompasses in a coherent way the thousand and one selves that constitute a "Self," and that the person whom one loves and the person one loathes also say "I."
> (30)

Our distinction between authentic and sincere is helpful here. The personal poet's sincere self can be seen as one, or part of one, of these many selves; it is the persona presented publicly as poetic voice and is confined to the poem exclusively. A poem's speaker is not wholly the poet and consequently cannot even represent the authentic self, the assemblage of selves.

This issue long has been moot, as Trilling's and Elliott's books recount. Yet concerning American personal poetry of the late 1950s through the following two decades, most critics often have disclaimed any meaningful separation of a poet from his or her speaker. My study addresses the speaker as persona in the personal poetry of this period, categorizing it into three modes of voice: the confessional, the persona, and the self-effacing. The poets I have chosen to represent these modes each rejected the authentic self and created another, sincere self in its place (to paraphrase Hugo), a self expressed as the persona-speaker of their personal poems. These poets are: Robert Lowell, James Wright, and Anne Sexton as reflective of the confessional mode; John Berryman, Weldon Kees, and Galway Kinnell of the persona; and Mark Strand, Charles Simic, and David Ignatow of the self-effacing. (Each mode will be defined at some length later in this chapter.)

My central argument regarding the voice as persona is predicated on my belief that a personal poem is distinguishable by its speaker and that all American personal poetry since the late 1950s has been written in one of the three modes I have identified. My discussions of the work of these poets will demonstrate personal poetry's widely varying styles and practices in presenting the sincere self as speaker. It will be important to regard always this speaker as sincere no matter how directly the experience may be brought to us, no matter how seemingly intimate or private the voice—even if a poem's subject derives entirely from the poet's autobiography, as it does in much of Lowell's, Sexton's, Wright's, and Berryman's work as we know. That readers may disregard consideration of the use of persona as speaker in poetry derived from autobiography is partially a result of this poetry's style of free verse, proselike diction, and other constructions—used to convey sincerity and thus verisimilitude. Robert Elliott makes note of this:

> Sincerity…can mean many things, but in most definitions it clashes inevitably with ideas of the persona, whether employed functionally by the poet or analytically by the critic. Masks, irony, dissimulation, artifice—all associated with the persona—are suspect when sincerity holds sway. (32)

In suggesting that personal poets use a mode of voice to present a sincere self in their poetry, I differ from the almost universally held notion that those poets whom we now call "confessional" are so because of their uncovering of the authentic self when using the "I" speaker. From the earliest commentary to the latest, the distinction between the poet's "I" and the poet has been ignored. M. L. Rosenthal (who well may have been the first to use the label "confessional") wrote in his 1959 *Nation* review of *Life Studies* that "Lowell removes the mask. His speaker is unequivocally himself, and it is hard not to think of *Life Studies* as a series of personal confidences, rather shameful, that one is honor-bound not to reveal" (154). Nearly a decade and a half later, in the first book-length study devoted solely to the confessional mode, Robert Phillips posited: "[A] true confessional poet places few barriers, if any, between his self and direct expression of that self, however painful that expression may prove" (8). And Diana Hume George in her 1987 book *Oedipus Anne*, writing about a decade and a half after Phillips's remarks, says that "Sexton had in her earlier collections included poems to and about her doctors (such as the superb 'You, Doctor Martin' and 'Said the Poet to the Analyst') ..." (146)—which statements will prove not quite right by my discussions of those poems in the next chapter; that is, "she," the authentic self, the poet, does not address anyone by a poem. Similarly, I would amend Phillips's statement to read "a *sincere*, confessional poet" or poet of the confessional mode in my terms, for it seems he used "true" as Trilling's sense of "authentic."

Sexton corroborated—as did many personal poets in statements concerning their poetic composition—my understanding of sincerity in personal poets. She considered herself the only "real confessional poet," as W. D. Snodgrass remarked, and as she told Stanley Kunitz in a letter. Yet she once illustrated for an interviewer (William Packard) her knowledge that the private self is not fully identical to the poet's public self as the speaker of a poem which recounts an autobiographical experience: "I've heard psychiatrists say, 'See, you've forgiven your father. There it is in your poem.' But I haven't forgiven my father. I just wrote that I did" (46). More appropriate to personal poets—writing in any of the three modes of voice—is the characteristic Phillips applied to the genre known collectively by then as confessional: "It uses the self as a poetic symbol around which is woven a personal mythology" (17). It is a mythology selective of experiences both autobiographical and imaginary, as Phillips observes (but then continues to assume those poets' authenticity):

> While a confessional poem is one which mythologizes the poet's personal life, it has its elements of fancy like any other. It does not constitute, certainly, a mere recitation of fact for fact's sake, nor should the "facts" recited be mistaken for literal truth. If they were, one would be positive that Anne Sexton had a brother killed in the war (she hadn't) and that Jerome Mazzaro has a twin sister who is a nun (equally untrue). (11)

Any personal poet assumes a voice—as Sexton and Mazzaro did—to present one's subjective experience focusing on self-exploration leading to self-definition. Personal poetry, then, is one of this created self, a poetry inclusive of that self's individual consciousness in relation to its subjective experience. The self of the confessional mode, as will be shown in the next chapter, usually attempts personal definition by means of a direct relationship to experience, the persona self by filtering experience through a mask, or persona—and I use the term here in Blackmur's sense—as will be discussed in chapter 3, and the self-effacing by removing itself from the context of experience, as the work examined in the fourth chapter will explain.

Personal poetry in our time marked a movement away from the modernist doctrine of impersonality (sketched in part by Hugo) which informed the New Critical view, the poetry of which had been foremost just prior to the popularity of poetry about the self. The modes of voice used by these new, personal poets convinced readers of their sincerity—as demonstrated by Rosenthal's remarks. This poetry had a new look, too, and a change in technique—necessary to its purporting sincerity, as Robert C. Elliott observed—so readers assumed it had abandoned also any use of persona, or speaker, other than the poet's authentic self. This, as I mentioned, is a faulty perception of personal poetry. Each mode developed as a consequence, not denial, of the persona aesthetic used in this century since the time of Pound's *Personae*. These modes, therefore, will be viewed with particular regard to their practices of voice as they have developed in America since the late 1950s when the publications of Allen Ginsberg's *Howl* (1956) and Robert Lowell's *Life Studies* (1959), and the subsequent notice these books received, marked a significant change in the direction of poetry in this country. These books' two most distinctive features, which proved lasting influences on the majority of poetry to date, were a return to the open forms the modernists had made acceptable earlier in the century and the extensive use of autobiography for matters of content, a subject which had been obscured by the New Critical insistence on objectivism.

That is, one reason for the reappearance of personal poetry within the past several decades was that it evolved, partially, from a reaction to the theories of impersonality which were entrenched in the poetry of New Criticism, or any poetry of the 1940s and 1950s which intentionally eschewed the personal self—of which poetry Eliot and Auden were the reigning masters. Some New Critics wrote personal poetry, certainly, and not all poetry in the "post–New Critical era" has been personal. Yet generally, New Critical poetry presupposed a critical "orthodoxy," as Donald Hall wrote, one which dictated "a poetry of symmetry, intellect, irony, and wit" (qtd. in *Cry of the Human* 3). Also it was one that had adopted Eliot's "Impersonal theory of poetry," as he titled it in "Tradition and the Individual Talent" (from the 1920 *Sacred Wood* essays). But this formal (stanzaic, metered) New Critical poetry did not incorporate Eliot's, or Pound's, *vers libre* aesthetics, as

Robert Lowell told Frederick Seidel (long after Lowell had abandoned his commitment to the New Critical style): "I feel Eliot's less tied to form than a lot of people he's influenced, and there's a freedom of the twenties in his work that I find very sympathetic" (365). It was Eliot's notion of how the self should—that is, should not, or only in an impersonal way—function as a matter of content for poetry which served the interests of such New Critical poets as John Crowe Ransom, Allen Tate, Robert Penn Warren, and Cleanth Brooks—poets influential on the early work of Lowell, Berryman, and, later, Galway Kinnell and James Wright, to name but few.

Literary historians have made note of the nexus between Eliot and the New Critics, and how both differ from those writing personal poetry. James Breslin, in *From Modern to Contemporary*, has written of Eliot's impact on the poetry of the time of the New Critics:

> ...the effect of Eliot went far beyond the supplying of manifest content for the dreams of younger poets. His influence was not so much specifically literary, in conveying rhythm, image, or voice, but one associated with a specific set of attitudes and values, subtly defining the expectations of many readers and editors as well as writers of poetry; and his influence was transmitted most powerfully by the New Critics. When the postwar period was not calling itself "the age of anxiety," it was calling itself (somewhat anxiously) "the age of criticism." Poetry and fiction might be floundering, but criticism flourished. In fact, while the second generation of modern poets often struggled against a sense of unrealized potentialities, the second generation of modern critics emerged as astonishingly successful. (15)

In the opening chapter of his *Cry of the Human*, Ralph J. Mills made the distinction between personal poets and those of the New Critical generation based on the degree to which "the personal element" informs the poem:

> ...both terms ["personal element" and "personality"] oppose the view handed down from Eliot and the New Criticism that poetry and the emotions it conveys are or should be, impersonal, and that an author's personality and life ought to be excluded from his writings. In many of their poems Eliot, Pound, Stevens, and others stress the poet's anonymity by employing fictional masks, invented speakers or *personae*, thus enforcing a division between writer and work. The original motive for such objectivity seems genuine enough: to rid poetry of biographical excesses and the residue of the Romantics' preoccupation with personality which had seduced attention from the true object of interest, the poem itself.... [T]he emphasis on the poet as an impersonal or anonymous "medium" (actually, as various commentators

have shown, to permit deeper, unconscious sources to aid in shaping poetic imagery and speech) passed out of Eliot's essay "Tradition and the Individual Talent" to become an important factor of the modern critical atmosphere. Subsequently, the poem came to be considered a neutral object, a vessel filled with the feelings of nobody, what Louis Simpson names "the so-called 'well-made' poem that lends itself to the little knives and formaldehyde of a graduate school." (4–5)

The New Criticism, of which Breslin and Mills write, espoused that "a work of art is an object in itself," and some of the criteria of this "objective poem" theory were: the autonomy of every poem, verbal ingenuity and wit, sustained objectivity, complex strains of irony, and aesthetic distance. The revolt against such New Critical ideas of verse—including also regular meter counts and rhymed stanzas, allusions to literature or other arts, subjects of ideation and philosophy (but not of one's subjective experience, which resulted in the consideration of the poem as "a neutral object")—informed the basis of contemporary personal poetry and its voices. As has been suggested, this "revolution in poetic taste"—to borrow a phrase of Louis Simpson—manifests itself in a verse of marked contrast in subject and style to that of the New Critical poetry, but some remnants of the modernists' personae were retained. Let us consider first the matter of subject.

T. S. Eliot is the only poet mentioned by Hugo in his list of theorists (who claimed that self-rejection is the means of poetry) whom, however tenuously, we can call American. His nationality is of note since this is a study of American personal poetry resulting from the seeming break with Eliot's followers—seeming, that is to say, because personal poetry, that which is seen opposing Eliot's impersonality theory, is in actuality another form of self-rejection, or the making of another self in Hugo's terms. And yet discernible periods in American poetry, as history has proven, need not result from a decision to eschew necessarily a countryman's influential work, but more likely a British poet's work, like Auden's as soon will be mentioned. Still, since Eliot's were the theories which ultimately led to the distinguishing voices of personal poetry—in that personal poets began writing in opposition to these theories—it will be useful to review his "Impersonal theory of poetry." Eliot's best expression of this theory is found in "Tradition and the Individual Talent." The poet, he wrote, "must be aware that the mind of Europe—the mind of his own country—a mind which he learns in time to be much more important than his own private mind—is a mind which changes, and that this change is a development which abandons nothing *en route*, which does not superannuate either Shakespeare, or Homer, or the rock drawing of the Magdalenian draughtsmen" (51). The collective mind of the country, then, takes precedence over the individual mind of the poet. "What happens [to the poet] is a continual surrender of himself as he is at the moment to something which is more valuable. The progress of an artist is a continual self-sacrifice, a continual extinction of personality" (52–3). Eliot's conception of impersonality, which shows in his own work of this time, begins with an understanding of the "universal" mind as having precedence over the individual mind, the personal self. Near the end of the essay, Eliot summarized his thesis as follows:

> Poetry is not a turning loose of emotion, but an escape from emotion; it is not the expression of personality, but an escape from personality. But, of course, only those who have personality and emotions know what it means to want to escape from these things. (58)

In "Hamlet and his Problems," he instructed the poet in the method of evoking emotions while restraining the poem from becoming "a turning loose of emotion":

> The only way of expressing emotion in the form of art is by finding an "objective correlative"; in other words, a set of objects, a situation, a chain of events which shall be the formula of that *particular* emotion; such that when the external facts, which must terminate in sensory experience, are given, the emotion is immediately evoked. (100)

Eliot was later to modify his idea of impersonality in poetry (as did Auden, who wrote personal poetry by the end of his career), claiming that a poet writing of "intense and personal experience is able to express a general truth," and he used Yeats's last poems as exemplary. Eliot said, in the first annual "Yeats Lecture" (delivered at the Abbey Theatre in 1940):

> I have, in early essays, extolled what I called impersonality in art, and it may seem that, in giving as a reason for the superiority of Yeats's later work the greater expression of personality in it, I am contradicting myself.... [T]he truth of the matter is as follows. There are two forms of impersonality: that which is natural to the more skillful craftsman, and that which is more and more achieved by the maturing artist. The first is that of what I have called the "anthology piece," of a lyric by Lovelace or Suckling, or of Campion, a finer poet than either. The second impersonality is that of the poet who, out of intense and personal experience, is able to express a general truth; retaining all the particularity of his experience, to make of it a general symbol. And the strange thing is that Yeats, having been a good craftsman in the first kind, became a great poet in the second. It is not that he became a different man...

But he had to wait for a later maturity to find expression of early experience... (1828)

But the poets of the New Critical school considered Eliot's first impression,
or theory, more germane to their purpose. Perhaps they regarded Yeats, as did
Eliot, as "unique," and that an expression of the personal—an expression of universal significance or "general symbol"—could be accomplished only by Yeats's
genius. That those of the New Criticism believed most poetry of personal experience could not evoke a "general symbol" separated them from the next generation
of poets who contended that any personal poetry, because it is naturally self-serving, speaks for the many, and they cited Whitman as their forefather, in both style
and content, in this versification.

Yet these disciples of Whitman were few in the 1950s, and the American
bard was very much out of favor with the literati of the time. The enormous popularity of the work of Auden, who had come to the United States, served to
strengthen the New Critical dominance of the principal current in poetry. Louis
Simpson writes of this in *A Revolution in Taste:*

> As long as Auden set the fashion—and this he was able to do, for he was a
> brilliant literary journalist as well as poet—the stream of experiment that had
> begun with the Imagist poets, especially that kind of writing of which William
> Carlos Williams was the chief exponent, receded into the background. Auden
> ruled with wit and a knowledge of verse forms; in comparison, the American
> poets who looked to Williams, or to a poet thought to be even more rudimen-
> tary, Walt Whitman, appeared to be fumbling provincials—certainly not
> worth the attention of readers who had been trained by the New Criticism to
> look for shades of irony and multiple, ambiguous meanings. (xv–xvi)

W. D. Snodgrass, whose book of personal poetry in the confessional mode,
Heart's Needle, appeared in 1959—the same year as *Life Studies*—has explained in
his *In Radical Pursuit* that he began writing in this atmosphere of New Criticism,
as described by Simpson, and that he patterned his early poems to the dicta of its
theories:

> ...we had been taught to write a very difficult and very intellectual poem. We
> tried to achieve the obscure and dense texture of the French Symbolists...by
> using methods similar to those of the very intellectual and conscious poets of
> the English Renaissance, especially the Metaphysical poets. I need hardly say
> that this was a very strange combination. My first published poem started like
> this:

June, and the Tigerlily swam our hedge
Like gold fish in the inmost sea's most green

Awakenings. Fondly, we gathered the bloom.
Thus: Dis. In our inquisitive, close room
The Lily parched and clenched to a fist
Which could then neither fierce nor pure subsist.

Of course you recognize that this is a poem about the loss of religious faith? The Tigerlily is meant to stand for Christ, who, like Persephone, was gathered away into the underworld by a dark god, Dis or Pluto.... one critic said this poem had no intellectual content; he said he wouldn't demand a metaphysical conceit (which, of course, the poem *was*), but he would like to have it talk about something besides plain old flowers. I had so packed my poem with intellection that he thought it had none! (42–3)

And Sylvia Plath's initial experiences with poetry, as Simpson reports in *A Revolution in Taste*, were similar to that of Snodgrass. Simpson defines further the poetry affected by New Criticism, and explains the extent of its influence on such young poets as Plath, as well as on the "generation of readers" trained by its school. He wrote:

In her attempt to write about history and culture in the manner of Auden, Plath diverged from her best subject—experience and what to make of it—as far as she would ever go. She was not alone: the influence of Auden was strong in these years. Young poets tried to write like Auden about history, with irony and wit, using traditional forms....

This elegance was very much of the period. New Critics emphasized the qualities in verse that lent themselves to "explication." Irony and ambiguity were especially favored. If the poem didn't fit the tools they kept the tools and threw away the poem. Cleanth Brooks' and Robert Penn Warren's *Understanding Poetry*, from which a generation learned how to read, contained six poems by Donne and not a single poem by Whitman.

...it would be another ten years before Ginsberg made an impression and Olson had a following. The admired poets...stood for poetry written in traditional forms and in a language removed from actual speech. (100)

Auden and the New Critics went beyond the modernists' deflection of the personal; they seemed to replace it entirely with a formal poetry using rarely the subject of one's personal history.

Yet Ginsberg arrived with his notion that autobiography—that which "you tell your friends about yourself," even—is the only proper subject for literature. Ginsberg said in an interview with *Paris Review*:

> So then—what happens if you make a distinction between what you tell your muse? The problem is to break down that distinction: when you approach the Muse to talk as frankly as you would talk with yourself or with your friends. So I began finding, in conversations with Burroughs and Kerouac and Gregory Corso, in conversations with people whom I knew well, whose souls I respected, that the things we were telling each other for real were totally different from what was already in literature. And that was Kerouac's great discovery in *On the Road*. The kinds of things that he and Neal Cassady were talking about, he finally discovered were *the* subject matter for what he wanted to write down. That meant, at that minute, a complete revision of what literature was supposed to be, in *his* mind, and actually in the minds of the people that first read the book.... It's the ability to commit to writing, to *write*, the same way that you...are! (288)

It was the poets' commitment to writing in a style which best suited their personal poetry ("to *write*, the same way that you...are!") that led in part to the rejection of the "objective school" represented by New Critical poetry. "So it was," writes Mills in *Cry of the Human*:

> that Stanley Kunitz, Richard Eberhart, Theodore Roethke, John Berryman, Robert Lowell, Karl Shapiro, Randall Jarrell, and others who began to write in the 1930s ... were freed as individuals from the demands created by literary movements to an energetic and single-minded concentration that brought, in due time, Roethke in *The Lost Son*, Lowell in *Life Studies*, Berryman in *Homage to Mistress Bradstreet* and *The Dream Songs*, and Shapiro in *The Bourgeois Poet*, for example, to the kind of poetic breakthrough James Dickey calls "The Second Birth"—an intense imaginative liberation, achieved at great personal cost, in which the poet, like a snake shedding his dead skin, frees himself of the weight of imposed styles and current critical criteria to come into the place of his own authentic speech. (3)

In 1958, Robert Bly was calling for a break with that tradition established by the New Critical thought of objectivism. In reference to the insistence on objectivity (as opposed to the more subjective personal self) in poetry, Bly wrote in his essay "Five Decades of Modern American Poetry":

> Why do so few poets write now of business experience, of despair, or the Second World War? One reason, I think, is that we write in the old tradition, and

it is impossible to write of these subjects in the old tradition. A new style is invented to deal with new subject matter, and if we continue to write in the old
style, we will cut ourselves off from the most important experiences of our
time. (38–9)

The books, besides *Howl* and *Life Studies*, which soon began appearing—and
which could be added to Mills's list—were Snodgrass's *Heart's Needle*, poems
about the complications arising from the poet's divorce, Bly's *Silence in the Snowy
Fields* (1962), which collected poems of his subjective experience he had written in
the 1950s, Plath's *Ariel* (1966), which showed clearly her change from an earlier
style (informed by Auden's influence) by revealing a personal verse mostly concerned with a suicidal protagonist, and many others—all poetry which took as its
subjects the self, the concept of selfhood, personal experience, the individual's relationship to his or her time in history. And most of it was written in the "new
style" (that is, not really "new" or inventive, but not in the formal style of the New
Critical school) since, as Phillips has remarked, "openness of language leads to
openness of emotion" and of subjective experience—which brings us to personal
poetry's contrasting style to that of New Critical verse.

The decade between 1959 and 1969 culminated with the appearance of two
major poetry anthologies: *Naked Poetry* and *The Contemporary American Poets*.
Stephen Berg and Robert Mezey, in their *Naked Poetry* (1969), called attention to
"open forms," a term first introduced into the vocabulary of criticism in the foreword of that anthology. Although several smaller publications such as the first issue of the magazine *Fifties* (1958), edited by William Duffy and Bly, encouraged
the poetic movement away from traditional prosody ("The editors of this magazine think that most of the poetry published in America today is too old-fashioned," that issue's epigraph read), *Naked Poetry* was the first anthology from a
major commercial publisher to receive wide observation, and acceptance, from
the literati. "Naked poetry," as it was, had supplanted that of the more traditional
verse forms as the main current of American poetry. Mezey and Berg remarked in
introducing the book: "We began with the firm conviction that the strongest and
most alive poetry in America had abandoned or at least broken the grip of traditional meters and had set out, once again, into the 'wilderness of unopened life.'"
The "open form" was somewhat defined by Mezey and Berg as "poems [that]
don't rhyme (usually) and don't move on feet of more or less equal duration
(usually). That nondescription gropes toward the only technical principle they all
have in common" (xi). *Naked Poetry* fairly represented verse in open form, which
by 1969 had become the preponderate mode of writing poems, even though the

content varied widely between the poets. Following each selection of poems, the living poets included a statement regarding his or her philosophy of the practice of open form poetry, resembling in manner some types of modernist manifestoes, many of which acknowledged an allegiance to the modern masters—Pound, Williams, Stevens, Roethke—and ignoring, except in a disparaging context, Warren, Brooks, Tate, and Ransom.

Parallel in importance to *Naked Poetry*, *The Contemporary American Poets* (1969), edited by Mark Strand, proclaimed to reflect the "rebirth" of poetry in this country. Whereas *Naked Poetry*'s primary objective was to display recent poetry's new look as differentiated from the adherence to forms common to the poetry written in the decade after World War II, Strand's choices, although the same at times as Mezey's and Berg's, reflected his concern for subject matter. To that end, he took as his starting date 1940, which included some poetry written in the New Critical style. That is to say, his anthology did not espouse a polemic of poetic form as did *Naked Poetry*. Strand wrote in his preface:

> Many of today's poets have made, if not a cult, at least a lifetime's work of the self, a self defined usually by circumstances that would tend to set it apart. In their energetic pursuit of an individual manner that would reflect a sense of self-definition, they have used what they wanted from various literary traditions. Helped on in recent years by the abundance of translations from almost every language, there are poets in the United States whose imaginative roots seem to have sprung from Neruda or Char or Cavafy or from Arthur Waley's versions of Chinese poetry quite as much as they have from Emerson or Whitman. (xiii–xiv)

Strand's remarks suggest that Bly's directive had become common practice, that "a new style is invented to deal with new subject matter" and that the "new style" could, presumably, borrow from the old. His remarks also support my earlier comment concerning the influence of foreign poets on the direction of American verse.

Statements by Adrienne Rich and Louis Simpson serve to confirm Strand's claim that some poets have made "a lifetime's work of the self." Rich has argued, in her essay "When We Dead Awaken: Writing as Re-Vision":

> Until we can understand the assumptions in which we are drenched we cannot know ourselves. And this drive to self-knowledge, for women, is more than a search for identity: it is part of our refusal of the self-destructiveness of male-dominated society. A radical critique of literature, feminist in its impulse, would take the work first of all as a clue to how we live, how we have

been living, how we have been led to imagine ourselves, how our language has trapped as well as liberated us, how the very act of naming has been till now a male prerogative, and how we can begin to see and name—and therefore live—afresh. A change in the concept of sexual identity is essential if we are not going to see the old political order re-assert itself in every new revolution. We need to know the writing of the past, and know it differently than we have ever known it; not to pass on a tradition but to break its hold over us. (278–79)

Although she speaks of "we" in the foregoing passage, Rich's personal "drive to self-knowledge" has brought her to the rejection of her authentic self and the projection in her poetry of her sincere, public self, as she told Stanley Plumly: "I am not interested in the poem as a way of revealing a self that I think I know about to the outer world. I am interested in, certainly, finding out more about that self, and I think of myself as using poetry as a chief means of self-exploration" (29–30). As Blackmur suggested, a persona voice can reveal about the self that which a poet "did not know she knew"; and—although Rich may disagree—she employs a persona as poetic voice (for this or other means) once she decides to write a personal poem.

Simpson speaks in a more general context than does Rich. His statement in *American Poets in 1976* included the following:

For some time American poets have been writing almost exclusively about their personal lives.... The present moment is everything—there is no sense of the past. Nor is there any sense of the community. If poetry is the language of a tribe, it seems there is no longer a tribe, only a number of individuals who are writing a personal diary or trying to "expand their consciousness." (332)

The problem of self-definition had been the focus of the poetry written in the period covered in Strand's anthology, and one solution, of course, was to write poems in a distinctive, individual manner, even if failing to represent an authentic self—one can learn about this self because of (not despite) the persona voice. That ambition, coupled with the subject of self, dictated which foreign poetry was to be translated—which further contributed to the influence of translations on American poets that Strand mentioned—and this in turn may have been responsible for poets' loss of "any sense of the community," as Simpson believes, in favor of an overwhelming obsession with their private experiences. Rich and Simpson, both writing in 1976, indicate how self-obsession had flourished since Strand's remarks of 1969 to the point where American poets wrote "almost exclusively about their personal lives," as Simpson complained. This level of saturation in contemporary poetry is due to the freedom open form allows and in part to the (over)reaction to New Critical objectivism. That these poets have "no sense of the past" is in deliberate disregard of Eliot's theory as stated in "Tradition and the Individual Talent." Yet my ensuing chapters will show that many personal poets could blend formal poetics, a sense of history, and the subjective self. The modes of voice give each the opportunity to retain some of the New Critical intention of objectivity.

Having published his first full-length collection (*Reasons for Moving*) just the year before writing the preface to his anthology, Strand was still developing his own aesthetic of voice and style, and therefore naturally was concerned with the personal styles of other, older poets, as he said in an interview with Richard Vine and Robert von Hallberg:

> We all require a certain amount of self-definition, and self-definition means being recognizable as someone different from the others. I think that poets, particularly young poets, really want that in their work. They don't want their poems to sound like someone else's. In the very beginning, of course, they do. It gives their poems authority. They want to sound like Eliot or Lowell because that's what poetry sounds like to them. If they write like established poets, their poems will sound like real poems. (131–32)

Strand, then, tried to determine these older poets' "imaginative roots," by which he seems to mean their forms as well as their subjects. And when subsequently breaking from them, he developed what he considered his own, idiosyncratic voice (as we shall see in chapter 4). It is understandable, too, that many of the poets represented in his anthology would turn to "self-definition," not because of the then increasing trend towards introspection, but also as an organizing principle for their poems in light of the absence of traditional prosody, as previously suggested, and as Bruce Weigl has written: "The most immediate reason for the common use of autobiographical detail, structure, context, or strategy within the contemporary tradition seems to be the increasingly widespread use of the free-verse form, especially in the latter half of the twentieth century. Given the absence of traditional prosody to organize and structure a poem, it became necessary for poets to look elsewhere for organizing principles, the most common of which presents private consciousness for public consumption: telling a story about oneself" (113).

David Ignatow explains more specifically, and in more depth, that the concentration on the self as subject matter is necessary in our age, and that a poet's notion of selfhood will ultimately dictate the principal structural means of the poem. More important to Ignatow, as he said in "A Dialogue at Compas," is the model (inclusive of the impetus of poetry written in intentional rejection of that model) Whitman provides for this kind of poem:

> ...the mainstream in American poetry derives from Walt Whitman. It's not so much a celebration of oneself, and not oneself as a self, but as a self which is a personification or a surrogate of another power transcending the individual power. And it's not so much a poetry of optimism as a poetry of self-identification with that which exists above and beyond us.... We question ourselves as being surrogates of any kind of divine energy, and American poets are sons and daughters of Walt Whitman. We are still arguing this problem with him. We are asking him, "Are you still viable?" We don't believe he's viable to the extent that he thought of himself as viable.... But to give up entirely is to let ourselves sink into something which we just don't want to imagine. So we are at a point now where we talk to him, argue with him, refute him, and when things become very desperate for us...we have an automatic reflex and fall back upon things that he said. We fall back upon the self once more. But that's still not adequate, which is the main problem. We're in a crisis...right now as poets. (62–3)

When poets "fall back upon the self," their poetry becomes more personal, in search of the proper definition, or re-definition, of one's self, marked by a distinctive style as Strand and Bly have mentioned. Yet Strand feels there should be limitations of subject in trying to create a poetry that is, as Ignatow said, a "celebration of oneself...a poetry of self-identification with that which exists above and beyond us." Eliot called for a poet, in "retaining all the particularity of his experience, to make of it a general symbol," but sometimes, Strand suggests, a poet does not have a personal experience that can be applied generally, as he said of Adrienne Rich's work. In response to Richard Vine's question: "Would it make sense for any poet today to address his readers the way Whitman addressed his?" Strand replied:

> It would be ridiculous.... It's very presumptuous, I think, of anyone to address himself to a whole nation. And it is a bit self-defeating to address yourself to the little sunbirds of poetry. But I'm not sure that one has to do either one of those things. I think all you can do is address yourself to ideas and issues that you yourself are concerned about. Hopefully, these exist at the very center of your culture and have to do with being human and being alive. Poetry doesn't usually address itself to specific issues. Such issues tend to diminish.... I am not sure that the issues to which Adrienne Rich addresses herself right now, and the terms in which she addresses them, are overriding.... A

poet must invite you out of yourself with what you yourself have. He can't bombard you with prejudice. Reading Rich one is participating in an assault, or one is defending one's self. I just don't believe, for example, that all women are lesbians. Some are. But the argument is: well, they all would be if they had the courage. That's like saying all men are killers, etc. (132–33)

In following Bly's directive, then, to write about "the most important experiences of our time" in a new style, Rich, Strand contends, has failed to make clear how the issue of her private self becomes "a general symbol." Rather, like the poets of whom Simpson wrote, Rich seems to feel that "the present moment is everything," that "there is no longer a tribe" to which she must address her personal poetry other than the community she has conceived. I use Strand's remarks about Rich to illustrate that although personal poetry was one result of the break from the New Critical "old style," it was not the only one; poetry written in open form does not make it personal nor does it represent a school uniform in theory or content. The various notions of selfhood we have seen indicate each poet's individual scope in constituting one's "subjective experience."

It was earlier suggested that personal poetry may have been an effect of the need for an organizing principle "in the absence of traditional prosody," but as Berg and Mezey write in their foreword of *The New Naked Poetry* (1976), this may not be:

One academic fellow who saw a preliminary version of this book wondered why the editors did not write a long essay defining the "genre" of open form and relating each poet to this "genre." That doesn't seem to be the right word. Listening to the sounds of Ethridge Knight and Robert Duncan, for example, we do not believe it means anything to say they are both working in the "genre" of open form. We would suggest the fellow have a look at "Some Notes on Organic Form" in the first *Naked Poetry.* Organic—the metaphor is of the living and growing thing. The rhythm and shape of the flower cannot be made clear as separate from or meaning anything different from the coming to be a flower. (xviii)

Whereas the more traditional poetry of New Criticism was, in fact, a seemingly unified school representing the dominant period style, poetry of open form, the "new style" (again, much of which is personal poetry) is neither uniform in subject nor technique, as evident by the disagreements cited by poets over the role of Whitman, the extent of personal, subjective experiences as matters for poetry, audience concern, and so forth. Further, not all personal poetry need be expressed in open form, as will be demonstrated with some of Lowell's work discussed in the next chapter and a few poems of Strand (forthcoming in chapter 4). About poetry of open form Strand wrote in his essay "Notes on the Craft of Poetry":

> It hardly seems worthwhile to point out the shortsightedness of those practitioners who would have us believe that the form of the poem is merely its shape. They argue that there is formal poetry and poetry without form, free verse in other words, and that formal poetry has dimensions that are rhythmic or stanzaic, etc., and consequently measurable. But if we have learned anything from the poetry of the last twenty or thirty years, it is that free verse is as formal as any other verse. There is ample evidence that it uses a full range of mnemonic devices, the most common being anaphoral and parallelistic structures, both as syntactically restrictive as they are rhythmically binding. I do not want to suggest that measured verse and free verse represent opposing mnemonics; I would rather we considered them together, both being structured or shaped and thus formal, or at least formal in outward, easily described ways. (344–45)

So far, then, all we have established is that personal poetry is not wholly without form—rather, it is usually in an ambiguous "open form" or, as Robert Phillips observed, in "the language... of ordinary speech, whether in blank verse or no" (9)—and that it represents a marked distinction from the more objective subject matter ("history and culture in the manner of Auden," as Simpson said of Plath's early work) of the poetry it succeeded. That is, its subject became more and more that of the subjective self. Yet this is not to presume that all poetry of the "new style" is personal poetry. Let us again turn to Strand for a general description of American poetry since the New Critical verse of the 1950s; he told Plumly:

> I'm not sure I would characterize recent poetry or post–World War II poetry as anti-poetry. We had a terrific resurgence of formalist poetry in the 50's, and what we had combating that, I guess, was "beat poetry"... anti-poetry is really modern poetry. Contemporary poetry isn't modern poetry, and it isn't anti-poetry. I feel very much a part of a new international style that has a lot to do with plainness of diction, a certain reliance on surrealistic techniques, a certain reliance on journalistic techniques, a strong narrative element, etc. Now I realize this doesn't cover all of contemporary poetry...(57)

But it does, I suggest, provide a broad summation of the arrival (and brief description) of the style of personal poetry.

Both *Naked Poetry* and *The Contemporary American Poets*, viewed in retrospect (it is interesting that neither book included the work of the editor, or editors, of the other), were important in identifying the poetic taste of the period in style and subject, a preference, once established, that has remained in fashion for the nearly three decades following their publication. Although Strand chose from among poems published since 1940—which is to say that some are in measured forms even though the "formal" verse in his anthology is often only very loosely, or irregularly, metered and rhymed—he betrays, by his selection of those poems, an explicit favor for those in open form. Most likely, then, the general consensus is that personal poetry is best presented in that way.

Louis Simpson's remarks lend support here. Writing of Auden's formal verse, which influence, Simpson believed, prolonged the reign of the New Critical school, he offers his version in *A Revolution in Taste* of how current poetry became so self-involved and written in open form:

> ...something was missing in Auden's concept of poetry, and what this was became evident when the Welsh poet Dylan Thomas began his American tours. The missing quality was passion. In Thomas this was expressed in music, the sound of words, over and above what they might be saying. A poem by Auden was an exercise in reason, listening to a poem by Thomas was an experience. At the boom of his voice from the platform the Audenesque facade began to crack, and a few years later Allen Ginsberg brought it tumbling down. The poet moved to the center of the stage and spoke his mind freely. This became the common stance for poets in the years that followed. "Most artists and critics," said Susan Sontag, writing in the sixties "have discarded the theory of art as representative of an outer reality in favor of art as subjective expression." (xvi)

The primary reason for the continuing emphasis on the self in poetry following the decades of the 1960s, Simpson would argue, is no longer an issue of form, or the need for passionate presentation of a verse no longer "objective," no longer Audenesque, but it is a consequence of the society which spawns it:

> If one considers the impersonality of the modern bureaucratic state it is likely that, more and more, poetry will be written to express the life of an individual....
>
> To most people living in the West, poetry has become almost exclusively a means of self-expression. This is bound to continue until the aim of education is changed, and this must wait on changes in society as a whole. (169)

Robert Penn Warren, in his prose work *Democracy and Poetry* (1975), presents a similar notion, but from a different perspective:

In the preceding essay I looked at our poetry as a record of the dwindling of our conception of the self. Then I was regarding poetry as "diagnostic," as a social document; I noted how it has analyzed and recorded a crucial ailment of our democracy: the progressive decay of the notion of the self. Now I am regarding poetry as "therapeutic"; I am trying to indicate how, in the end, in the face of the increasingly disintegrative forces in our society, poetry may reaffirm and reinforce the notion of the self. Though I hasten to say that the end of poetry is to be poetry, and that only insofar as it fulfills that end may it properly serve either diagnostic or therapeutic ends. (42)

But Richard Hugo thought a democratic society allows poetry—no matter what its purpose—to flourish, as he stated in "Stray Thoughts on Roethke and Teaching":

Mark Strand remarked...that American poetry could not help but get better and better, and I'm inclined to agree. I doubt that we'll have the one big figure of the century the way other nations do, Yeats, Valéry. Giants are not the style of the society, though the wind knows there are enough people who want to create them, and not just a few who want to be them. I think we'll end up with a lot of fine poets, each doing his thing. (33)

That the subject of self—whether "the progressive decay of the notion of self," as Warren said, or the representation of "art as subjective experience," as did Sontag—is the predominant one in our current poetry supports the argument of a lingering Romantic tradition. Leonard Nathan believes that the personal "I" introduced by William Wordsworth in his "There was a boy" (Nathan writes: "Only a critic defending a theoretical position could doubt that the Wordsworth in 'There was a boy' is the real Wordsworth,") continues now in the form of our "confessional" verse, and he cites other characteristics of Romanticism in today's personal poetry:

The third new element in poetry, besides the private "I" and the importance of pathos, is the loosening of form and structure, which follows from the fact that poems are in some sense—in theory if not in practice—the spontaneous overflow of feeling, in other words, the individual awareness actually in the process of discovering or experiencing its own deepest emotions.... [T]he exaggeration I have presented as Romantic poetic practice and theory is more or less the reality today. It is as if a certain logic based on Romantic premises had worked itself out to its conclusion, a conclusion which no contemporary poet is spared, no matter how anti-Romantic he may think himself. (88)

The self is certainly not a contemporary notion for poets, as Edmund Wilson argued rather succinctly in his *Axel's Castle*. Its most recent ancestor—which is to say that the self has been a subject for verse periodically throughout history (one discussion of confessional poetry began with a sonnet from Shakespeare; others have traced the mode from Sappho through Catullus, Augustine, and Rousseau)—is nineteenth century Romanticism, which, Wilson said,

> was a revolt of the individual.... [The Classical poet] would consider it artistic bad taste to identify his hero with himself and to glorify himself with his hero, or to intrude between the reader and the story and give vent to his personal emotions. But in [Romantic poetry] the writer is either his own hero, or unmistakably identified with his hero, and the personality and emotions of the writer are presented as the principal subject of interest.... Byron and Wordsworth ask us to be interested in themselves by virtue of the intrinsic value of the individual: they vindicate the rights of the individual against the claims of society... it is always, as in Wordsworth, the individual sensibility, or, as in Byron, the individual will, with which the Romantic poet is preoccupied. (2–4)

Wilson has separated "the poet as his own hero" from a "created" hero with whom the poet is "unmistakably identified," a distinction which can be made in contemporary personal verse, particularly that of the confessional and persona modes of voice.

Alan Williamson suggests that the need for poets to be their own artistic heroes is cultural, and that introspection is a result of historical and sociological sequences:

> The diffusion of psychoanalysis in the general culture, and the sheer amount of inner conflict and turmoil experienced by some of the most talented poets of the period, are factors that should not be underestimated. But the larger political history may have been even more important. The poets who shaped contemporary poetry all came of age sometime between the rise of Hitler and the fall of Joe McCarthy—that is to say, during a time when the relative influence of irrational hatreds, fears, and identifications, as against pragmatic interests, in political life seemed more disproportionate than it had, perhaps, for several centuries. The responses of the great Modernist writers to this history—wrongheaded, symbolic, and personally driven as they often were—I suspect helped later poets conclude that a psychology beginning at home was a necessary middle term between poetic sensibility and impersonal or ideological judgment. (2)

Whether certain Romantic tendencies emerged again in poetry since the 1950s, or cultural conditions influenced the subject matter of poetry—whatever the reasons—poets became more personal than objective, more inward directed than outward. And although, as Wilson traced for us, history shows this not to be unique, never has the concern for self so completely dominated any period of poetry, any style, as it has our present one.

Yet, be that the personal poem's reliance on self as principles of theme and structure is predominant, it is somewhat surprising that much academic commentary of contemporary poetry has been focused on other subjects. At present, the critical fashion is to find meaning between the texts (or to find no meaning at all). Some French theorists have deconstructed "I," showing language's disengagement from reality. The self in the poem is but an illusion in this regard. "There are *no* texts, but only relationships *between* texts" (3), Harold Bloom tells us in *A Map of Misreading*, which de-emphasizes the author's work as a distinctive object of art and removes the focus from the author of (and very much in) the work. Indeed, Roland Barthes (in "The Death of the Author") would have us believe there are no poets either, in addition to there being no texts. And Helen Vendler has minimized the importance of autobiography in Robert Lowell's most personal poetry, preferring instead to concentrate on the objects he describes, his external stimuli. She has written of the Lowell of *Life Studies*: "[F]or all his learning and his intellectuality, for all his interior 'autobiography' even, Lowell is a poet essentially externalized—in data, in description, in scene, in action, in history" (351).

Despite the critical preference of the most famous literary theorists and commentators, a few younger critics in this country, not yet widely known and oftentimes poets themselves, have begun to argue the significance of personal poetry and to examine more closely the poets' personalities and lives in relation to their poems, as this study must do in contending for the modes of voice in current practice. Alan Williamson has pointed towards the critical bias against the examination of the self, stating: "[A]lthough the importance of subjectivism in the development of contemporary poetry is universally acknowledged, there seems to be a certain resistance to making it the main focus of critical scrutiny—especially an implicitly approving scrutiny" (5–6). And the poet Dave Smith, in reference to the poetry of James Wright, has written in *The Pure Clear Word*:

> We live in a time when critical theory has called into question not merely the function of art but the very existence of art. Theorists deny there can be an author. From Derrida to Culler to Fish, the talk is of the *text*, an impersonal object neither story nor poem. The desire of such criticism, whatever its Archimedean point, is to bring to literature the objectivity of scientific

inquiry; that is, to codify what and how literature knows. This is the direction and legacy of New Criticism in part, of modernist rebellion in part—but it is largely the temperament of the industrial world. While criticism fabricates objectivity and impersonality, becoming at last not a way of experiencing art but a kind of parodic extension of Robert Frost's remark about free verse— that is, a game played without net, racket, or balls—poetry has gone in the opposite direction. To understand and to follow James Wright's development as a poet we have to search for the man in the poems. (xii)

Consequently, there has not been a study of the self as subject, particularly in relation to the contemporary poem's use of a voice persona, the modes of which are defined as follows:

The Confessional Mode, which employs "I" as the principal speaker, relates a personal incident of the poet's public self—an incident either actual, that is, autobiographical, or created from the imagination—usually intended as a means of self-identification, self-definition, and which often evokes pathos in the reader, although the incident depicted in a poem of this mode can be joyous as well. This "I" is the sincere voice of the poet (intended or not), one used as the primary instrument in presenting the poem. The poet who writes in the confessional mode of voice attempts to present the "I" as the self he or she wishes to define by the poem.

The Persona Mode, which combines the seemingly veracious elements of the subjective voice of the confessional mode with the apparent objectivity of the self-effacing poem, invents a character as the narrator of a personal incident (again, real or imagined by the poet). This character is closely associated with the poet's public self. It is his or her mask through which a personal experience can be related with both the subjective (and often pathetic) expression of the confessional voice and the objective stance a poet takes when narrating an account of an imagined character. The modernist archetype for this mode is Pound's "Hugh Selwyn Mauberley."

The Self-Effacing Mode, which also uses "I" as its principal speaker, attempts to depersonalize the voice of the poet's public self in order to render a seemingly objective account of a personal experience (actual or invented) of that self. The depersonalized voice acts to control the tone of the poem so that if pathos is evoked in the reader, it derives from the incident depicted by the poem, not the voice (as it often does in the confessional mode). More commonly, however, the poem will contain themes of absence, self-alienation, and its "I" speaker will attempt to define himself or herself within the context of these themes. The poet who writes in this mode attempts not actually to obliterate his or her public self from the poem, but to transcend that public, sincere voice in order to become inconspicuous so to effect a seemingly objective voice, one illustrative of the world this public self finds alien.

Poets covered in the period of this study (roughly, the late 1950s to the present, with the exception of the poetry of Weldon Kees which precedes that date) tend to write in all three modes. Most betray a marked preference for one mode over the other two, but it is rare for a poet to practice one voice exclusively. I intend to illustrate my thesis by examining the work of three poets major to this study, one for each mode, and also show how each poet writes in all three modes. In addition, for each mode I will analyze the work of two other poets whose verse I will treat only in the mode of voice I have chosen it to exemplify. As mentioned, Robert Lowell will serve as the major figure for the confessional, John Berryman for the persona mode, and Mark Strand for the self-effacing.

Of particular note: My definition of "confessional" (that it is one type of persona) may vary from its current usage—but that varies widely too. Phillips wrote that "Lowell and Allen Ginsberg eschew *personae* altogether" (9) and so are confessional, but to the contrary, each adopts the persona of his public self as the speaker of his confessional verse, so that James Merrill is right in observing that confessionalism "is a literary convention like any other, the problem being to make it *sound* as if it were true," that is, to sound sincere, as I would amend Merrill's remark. Simpson properly identifies Lowell's and others' work of the confessional mode as "deliberate self-portraitures," however misguided he may be in agreeing with Rosenthal about Sexton's placing "the literal [authentic] self…at the center of the poem."

David Ignatow, one of the self-effacing poets, wrote in his *Notebooks*: "Obviously, I'm not a confessional poet. I feel no guilt or hatred or consuming love that must be allowed to spill over" (qtd. in *New Naked Poetry* 112). And Snodgrass has said to David Dillon: "…my poems aren't confessional. That has to imply that one is talking about some kind of forbidden activity and doing it in a rather lurid way—like a confessional magazine" (219).

Simpson, Ignatow, and Snodgrass have differing conceptions of the term "confessional poet," and each differs from mine. A poem using the mode of persona as voice which I term confessional does not have to "confess" anything as Ignatow suggests it must—particularly "in a rather lurid way" as Snodgrass thinks—nor does the poem's subject need to be autobiographical. But the voice requires, at the least, a semblance of a personal experience that is plausible, and it must be sincere in the presentation of that experience in Lionel Trilling's sense— that the poet must represent his or her speaker and experience to us in believable fashion. The confessional voice may be closely associated with the poet's private self, as I have defined it, but it is the poet's public voice used with the knowledge that his or her poems' audience is the public. The poet successfully evoking pathos, then, is the confessional poet "weeping with one eye on the camera," as Simpson remarked. Sincerity will distinguish, ultimately, the confessional mode of voice from the self-effacing, as we shall see.

This study is one of criticism. That is, it asserts a theory I will attempt to prove by my analysis of the work of representative poets. The reasons for my selecting these poets are stated in the chapters in which their works are treated. As indicated previously, not all poetry of this country since the late 1950s concerns the self, or is personal poetry, one attempting answers to what Emerson called the "burden" of the individual: to define himself in relation to his immediate surroundings, his community, and the age in which he finds himself belonging. Consequently, many of the best-known poets of our day are not mentioned in the following chapters, or if they are, only briefly and usually derogatorily by the poets whom I do include—for poets concerning themselves with the self are often not sympathetic to those whose primary focus is on form, say, or the direction of "the lyric," or popular philosophy, or anything else besides the self. Bly, therefore, will derogate the work of John Ashbery, as he did in an interview with Wayne Dodd: "Ashbery has become an utterly academic poet. Academic poetry in the fifties was recognizable by emotional anemia and English meter. Now it is recognizable by fake French surrealism and emotional anemia. In Ashbery there is no anger, there is no world" (299), and David Ignatow will say things like: "John Ashbery is not dealing with this subject [self] at all. Neither is a critic like Harold Bloom. They are critics of literature, they are writers of *literature*; they are not writers of life" (*Open Between Us* 63).

Disregarding aesthetic favoritism, I have excluded such well-known poets as Ashbery, Kenneth Koch, and James Merrill from this study simply because they have not written enough about the self. Nor do these poets have, in most of their work, an identifiable voice as persona. In their poetry of images, or ideas, or lyricism, the voice is indeterminate and therefore cannot be traced to any mode. W. S. Merwin is excluded for this reason, even though Strand, Kinnell, and others speak well of his work. This may raise the issue of my exclusion of poets who do write of the self and whose voice is clearly distinguishable in their work. But this study is not a survey of the poets of personal verse. Rather it posits the critical assumption that any woman or man writing of the self does so in one of the three modes of voice I have identified, and that the poets I do use in the study are exemplary of anyone writing in these modes. In this regard, then, I have not excluded any poet, for her or his aesthetic, or technique of voice, is represented by the work I have chosen to discuss. My only criteria of selection were that the poets clearly reflect the practice of the mode (which I believe they do) and that their national identity was American—not origin, that is, for Strand was born in Summerside, Prince Edward Island, Canada, and Simic in Yugoslavia.

A final word before turning to those poets: Since Lowell, Wright, Sexton, Berryman, and Kees are deceased—more than half the poets whose work I discuss in the ensuing pages—I have concluded with a chapter which examines a few younger poets presently writing personal poetry to determine whether the use of voice in the confessional, persona, and self-effacing modes has continued in today's practice, or has died with the older poets. In addition, I have updated the work of the poets I treat in chapters 2 through 4 who are still living—that is, I discuss their most recent poems—in order to comment on their continuing, or discontinuing, uses of voice in their personal poetry through the 1990s. But enough of what is to come. It is time to let the poets and their poems speak for themselves and to make their voices and personae known.

Two

⁓

The Confessional Mode

Robert Lowell's troubled life—his personal, private, and public confrontations stemming from his manic depression (which was improperly diagnosed at first, and thereafter poorly treated)—is closely linked to much of his poetry. And this interesting life, rich in political, poetic, and religious concerns, has proven to be of continuous fascination, the source of numerous biographies, memoirs, and sketches which began appearing shortly after Lowell's somewhat premature death in 1977 at age sixty. Within the last decade or so, two lengthy biographies have been published: Ian Hamilton's *Robert Lowell* (1982) and Paul Mariani's *Lost Puritan: A Life of Robert Lowell* (1994). Other books include *Manic Power: Robert Lowell and his Circle* (1987) by Jeffrey Meyers and a collection of anecdotal writings about Lowell, *Robert Lowell: Interviews and Memoirs* (1988)—to name but two of very many.

Consequently, the confessional voice of personal poetry is best represented by Robert Lowell's work. Not only did Lowell admit that his personal poems were autobiographical, but—given the amount of factual evidence concerning his life that is available—these poems often can be documented as representing some of his personal experiences. The voice of these poems, therefore, is confessional in the sense that it acts as the voice of the public Lowell who is narrating parts of his autobiography in verse. Also, in order to create a tone of sincerity—which is, as

we learned from Trilling in the previous chapter, the presentation of personal experiences as believable, plausible, even though the speaker of these poems depicting such experiences may not be representative of the poet's authentic (private)
self—Lowell used certain rhetorical techniques in his verse such as a simple-sentence syntax common to prose (personal pronoun subject, verb, object), a more
conversational diction, and a narrative structure. We find the following lines in a
random selection from the first few poems of *Life Studies*: "I saw our stewards go /
forward..." "I left the City of God..." "I heard the El's green girders..." "I char-
tered an aluminum canoe..." "I sat on the stone porch..." Within the context of
each poem from which these lines have been culled, the speaker is the sincere
Lowell. Once we have accepted the speaker's integrity—that is, the sincerity, honesty, candor—we can accept a poem as confessional even if our assumption cannot be supported with biographical data. The assessment of the speaker's sincerity
must be approached through the poem's technique, not the poet's intent.

Lowell's poems of the confessional mode which can be traced to an autobiographical origin are constructed in much the same way as those which cannot.
Consequently, the technique of craft, the principle of his aesthetic, rather than a
"source," serves to indicate whether his poems are confessional. This means of determination is the primary basis for my analysis of the poetry of James Wright
and Anne Sexton, whose personal poems—together with Lowell's—will help sub-
stantiate the conclusions I reach about the confessional mode.

Lowell uses the confessional voice in his personal poems as a method of
self-exploration. In some poems, the voice, the "I" in the poem, acts as the principal catalyst necessary for the representation of the poem's theme, or acts as the
central character in the dramatic situation of a poem. In others, the voice is an
observer of events or landscapes that do not include the "I"—either as a catalyst
or character—within the context of the poem. In these poems the basis for self-
exploration derives from the peculiar manner in which the voice (the speaker of
the poem) observes the event or landscape. This, too, can reveal the self that is defined by such observation. In either type of use, though, the confessional voice is
that of the poet chronicling his public self's personal history, using that self—as
Phillips informed us—"as a poetic symbol around which is woven a personal mythology," a work Lowell emphasized when he altered his poetic style from formal
versification to *vers libre*.

ROBERT LOWELL

LOWELL'S CHANGE IN HIS AESTHETIC approach was correlative with his concern for the self, as Jay Martin has suggested:

Settling in Boston in 1954 with a view toward rediscovering some roots, he made a start on a prose autobiography. He became interested in psychoanalysis, particularly in Freud. Now, "Freud seemed the only religious teacher" to him. He began giving poetry readings, and "more and more [he says] I found that I was simplifying my poems...." His readings loosened his tight, difficult forms; and his interest in autobiography and self encouraged respect for prose ("less cut off from life than poetry is") and diminished his interest in highly rhetorical poetry. In short, he became interested in the discovery, the invention, and the definition of his self; and he attempted to incorporate into his work the contemporary forms, myths, and metaphors which describe the individual imagination. (230–31)

So it was that five years after this initial period of acute interest in "the discovery, the invention...of the self" *Life Studies* was published, a book when reviewed by Rosenthal that received such criticism as: "...my first impression while reading *Life Studies* was that it is impure art, magnificently stated but unpleasantly egocentric—somehow resembling the triumph of the skunks over the garbage cans. Since its self-therapeutic motive is so obvious and persistent, something of this impression sticks all the way" (154). But for Lowell, his poetry written in a new (to him) style—even if intended as a kind of psychoanalysis as both Martin and Rosenthal propose—was foremost the appropriate manner by which to render his autobiographical accounts in verse. He said to Frederick Seidel: "...if a poem is autobiographical you want the reader to say, this is true.... [T]he reader was to believe he was getting [in *Life Studies*] the *real* Robert Lowell" (349), the *real* Robert Lowell, that is, which is the poet's self as represented in those same poems. That Lowell intended this self as sincere (as opposed to authentic) is evident by his suggestion that "the reader was to believe" it was truth he or she was reading. These experiences based on Lowell's autobiography, then, had to be veracious— they had to present an "illusion of veracity" (as Dave Smith will remark about James Wright's poems later in this chapter).

Lowell's change in style from *Lord Weary's Castle* (1946) may have been to ensure that his concern for self ("his interest in autobiography," as Martin wrote) would not be obscured by the poetic forms of that book, even though those poems—written more than a decade before the publication of *Life Studies*—showed Lowell's early predilection for self-definition. "The major modes of *Lord Weary's Castle*," Martin has argued, "are (1) the definition of the individual through suprapersonal structures and (2) the dramatization of the self's terrifying alienation from these through the divorce of observation from feeling and of sensibility from culture" (221).

Yet Allen Tate focused his remarks on the obvious surface changes in form in the poetry of *Life Studies* from that of *Lord Weary's Castle*, and when he read it in manuscript, admonished Lowell not to publish the book:

> ...*all* the poems about your family, including the one about you and Eliza-beth, are definitely bad. I do not think you ought to publish them. You didn't ask me whether they ought to be published, but I put the matter from this point of view in order to underline my anxiety about them.... The free verse, arbitrary and without rhythm, reflects this lack of imaginative focus. Your fine poems in the past present a formal ordering of highly intractable materi-als: but there is an imaginative thrust towards a symbolic order which these new poems seem to lack. The new ones sound to me like messages to your-self...and you are letting these scattered items of experience have their full impact upon your sensibility. (Qtd. in Hamilton 237)

Tate's remarks illustrate the apparently unresolvable disparities between the po-etic sensibilities of the New Critical school and personal poets of open form that were discussed in the first chapter. Tate and John Crowe Ransom had significantly influenced the younger Lowell. Ransom, Martin writes, "set the self-consciously Aristotelian, anti-Romantic, ceremonious, and politically orthodox intellectual tone. Ransom's New Critical emphasis on wit and paradox, Tate's 'attempts to make poetry much more formal...to write in meters but to make the meters look hard [as Lowell said] and make them hard to write'"—among other influences— "permanently affected" Lowell's poetry (213–14). Tate, then, was correct in ob-serving that Lowell's more pronounced concern for autobiography altered his ar-tistic sensibility. Lowell had to find a way to order his poetry now that form alone could not dictate "when to stop rambling," as he remarked to William Carlos Wil-liams. However, the narrative structure—an organizational method implicit in any autobiographically based work—often provided the closure he sought, a structure which thwarted his reliance on the more "symbolic order" Tate urged, but also one which helped to establish the sincerity of the piece—essential for the success of any poem of the confessional mode, as already has been noted.

Poems from *Lord Weary's Castle* such as "Winter in Dunbarton," "Mary Winslow," and "In Memory of Arthur Winslow" are personal in that they express the poet's familial loss. The speaker of "In Memory of Arthur Winslow"—using "Arthur" as the initiating impulse for self-contemplation—"achieves," as Martin has noted, "a dramatic ecstasy of awareness; and mediating between the closed and open worlds, he speaks for himself" (222), so that even the more formal verse of this volume could include Lowell's personal analysis of selfhood, of the self in relation to Arthur Winslow—*as* Winslow even. Yet Eliot's impersonality theory—

as adapted by Tate and Ransom—informed Lowell's aesthetic at this point, it seems (even in these more personal poems), to the extent of relegating the importance of the speaker's role in the poem as secondary to its subject, and often to the syllable count. Eliot's other dictum—that "poetry must not stray too far from the ordinary everyday language which we use and hear"—was pretty much ignored by the Lowell of *Lord Weary's Castle*. The following descriptive passage from "Winter in Dunbarton" serves as illustration:

> With muck and winter dropsy, where the tall
> Snow-monster wipes the coke-fumes from his eyes
> And scatters his corruption and it lies
> Gaping until the fungus-eyeballs fall
> Into this eldest of the seasons....

In contrast to this earlier style, here are passages from the poem "Dunbarton," one of the many poems based on Lowell's autobiography included in *Life Studies*. Some people mistakenly referred to Lowell's grandfather as his father, about which the poem's confessional speaker says:

> They meant my Grandfather.

> He was my Father. I was his son.
> On our yearly autumn get-aways from Boston
> to the family graveyard in Dunbarton,
> he took the wheel himself—
> like an admiral at the helm....

> We stopped at the Priscilla in Nashua
> for brownies and root-beer,
> and later "pumped ship" together in the Indian Summer....

> Grandfather and I
> raked leaves from our dead forebears,
> defied the dank weather
> with "dragon" bonfires....

> In the mornings I cuddled like a paramour
> in my Grandfather's bed,
> while he scouted about the chattering greenwood stove.

The setting of this poem is clear. We are told it is a particular autumn at Dunbarton and the family burial site, the autumn "when Uncle Devereux died." The season in this poem is marked by raking and burning the fallen leaves. In "Winter in

Dunbarton" from *Lord Weary's Castle*—a poem of similar setting (although, as the poem's title informs us, the season is different and it is the object of the poem)—winter was seen as "fat with muck and winter dropsy." One difference between the two poems (which marks their contrasting styles) is that in "Dunbarton" Lowell relies on action to make the setting more visual; he uses action verbs rather than nouns such as "muck" and "dropsy."

The speaker of "Dunbarton," who is the adult Lowell—represented by the confessional "I"—remembering a childhood experience, conveys the world of Dunbarton as seen by Lowell the child. This is accomplished partly by the narrative structure of the poem. The story begins with the drive from Boston to Dunbarton, mentions the stops along the way, and ends inside Grandfather's house. Each of these points in the narrative is characterized by an action exciting and impressionable to a child. During the car ride, Grandfather (the child's father substitute; Lowell's father was a naval commander—here Grandfather is "like an admiral at the helm"), "chuckling over the gas he was saving, / ...let his motor roller-coaster / out of control down each hill," and once they stop for brownies and root beer; at Dunbarton they make bonfires, the child captures salamanders, and so forth. Unlike "Winter in Dunbarton" in which the time of the cat's death—the central catalyst for that poem's objective correlative—is unclear (we are not certain whether an adult speaker is remembering back when, in childhood, the cat died, or if in adulthood the cat's death spawned memories of the past—nor is this necessary, for the poem's intention is to present the cat as the principal object acting to evoke a certain winter), the dominating presence of the speaker in "Dunbarton"—often as the center of action—defines the poem's dramatic situation, which is the uncle's death and the absence of the child's real father.

Scene and object, then, are the foci of "Winter in Dunbarton" whereas the speaker is the primary focus of "Dunbarton" in that the poem's drama ultimately relates to the speaker's reaction to it. "Dunbarton" is a poem which takes the speaker's self as its subject; the story and concerns presented in the poem are the speaker's. (In "Winter," the cat and the season are the poem's bi-focus.) The speaker Lowell, as the child in "Dunbarton," was affected by the death of his favorite uncle, who died just when his father was away. His grandfather, therefore, provided the love he needed ("I cuddled like a paramour / in my Grandfather's bed"), and the Lowell speaker felt that he, in return, solaced his grandfather in the time of mourning the loss of a son: "My grandfather found / his grandchild's fogbound solitudes / sweeter than human society." This bond between grandfather and grandchild, coupled with the child's "Daddy on sea-duty in the Pacific," led the adult Lowell speaker to conclude that his grandfather was, just then, "my

Father. I was his son." Since "Dunbarton" is personal, self-exploratory, the voice—recognizably "the *real* Robert Lowell"—is the center of the poem, not scene or form or symbols as in "Winter." That is, "Dunbarton" serves as our first example of the expression of Lowell's "*real*" public self. The voice is of the confessional mode because the narrative structure, the poem's dramatic focus resting on the speaker, and the speaker's sincerity of tone both contribute in recounting an experience of seeming veracity. "Dunbarton" is confessional not solely because the poem's subject is inextricably linked to Lowell's autobiography. The poem, which relates a believable personal incident, uses "I" as its speaker so that the speaker is directly identified with that which he depicts—which is the premise of any poem of this mode, as suggested by the definition explained in chapter 1.

Although Lowell is now regarded as a poet of autobiography, few poems written before *Life Studies* clearly betray his exploration of self (as does "Dunbarton"), even though many moved toward such personal examination—the poems from *Lord Weary's Castle*, for example, previously mentioned. As he became more preoccupied with his "self-therapeutic motive," Lowell increasingly emphasized the proselike clarity of his poetry, as Martin has informed us and as seen by his change in diction from "Winter in Dunbarton," published first by Ransom in a 1945 issue of *Kenyon Review,* to "Dunbarton" from the 1959 *Life Studies.* Regarding the work of Williams as the influence for his new style (he wrote to Williams: "I feel more and more technically indebted to you..."), Lowell reduced significantly the number of symbolic allusions in his poems, and his diction moved closer to Eliot's call for "ordinary everyday language." He made these alterations in his aesthetic to free his work of the complexities common to what he termed as his "old New Critical religious, symbolic poems, many published during the war." He found that "audiences didn't understand" these poems and confided that: "I didn't always understand myself while reading [others' poems]." Specifically, as he gave readings, Lowell changed some of the components of prosody such as line measure in those New Critical poems he had published years before. These changes came at a time when "poetry reading was sublimated by the practice of Allen Ginsberg.... Much good poetry is unsuited to audience-performance; mine was incomprehensible" (25), he told Ian Hamilton in an interview. Lowell explained to Seidel what he then did: "I went on a trip to the West Coast and read at least once a day...and more and more I found that I was simplifying my poems. If I had a Latin quotation I'd translate it into English. If adding a couple of syllables in a line made it clearer I'd add them, and I'd make little changes just impromptu.... I began to have a certain disrespect for the tight forms. If you could make it easier by just changing syllables, then why not" (345)?

This is not to argue, however, that one style is superior to the other (as many commentators have done), or that—as already noted—Lowell's more formal verse could not be personal. Robert Hass remarked:

> ...I still find myself blinking incredulously when I read—in almost anything written about the poetry—that those early poems "clearly reflect the dictates of the new criticism," while the later ones are "less consciously wrought and extremely intimate." This is the view in which it is "more intimate" and "less conscious" to say "my mind's not right" than to imagine the moment when
>
> > The death-lance churns into the sanctuary, tears
> > The gun-blue swingle, heaving like a flail,
> > And hacks the coiling life out...
>
> which is to get things appallingly wrong. (6)

And Jay Martin properly asserts:

> Lowell's poetic manner has changed drastically... His earliest verse was characterized by a tone of baroque exaltation... By the sixties, Lowell's poetry had experienced many modifications. No longer oratorical and less pointedly symbolic, it might be dramatic... Or intensely personal, even confessional—as in "Fourth of July in Maine"... Despite such striking external shifts, all of Lowell's work exhibits the same preoccupations. His basic subject has always been the fate of selfhood in time, and his basic method the examination of the convergence in man of past history and present circumstance. (210–11)

I would add to these remarks that the Lowell of *Life Studies*, and after, increasingly explored the convergence in himself of his own past history, and therefore used the confessional mode of voice to define that self in verse.

Because Lowell's blatant aesthetic transformation accompanied his interest for self—work which many poets, who came into prominence after Lowell, regarded as the precursor of their personal verse of the confessional mode—it will be useful to trace briefly the development of this aspect of his technique. Both the poetic climate of the late 1950s and Lowell's introspection contributed to his style change. Contrary to Tate's argument that the personal poetry written in open forms lacked an "imaginative focus," Lowell's subject—his self—provided the imaginative impulse for his work, and the loosened forms helped to shape it into the type of "understandable" poetry he wanted to write. The poetry of *Life Studies* originated from autobiographical prose pieces Lowell began in 1955—at his therapist's suggestion—to help him recover from the breakdown he experienced the year before. The idea was that prose was more relaxing for Lowell to write; he was to avoid the long periods of unrelieved excitement that usually accompanied his writing poetry. "His new therapist had encouraged him to adopt a strict daily regime.... The prose 'reminiscences' were a way of cementing Lowell's new, time-tabled calm—prose, Lowell found, need not thrive on bouts of high 'enthusiasm,'" reports Hamilton (220). So Lowell originally intended to present in prose all the autobiographical material of *Life Studies*. But he "found it got awfully tedious working out transitions and putting in things that didn't seem very important but were necessary to the prose continuity. Also," he told Seidel, "I found it hard to revise" (346). The surviving prose piece is "91 Revere Street," part 2 of *Life Studies.*

Later, in 1971, he was to reflect on what he termed "meter and matter." When the matter of his poetry was autobiographical recollection, he chose a "formless," proselike construction, but when it encompassed public affairs, he required a "fixed form." He told Hamilton: "Much of *Life Studies* is recollection; *Notebook* mixes the day-to-day with the history...." And referring to his fourteen-line stanza units of *Notebook* (revised version 1970), he stated, "I didn't find fourteen lines handcuffs. I gained more than I gave. It would have been a worry never to have known when a section must end; variation might have been monotony. Formlessness might have crowded me toward consecutive narrative" (13). Lowell's implication is that his autobiographical poetry, which is written in open forms, is "formless" and therefore requires a narrative structure to order it. Of course since his intention in *Life Studies* was to tell part of his life's story in verse, he had to assume the narrative approach—often, as it is applied to certain groups of poems in *Life Studies*, a "consecutive narrative" sequence, though not necessarily a day by day account. Because he wished to keep the "public" subjects of *Notebook* from becoming a type of narrative, daily journal, Lowell believed that his consistent use of the more regular stanza units, rather than his narrative, would provide the form.

So the choice of subject dictated the form of his poetry written after the early collections. Concerning the personal poems of *Life Studies*, Lowell made this comment in his essay "After Enjoying Six or Seven Essays on Me," written just before his death in 1977:

> I found I had no language or meter that would allow me to approximate what
> I saw or remembered. Yet in prose I had already found what I wanted, the
> conventional style of autobiography and reminiscence. So I wrote my auto-
> biographical poetry in a style I thought I had discovered in Flaubert, one that
> used images and ironic or amusing particulars. I did all kinds of tricks with
> meter and the avoidance of meter. When I didn't have to bang words into

> rhyme and count, I was more nakedly dependent on rhythm. After this, in the
> *Union Dead*, I used the same style but with less amusement, and with more
> composition and stanza-structure. Each poem was meant to stand by itself.
> This stronger structure would probably have ruined *Life Studies*. Which
> would have lost its novelistic flow. Later on in *For the Union Dead*, free verse
> subjects seemed to melt away, and I found myself back in strict meter, yet
> tried to avoid the symbols and heroics of my first books. (114)

These remarks are particularly insightful because they are made from the advantageous perspective of Lowell's reflecting back on the body of his work after he was some years distant from it. He reaffirms that metered verse would not accommodate his autobiographical subject matter which he wanted conveyed in the conversational manner of prose, and structured in a narrative of "novelistic flow." And when his subjects shifted to something less personal—as in some of the poems in *For the Union Dead* (1964)—he returned to "strict meter." This practice further supplements his theory regarding the use of the fourteen-line stanza in *Notebook*. As he commented in his essay in *Naked Poetry*: "The joy and strength of unscanned verse is that it can be as natural as conversation or prose, or can follow the rhythm of the ear that knows no measure. Yet often a poem only becomes a poem and worth writing because it has struggled with fixed meters and rhymes. I can't understand how any poet, who has written both metered and unmetered poems, would be willing to settle for one and give up the other" (124).

The "rhythm of the ear" that Lowell mentioned relates back to his conclusion (as stated in the passage about *Life Studies*) that his "avoidance of meter" and of "rhyme and count" resulted in a dependence on rhythm—which is to note that his verse in open forms remained "poetic," artful, as opposed to being "bad prose hacked into arbitrary line-lengths," to use Ezra Pound's phrase. In his interview with Seidel after *Life Studies* was published, Lowell remarked that his poems in that book were no less crafted than his earlier poems in meter and rhyme, and no less hard to write:

> They're not always factually true. There's a good deal of tinkering with fact.
> You leave out a lot, and emphasize this and not that. Your actual experience is
> a complete flux. I've invented facts and changed things, and the whole balance of the poem was something invented. So there's a lot of artistry, I hope,
> in the poems. Yet there's this thing: if a poem is autobiographical...you want
> the reader to say, this is true. (349)

The effect of presenting the "real Robert Lowell," then, sometimes required straying from the autobiographical facts. It seems Lowell knew what Bruce Weigl—a contemporary personal poet—contends: that "for a poet, relying too heavily upon autobiographical detail, structure, context, or strategy can be a dangerous thing. Such a dependence can lull the writer into focusing too much attention on being true to actuality and not enough attention on the poem itself: on the language and on the possibilities of surprise that should always accompany the act of writing poems" (113). These remarks of Weigl, when writing of a book of personal poems by another contemporary poet, illuminate Lowell's reasoning. At present, it is common for poets working in open forms to comment on how grammatical phrases should mark line-breaks: Do not, they contend, end a line with a preposition. Others rely on the "breath line," practicing their theory that a line only should be as long as can be read aloud in a single breath; some argue for more complex syntactic units to measure the line, and so forth. Consequently, contemporary personal poetry—much of which betrays Lowell's influence—really is not completely "free," but is often restricted to these technical principles. Yet it remains "open," not confined to specific rhyme and meter schemes. These aesthetic guides originated in part from Lowell who governed his personal poetry with his special artistry, the "rhythm of his ear"—which many *Life Studies* reviewers failed to notice—and in order to maintain this rhythm at times meant sacrificing or altering his autobiographical details. This is why Lowell's personal voice is sincere, but hardly authentic.

Lowell sensed that by abandoning the meter and rhyme forms, he would become "nakedly dependent on rhythm," and he trusted to his ear to regulate the sound of his personal poetry. But—although many reviews were favorable—several critics felt that the *Life Studies* poems had neither form nor rhythm, and some were reluctant even to call it poetry. The book was first published in England by Faber and Faber and most of the British reviewers felt that Lowell's verse suffered by the style change from his earlier work. Frank Kermode, in his essay in *The Spectator* (May 1, 1959), remarked that "the sequence 'Life Studies,' which is the greater part of this book, strikes one as the work of a poet so sure of his powers that he does not recognize the danger of lapsing into superior doggerel when he too luxuriously controls it." And Philip Larkin wrote that the poems of the "Life Studies" section of the book were "curious, hurried, off-hand vignettes, seeming too personal to be practised..." (*The Manchester Guardian Weekly*, May 21, 1959). When the book was published in the United States, most reviews were cautious to endorse Lowell's new style of "prosaic quality," as Richard Eberhart termed it, even though he praised the book in general. Rosenthal (in *The Nation*, September 19, 1959) called it "impure art." I write of these comments to illustrate how critics assumed that Lowell's personal poetry in open forms was a lessening

of the art; and, aided by Lowell's own remark about the "formlessness" of his autobiographical poetry, many believed that matters of the self were best left to
prose.

Conversely, however, in studying the art of the poetry in *Life Studies*, we see
that personal poetry can in fact be "formed" by language rhythms and by the use
of a confessional voice. We know that Lowell made poetry from his autobiographical prose. Not only did he transform that prose into verse, but his first drafts were
often in traditional forms. He said to Seidel:

> ...when I was writing *Life Studies*, a good number of the poems were started
> in very strict meter, and I found that, more than the rhymes, the regular beat
> was what I didn't want. I have a long poem in there about my father, called
> "Commander Lowell," which actually is largely in couplets. Well, with that
> form it's hard not to have echoes of Marvell. That regularity just seemed to
> ruin the honesty of sentiment, and became rhetorical; it said, "I'm a poem"—
> though it was a great help when I was revising this original skeleton. I could
> keep the couplets where I wanted them and drop them where I didn't; there'd
> be a form to come back to. (345–46)

Lowell made at least two significant points here about the style of his personal poetry: His foremost intention was to preserve the integrity of the poem (the "regularity" of a fixed form "just seemed to ruin the honesty of sentiment"), and his
work in open forms did not disregard entirely some elements of the fixed form—
the rhymed couplet for example—which he considered useful in crafting the
poem. Here are two passages from the first stanza of the final version of "Commander Lowell":

> There were no undesirables or girls of my set,
> when I was a boy at Mattapoisett—
> only Mother, still her Father's daughter....
> And I, bristling and manic,
> skulked in the attic,
> and got two hundred French generals by name,
> from *A* to *V*—from Augereau to Vandamme.
> I used to dope myself asleep,
> naming those unpronounceables like sheep.

The "four-foot" measures are gone; the syllable count varies greatly from one line
to the next—from fifteen to five—and Lowell does not adhere to any regular foot
stress much more than a line at a time. But he does retain many of his end-
rhymes, and most of the poem is written in these modified couplets. The rhymed

couplet is the most obvious argument to disclaim the charge that Lowell's use of language in *Life Studies* is without rhythm, that it is the language of prose, not poetry. Yet these rhythms do not detract from the speaker's sincerity in presenting the poem either.

Lowell also sustained rhythms in other poems in the book by the more subtle methods of internal line rhymes, alliteration, and assonance. The third stanza of "Skunk Hour" uses all three:

> The season's ill—
> we've lost our summer millionaire,
> who seemed to leap from an L. L. Bean
> catalogue. His nine-knot yawl
> was auctioned off to lobstermen.
> A red fox stain covers Blue Hill.

The "ill/Hill" rhyme neatly encloses the stanza, and also correspondingly rhymes with "millionaire," "L. L. Bean," and "yawl." Lowell's heavy use of the alliterative "l" sound in "lost," "leap," "catalogue," and "lobstermen" also relates to the "ll" rhyme pattern. And the "a" and "o" assonance of "His nine-knot yawl / was auctioned off to lobstermen" creates the sound of speech of the summer millionaire with his New England accent. Speaking aloud "nine-knot yawl" is difficult to do *without* sounding like a New Englander, in fact. And "Skunk Hour" nearly forces one to read it aloud. The "s" sounds in "season's," "summer," and "seemed" running through the stanza—ending with "fox stain covers"—paces slowly one's enunciation and thereby forces the resemblance to Maine speech. So Lowell's aesthetic provides his readers with a better sense of his subject as well as gives his poem the "form" of sound and rhythm he felt it needed. "Skunk Hour" exemplifies Robert Frost's theory of "sound and sense"—that sound can engender or augment meaning. Sometimes for Lowell, his poem's subject dictated a form which utilized these devices of sound—devices which establish the tone of sincerity.

He could never make his poems completely "naked." That is, he could not write without some use of sound or rhyme because, as Hamilton has written, "rhyme and meter were for him very close to *being* the 'natural speech' that William Carlos Williams and his followers were always calling for. The iambic pentameter was not an external, imposed literary method; after three books, it had become compulsive utterance. And it was probably harder for Lowell to discard rhymes than to invent them" (231–32). All his theorizing over "meter and matter" may be misleading then. Although his distinction is sound, Lowell's personal poems are not quite formless—even if they are without strict meter—nor are they less artful than his public poems. He said: "the style of autobiography...used images and ironic or amusing particulars...tricks with meter...." The careful diction of his personal poems—the sounds created by the order of words, the conversational tones of the language—helps to identify the voice.

The form Lowell's poetry takes often is determined by its content. So a poem from *Life Studies* in open form with an "I" narrator usually has a confessional voice, relating an experience derived from Lowell's personal history—even if some of the details are not wholly factual. As we have seen from the comparison of "Winter in Dunbarton" to "Dunbarton," it is Lowell's direct use of autobiography as part of his aesthetic as well as his language use that ultimately formulates the voice of his personal poetry. Rhyme and sound are used in his personal poems to help clarify the meaning and to center the poem around its speaker.

Both "Commander Lowell" and "Skunk Hour" reveal highly personal matter, and both use different poetic devices to create their particular sounds. In "Skunk Hour" Lowell used the sound of the poem as part of his subject in order to evoke a better sense of his characterization; in "Commander Lowell" he relied on the rhymes to help form the poem. In either case, all parts of his aesthetic— the forms, rhythms, etc.—contribute to the making of a distinctive voice in his poetry of "autobiography and reminiscence."

The various components of Lowell's open form aesthetic all work toward the common concern of conveying his autobiography, and it is this purpose that distinguishes the voice of his personal poetry from the voices of his earlier work, his "American version of heroic poetry." Lowell wrote in "After Enjoying Six or Seven Essays on Me":

> Looking over my *Selected Poems*, about thirty years of writing, my impression is that the thread that strings it together is my autobiography, it is a small-scale *Prelude*, written in many different styles and with digressions, yet a continuing story—still wayfaring. (113)

His concern for a personal history returned Lowell back again and again to the writing of autobiographical poetry. After *Life Studies* was completed, he said: "I don't think that a personal history can go on forever, unless you're Walt Whitman and have a way with you. I feel I've done enough personal poetry. That doesn't mean I won't do more of it, but I don't want to do more now." But *For the Union Dead*, his next book, opens with such personal poems as "Water," "The Old Flame," and "Middle Age." It is true that *For the Union Dead* is less intimately autobiographical than the section of "Life Studies" poems in the previous collection, but the voice in most of the poems in *Union* remains sincere, "the *real* Robert Lowell."

In a reading he gave at the Poetry Center of the New York YM-YWHA in April 1968, he said: "The poems I'm going to read have this peculiarity: that they're all in the first person and the first person is me, not an imaginary me though you always lie a bit and invent." He then proceeded to read the following poems from *Union*: "The Mouth of the Hudson," "July in Washington"—in both, he said, "the person isn't very important, it's an observer.... There's two things I like very much: an 'I' that's yourself more or less so you can feel what you're saying, possibly, and the place that is a place you can take in in some way"—and "Middle Age," a poem, he said, "about my father. And I think when someone's died, when your father's died, that perhaps your different memories you have of him merge into one theory. He was in his early thirties when I first remember him, and he was sixty-two when he died. But I remember him as something—as some composite age which would have been forty-five. When I wrote the poem I was forty-five myself, and then it's very easy... to identify with him, to feel I was walking in his shoes and sort of doomed to the same advantages and disadvantages in character." So his practice of personal poetry continued in *Union*; some poems were personal in the sense that he knew well the places described in them, and some were more directly personal like "Middle Age" in which Lowell's seeing himself in his father's role engenders the impetus for what finally becomes a type of self-definition.

Lowell's distinction between the "I" as observer of place and the "I" as the primary focus of the poem provides an effectual starting point for an analysis of his confessional voice in the autobiographical poetry of *Life Studies* and *For the Union Dead*. Let us begin with two poems that have Lowell's personal voice as their centers, both from *Life Studies*: "Waking in the Blue" and "Memories of West Street and Lepke." Begun in early 1958 during his first week in the locked ward Lowell occupied at McLean's Mental Hospital outside Boston, "Waking in the Blue" initially describes the attendant and other occupants of the ward, then in the final stanzas fixes on the Lowell speaker, the voice of the poem:

> Absence! My heart grows tense
> as though a harpoon were sparring for the kill.
> (This is the house for the "mentally ill.")...
>
> I grin at Stanley, now sunk in his sixties,
> once a Harvard all-American fullback...
> still hoarding the build of a boy in his twenties...

with the muscle of a seal
in his long tub...
he thinks only of his figure,
of slimming on sherbert and ginger ale—
more cut off from words than a seal.

This is the way day breaks in Bowditch Hall at McLean's;
the hooded night lights bring out "Bobbie,"
a replica of Louis XVI
without the wig—
redolent and roly-poly as a sperm whale,
as he swashbuckles about in his birthday suit...

    Cock of the walk,
I strut in my turtle-necked French sailor's jersey
before the metal shaving mirrors,
and see the shaky future grow familiar
in the pinched, indigenous faces
of these thoroughbred mental cases,
twice my age and half my weight.
We are all old-timers,
each of us holds a locked razor.

Again, the rhymes and off-rhymes are present in some of the unmeasured couplets—kill/ill, ale/seal, faces/cases, and the triplet mirrors/timers/razor. And some lines also contain sounds of alliteration and assonance, though occasionally just barely (the "s" and "t" rhythms of "I strut in my turtle-necked French sailor's jersey," for example, are not as apparent perhaps as the "ol" sound in "redolent and roly-poly as a sperm whale"). Yet the effect of the poem is close enough to Lowell's desired conversational prose of novelistic flow: "roly-poly" and "cock of the walk" typify the clichéd speech abundant in conversation.

The narrative—Lowell waking in the morning, observing the others, having breakfast—structures "Waking in the Blue"; there is a gradual progression toward the poem's climax, which is Lowell's realization that "each of us holds a locked razor," a direct comparison between himself and his fellow patients whom he has just depicted rather disparagingly. Even though the final two lines nearly make a measured, end-rhymed couplet, they retain the conversational manner which creates an intimate communication between Lowell and us; we are privy to his new self-awareness—here he "weeps with one eye on the camera" as Simpson remarked of confessional verse in general. "Each of us" could then mean that everyone is mentally imbalanced in some way; no one is perfectly sane.

Because we know that the voice is that of Lowell's public self, the situation he describes at McLean's and his assessment of his mental condition at the time of his stay there are sentimental, and this establishes, in part, the sincerity of that voice. The proselike qualities of conversational tones of language and narrative progression, which allow for the presence of the speaker in the poem (just as they did in "Dunbarton"), create the intimacy between the voice and reader upon which the success of the poem's climax is dependent. These qualities, then, help to make the voice of the confessional mode—the "I" speaker's direct expression to us of a seemingly veracious experience.

In the poetry about the self written in the confessional mode, the aesthetic principles—such as conversational language and narrative—work together to illuminate the personal voice. And, more particularly, in the personal poems of Lowell, we know enough of his life to recognize his experience in them which, combined with his admission that his "I" is not an imagined narrator but himself (albeit his public self), reveals a confessional voice: the poet, who is the voice of the poem, speaking as himself, his sincere self. It is part of Lowell's aesthetic, too, to select carefully which autobiographical details to include in "Waking in the Blue." He does not, certainly, portray all the patients who were with him in the ward, but only those who best reflect certain physical aspects of himself or his own behavioral tendencies: Stanley, who "thinks only of his figure," is "more cut off from words than a seal"; and "roly-poly" Bobbie "swashbuckles about" naked. Although—as I have mentioned—Lowell started this poem in his first week at McLean's, he was frustrated with his attempts. The language was too relaxed, chatty, and lacking the fine rhythm of the published version which he did not complete until months after his release. Consequently it would have been easy for Lowell to regard himself, at least momentarily, "cut off from words" like Stanley. And Lowell struts in front of the shaving mirrors, regarding himself as the "cock of the walk" when earlier he calls Bobbie's swashbuckling a display of "bravado." Stanley is vain about his figure; Lowell is proud to be a strong two hundred pounds, able to put away "a hearty New England breakfast." Lowell, in the final stanza, realizes his "shaky" future which he sees reflected in his fellow patients' "pinched, indigenous faces": He is one of them, revelling in youthful accomplishments (one of the "victorious figures"), every bit as "thoroughbred" as the other mental cases from Harvard and the Porcellian Club. In the final lines, then, the speaker Lowell is as "naked" as Bobbie. That is, he stands before himself stripped of the illusion that, because he is half their age and twice their weight, he is better off. Neither his sense of humor nor how he views others can set him apart from them. Each mental patient must shave before a metal mirror, not glass, and each "holds a locked razor"; no one is regarded more sane than another. Lowell balances this poem (recall his statement that he altered the facts in his autobiographical verse so that "the whole balance of the poem was something invented") between Stanley, Bobbie, and the self he depicts in the poem, the result of which is a final centering on the personal voice—the speaker—of the poem. So the last lines are acutely personal, intense, pathetic even, because of their tone of honesty as well as their placement at the end of a balanced narrative—both resulting from Lowell's aesthetic decisions while composing the poem. This point will become even more important later in the chapter when I discuss Wright's and Sexton's personal poetry without the aid of the extensive biographical information that is available on Lowell.

"Memories of West Street and Lepke" is constructed in a similar manner as "Waking in the Blue." Lowell's recollection in verse of his (factual) imprisonment at West Street begins with his fellow inmates, and his relationship to them:

> Given a year,
> I walked on the roof of the West Street Jail, a short
> enclosure like my school soccer court,
> and saw the Hudson River once a day
> through sooty clothesline entanglements
> and bleaching khaki tenements.
> Strolling, I yammered metaphysics with Abramowitz…
> so vegetarian,
> he wore rope shoes and preferred fallen fruit. He tried
> to convert Bioff and Brown,
> the Hollywood pimps, to his diet.…
> they blew their tops and beat him black and blue.
>
> I was so out of things, I'd never heard
> of the Jehovah's Witnesses.
> "Are you a C. O.?" I asked a fellow jailbird. "No," he
> answered, "I'm a J. W."
> …*Murder Incorporated*'s Czar Lepke,
> there piling towels on a rack,
> or dawdling off to his little segregated cell full of things
> forbidden the common man:
> a portable radio, a dresser, two toy American flags tied
> together with a ribbon of Easter palm.…
>   lobotomized,
> …no agonizing reappraisal
> jarred his concentration on the electric chair—

hanging like an oasis in his air
of lost connections....

It is necessary to recount some history before discussing the poem. Lowell's date for his induction in the army was September 8, 1943. As early as December 1941, he had been trying to enlist but had been turned away on six separate occasions because of his poor vision. Yet after the seventh physical examination—and with the United States now in the middle of the war—the army found Lowell fit to serve. The day before he was to report, however, he wrote to President Roosevelt refusing "the opportunity," he said, "you offer me...for service in the Armed Forces," and he filed a Declaration of Personal Responsibility as a conscientious objector with the U.S. District Attorney in New York. He told the President: "You will understand how painful such a decision is for an American whose family traditions, like your own, have always found their fulfillment in maintaining, through responsible participation in both the civil and the military services, our country's freedom and honor." He expounds these sentiments in his Declaration. Claiming that his participation in the war would not be "responsible," he argued:

> ...members of my family had served in all our wars since the Declaration of Independence: I thought—our tradition of service is sensible and noble; if its occasional exploitation by Money, Politics and Imperialism is allowed to seriously discredit it, we are doomed.... In 1941 we undertook a patriotic war to preserve our lives, our fortunes, and our sacred honor against the lawless aggressions of a totalitarian league: in 1943 we are collaborating with the most unscrupulous and powerful of totalitarian dictators to destroy law, freedom, democracy, and above all, our continued national sovereignty.... I cannot honorably participate in a war whose prosecution, as far as I can judge, constitutes a betrayal of my country. (Qtd. in Hamilton 86–9)

These last remarks help to explain Lowell's change in attitude from two years earlier concerning his service in the army.

As a consequence of his refusal, Lowell was sentenced to one year and one day in the Federal Correctional Center at Danbury, Connecticut. He was held for a few days in the West Street Jail in New York before being transferred to Danbury, and the tough jail proved to be a shocking and lasting experience for the "American whose family traditions" resembled Roosevelt's. An inmate of West Street at the time Lowell was there remembers:

> Lowell was in a cell next to Lepke, you know, Murder Incorporated, and Lepke says to him: "I'm in for killing. What are you in for?" "Oh, I'm in for

refusing to kill." And Lepke burst out laughing. It was kind of ironic. (Qtd. in
Hamilton 91)

Knowing this history augments one's understanding of "Memories of West
Street and Lepke," just as the biographical documentation supplemented the
reading of "Waking in the Blue." It suggests a confirmation that the voice of the
poem is narrating an experience from the poet's autobiography. Knowing something of Lowell's upbringing also illuminates his choice of details in the poem:
Boston's "hardly passionate Marlborough Street," the "bull pen," the Republican
filth scavenger, and the "Negro boy with curlicues of marijuana in his hair," a pac-
ifist, the pimps, a Jehovah's Witness, Lepke—a varied assortment of places and
characters. In an early draft of the prose autobiography he worked on in 1955—
material that he later drew from for his *Life Studies* poems—Lowell wrote that he
reflected on his rather privileged childhood while recovering from one of his
breakdowns:

> …after six or seven weeks at the Payne-Whitney Clinic, my bluster and manic
> antics died away. Images of my spoiled childhood ached inside me, and I
> would lean with my chin in my hand, and count the rustling poplars below
> me, which lined the hospital driveway and led out to the avenues of Manhat-
> tan, to life. (Qtd. in Hamilton 221)

In "91 Revere Street," writing of one of those images of his childhood, Lowell described his physical education at the private Brimmer School he attended: "On
the roof of our school building, there was an ugly concrete area that looked as if it
had been intended for the top floor of a garage. Here we played tag, drew lines
with chalk, and chose up sides for a kind of kids' soccer" (26). Although Joseph
Bennett in *Hudson Review* (1959) thought Lowell's poems betrayed a snobbishness ("…we visit an insane asylum for Porcellian members; our jail in New York
reminds us of the soccer court at St. Mark's school"), one of Lowell's intentions—
in these "self-therapeutic" poems—was to contrast his privileged upbringing with
what he experienced in adulthood, and thereby learn, as he did finally in "Waking
in the Blue," that being educated in private schools cannot prevent mental collapse, nor, as "Memories" indicates, prepare one for sharing a cell with pimps and
murderers. Rather than betray a snobbishness, the poems show how Lowell
changed, how these experiences of incarceration helped to "unspoil" him, so that
as he reflected back on them while at the Payne-Whitney Clinic, his "spoiled
childhood ached inside" him in contrast.

Aside from these facts of biography, his poetry tells us that he was trying to
overcome a spoiled childhood whose trappings extended to adulthood: in "Home

After Three Months Away," he says "I keep no rank nor station"; and a close reading of "Memories" reveals that Lowell acknowledged the contrast between his privileged lifestyle and that of others not listed in the Boston Social Register, as Lowell's family was. The narrative of "Memories," formed in part by a flashback, allows for a reverie which concludes with the speaker's understanding that he has matured because of his time in jail. So that now, long since freed and back in his Boston home, he can appreciate his privileges, but not as a spoiled child might. The biographical material on Lowell, then, regarding this instance, is superfluous; the poem's narrative structure allows for the inclusion of any background information necessary to understand "Memories."

As the poem begins, the narrator Lowell is at leisure: Only teaching one day a week, he has sufficient time to read and lounge in his pajamas in a large house he "hogs" in a (then) fashionable area of Boston ("hardly passionate Marlborough Street" is a line of William James). This situation initiates the speaker Lowell's memory of the time he spent in prison where his cramped living quarters were not so ideal. He reflects on his "seedtime" (from book 1 of Wordsworth's *Prelude*: "Fair seed-time had my soul, and I grew up / Foster'd alike by beauty and by fear"), his time of growth, which—now that he is forty—he can be "positively ironic about," as Louis Simpson suggested in *A Revolution in Taste*. (Simpson regarded *Life Studies* as Lowell's "portrait of an artist as a young man," and "Memories" makes this claim reasonable.) Lowell's description of his seedtime, dating from the 1940s which were more turbulent for him than the "tranquillized *Fifties*" (an allusion to a phrase of John Foster Dulles who called the era a tranquil time), includes calling himself "a fire-breathing Catholic C. O.," making a "manic statement, telling off the state and president"—the reasons for his being jailed. The roof of the West Street Jail, he remembers, was "a short enclosure," which he compares to Brimmer's soccer court ("an ugly concrete area"), not St. Mark's grass field as was suggested. Here, Lowell's reverie not only takes him through the steps of his seedtime maturation but, much like Henry Adams, attempts to link his education (both in and out of school) with his experience—jail, in Lowell's case. The contrast shows that very little of Lowell's education prepared him for West Street and the events that led him there. Lowell "yammered metaphysics with Abramowitz," which provides the clue indicating that he was concerned with the ontological knowledge claims of Aristotelian metaphysics, with the "connections" of how he arrived at one place from another. And this sets up the contrast between himself (the self of the poem) and Lepke: Lowell sits in a large house with plenty of books and other possessions; Lepke is satisfied with "his little segregated cell" with his "portable radio, a dresser, two toy American flags tied together with a ribbon of Easter palm"—this last detail contrasts with Lowell's using religion to break from his country rather than "tying" the two together as Lepke has done. Lobotomized, Lepke cannot remember his seedtime so he drifts "in a sheepish calm" unable to reappraise his past, but only looks forward to the future of the electric chair which for him is an "oasis in his air of lost connections"; Lowell, unlike Lepke, is able to retrace his development, and regards his own reappraisal as "agonizing" but ironic in comparison to the fate of Lepke. In stating that Lepke is not bothered by any "agonizing reappraisal," the insinuation following is that Lowell is so burdened, which is one of the poem's themes. That by tracing his personal history in the poem, the self depicted hoped to better define his present circumstance—a first time father at age forty—but instead this exploration uncovered his "spoiled" upbringing. The speaker tells us that he told off the president, that he had never heard of the Jehovah's Witnesses so consumed, as he was, by his own Catholic conversion, that he did not know how to make his bed properly, and so forth. So his seedtime, the speaker Lowell realizes, was about as pampered as that of the "man scavenging filth in the back alley trash cans" who "has two children, a beach wagon, a helpmate, and is a 'young Republican.'" But the fact that he is now able to see it as such, as an image of his "spoiled childhood aching inside" him, indicates that he has matured by the experiences, making him less spoiled. The flashback technique of "Memories" helps us to read the poem in this way. Like "Waking in the Blue," the poem concerns the speaker Lowell in the process of defining himself; the narrator of "Waking" comes to a sudden self-revelation, whereas the narrator of "Memories" is in the act of discovery. Lowell's "confession"—if any—in "Memories" is confiding in us that he considers his past agonizing. The final image of Lepke concentrating on his execution—which he finds as refreshing, beautiful, and sustaining as an oasis—contrasts with the speaker's memories of the past. Lepke doesn't remember his past, and this the Lowell speaker envies. In these "self-therapeutic" poems of Life Studies, the self depicted by Lowell has progressed from overcoming an attitude of smugness towards the other mental patients to realizing he is their equal (in "Waking in the Blue") to envying a fellow inmate, desiring perhaps his own "sheepish calm" (in "Memories").

It is this sense of self-therapy in Life Studies that forces the voice into confession, which implies of course, that someone—a reading audience—is listening. The expressions of self-analysis, then, are necessarily confessional: "What use is my sense of humor?" and "We are all old-timers, / each of us holds a locked razor" ("Waking"); "Ought I to regret my seedtime?" and "I was so out of things..." ("Memories"); "I keep no rank nor station. / Cured, I am frizzled, stale and small"

("Home After Three Months Away"); and "My mind's not right…. I myself am hell…" ("Skunk Hour") are a few examples. In each of these poems, the confessional tone of voice is accomplished by its use of "I," the narrative structure and the conversational language working to create the intimacy and sincerity necessary for the success of any personal poem of the confessional mode. We accept these pronouncements as sincere even though many are poetic artifice taken from other poems. "I keep no rank nor station" is an allusion to *Hamlet* and "I myself am hell" is what Satan says in *Paradise Lost*. These principles of aesthetics separate the private, authentic Lowell (who in actuality did spend time at McLean's and West Street) from the public representation of the self—a sincere one—who consciously makes these aesthetic selections in this verse of self-exploration. This distinction becomes especially important in identifying a confessional voice if the poet's biography is unknown. The narrator of "Memories"—whether or not we accept him as Lowell speaking in his own, private voice—makes simple prose statements such as "I hog a whole house," "I have a nine months' daughter," "I am forty," "I was a fire-breathing Catholic C. O.," etc. Given the reference to being Catholic, these statements assume a tone of delivery that one might make to a priest in the confessional: "I confess that I hog a house, I am forty…." Nevertheless, this speaker confesses these things with a sincere attitude, in "ordinary everyday language," which draws us close to him. And we get even closer when he allows us in on his reverie, the flashback to the past. So that even if we knew nothing of Lowell's life, "Memories" would remain a poem of the confessional mode because the speaker openly reveals personal details which we accept because he has won our trust through his diction, sentence syntax, and use of narrative.

In both "Waking in the Blue" and "Memories," the focus is, ultimately, the narrator: how he assimilates into his self-definition the experiences he depicts in the poems. This is one use of the confessional voice in personal poetry. Another is having the voice act as an observer, a recorder of an incident or scene, but without comment as to how it relates to the narrator's sense of himself. In this way, the poem unveils something of how the confessional speaker thinks by revealing what he chooses to observe. These poems are of the confessional mode because they present clearly the unsheathed perceptions of the narrator, the poet's public self, even though Lowell said he changed many actual details for the poem's sake. Two examples provided by Lowell, both from *For the Union Dead*, are "The Mouth of the Hudson" and "July in Washington." In "The Mouth of the Hudson," the narrator is completely removed from the landscape and the people he describes:

A single man stands like a bird-watcher...
He cannot discover America by counting
the chains of condemned freight-trains
from thirty states....
His eyes drop,
and he drifts with the wild ice
ticking seaward down the Hudson...

A Negro toasts
wheat-seeds...
Chemical air
sweeps in from New Jersey,
and smells of coffee.

Across the river,
ledges of suburban factories tan
in the sulphur-yellow sun
of the unforgivable landscape.

As Lowell has informed us, this poem is written "in the first person and the first person is me...an observer," his public self as represented by the poem. The view from the mouth of the Hudson River is not that of the "single man" whose presence begins the poem; rather the poem's voice is Lowell's watching this man, then the "Negro," the chemical air, and the factories. The single man, who "stands like a bird-watcher," drops his eyes and follows the ice downriver while the voice continues to observe other people and aspects of the landscape.

"The Mouth of the Hudson" explores Lowell's relationship to the land in which he finds himself. He interprets the "counting the chains of condemned freight-trains" as the single man's attempt to "discover America." Yet since the poem is in the first person, we are not allowed the opportunity to hear the single man think for himself. The psychology of counting the freight-trains in order to find America, then, is the voice's psychology imposed on the single man. So the concern expressed in the poem by the speaker is his concern for the country whose landscape has become one of "condemned freight-trains," "chemical air," and "a sulphur-yellow sun."

That the landscape affects the narrator, the confessional voice, is shown more directly in "July in Washington," in which the first person observer enters the poem:

The stiff spokes of this wheel
touch the sore spots of the earth....

The elect, the elected…they come here bright as dimes,
and die dishevelled and soft.

We cannot name their names, or number their dates—
circle on circle, like rings on a tree—

but we wish the river had another shore,
some further range of delectable mountains,

distant hills powdered blue as a girl's eyelid.
It seems the least little shove would land us there.…

This poem, which expresses a disillusionment with the Eisenhower administration, is constructed to allow the voice directly into the dramatic situation about halfway through. The city of Washington, D.C., planned in concentric circles, is described as the speaker sees it in midsummer: the Potomac, otters and raccoons, and, "above the breeding vegetation," equestrian statues where some of the circled streets intersect. This is the setting for our country's policy makers, "the elect, the elected" (a sardonic pun on Puritan leaders) who "come here bright as dimes, and die dishevelled and soft." These are the people who have come to Washington excited with new ideas for change, but, in these "tranquillized *Fifties*," they actually accomplish very little and eventually lose their enthusiasm. But the large wheel of government remains, touching "the sore spots of the earth," which of course alludes to the "wheels" of the planned circles of D.C. and also to Dante. So the landscape, seemingly pastoral and apart from the throngs of politics, becomes the metaphor for the current administration from which the Lowell speaker would like to be removed. "We wish the river had another shore…of delectable mountains"—another pun on Bunyon—which he claims is within reach if only something could awaken them from tranquillity, give them "the least little shove." In this way, the voice is able to relate the landscape to the men who govern it, and he can define better his place and power within this environment. The people can remain in the dreamland of "distant hills powdered blue as a girl's eyelid" until, the voice tells us, "only the slightest repugnance of our bodies / we no longer control could drag us back." In this world where a mediocre administration endlessly grinds on, serving a public so tranquil they do nothing to change it, people have no control over their destinies, are no longer in control of their bodies even.

The speaker as an observer of landscape, then, whether a character in the poem (as in "July in Washington") or not (as in "The Mouth of the Hudson"), provides a way for the personal voice of Lowell to explore an area of self-definition without using a narrative of an autobiographical experience that can be documented as such, as was the case in "Waking in the Blue" and "Memories of West Street and Lepke." Lowell's aesthetic, then, identifies the voice of his personal poetry as confessional. His biography clarifies certain references in the poems' text, and it corroborates our reasoning. Yet Lowell's use of an "I" speaker— one that is sincere, one that recounts plausible personal experiences—to define his public self by means of the poem (in that the poet's public self defines itself by the experience it relates) is finally that which determines the use of voice in the confessional mode. The poetry of James Wright will illustrate further this concept.

JAMES WRIGHT

JAMES WRIGHT BEGAN USING a more personal voice in his books *The Branch Will Not Break* (1963) and *Shall We Gather at the River* (1968). Like Lowell, Wright first wrote poems—collected in *The Green Wall* (1957) and *Saint Judas* (1959)— that displayed his concern for literary diction, an intellectualized surface of elegance and irony, and which exhibited a traditional use of meter, rhyme, and stanza patterns. He commented to William Heyen and Jerome Mazzaro in 1972: "I was trying to learn how to write in what I call a classical way, and I wanted to subordinate whatever devices of language I could control to a single theme in each poem" (137). However, these early poems seem to betray that content and theme apparently were of secondary importance to Wright. He concentrated, rather, on portraying an objective tone of speaker in relating his subject. In those poems in which the speaker was identifiable (that is, having a presence in the poem as opposed to an omniscient voice alone), Wright used either an "I" narrator possessing a distanced voice and taking a formal stance, or a persona. But his poetry of the 1960s shows a move inward, toward a confessional voice. These poems were now more concerned with theme and content, which necessitated a clarity of expression to be attained even at the expense of the formal verse he had been practicing. This echoed the situation Lowell had come to with his personal poetry.

In a 1975 interview with *Paris Review*, Wright spoke of the change in his style as a result of his struggles—both personal and artistic:

> After I finished [*Saint Judas*] I had finished with poetry forever. I truly believed that I had no more to do with this art....
>
> At that time I had come, for personal reasons but also for artistic reasons, to something like a dead end. I was in despair at that time, and what usually has consoled me is words—I've always been able to turn to them. But suddenly, it seemed to me that the words themselves had gone dead, I mean dead in me, and I didn't know what to do. It was at that time Robert Bly's

magazine, which was then called *The Fifties*, appeared.... He made it clear to
me that the tradition of poetry which I had tried to master, and in which I'd
come to a dead end, was not the only one. He reminded me that poetry is a
possibility, that, although all poetry is formal, there are many forms, just as
there are many forms of feeling. (48–9)

His poetry following *Saint Judas* broke, as he says, from "the tradition of
poetry which I had tried to master," yet the penultimate poem of that book, "At
the Executed Murderer's Grave," which is formally end-rhymed—albeit irregularly—points toward the examination of self that was to come in his poetry following it. The "grave" in the title belongs to George Doty, a rapist and thief who
was executed for murdering one of the girls he attacked. But as Wright's personal
speaker recounts this story for us in his poem, he tries to understand his relationship to Doty and, particularly, the reason for his own guilt over Doty's execution:

> 1
> My name is James A. Wright, and I was born
> Twenty-five miles from this infected grave,
> In Martins Ferry, Ohio, where one slave
> To Hazel-Atlas Glass became my father.
> He tried to teach me kindness....
>
> 2
> Doty, if I confess I do not love you,
> Will you let me alone? I burn for my own lies....
>
> 3
> I pity myself, because a man is dead.
> If Belmont County killed him, what of me?
> His victims never loved him. Why should we?
> And yet, nobody had to kill him either....
>
> 6
> Staring politely, they will not mark my face
> From any murderer's, buried in this place.
> Why should they? We are nothing but a man.
>
> 7
> Doty, the rapist and the murderer,
> Sleeps in a ditch of fire, and cannot hear;
> And where, in earth or hell's unholy peace,
> Men's suicides will stop, God knows, not I....

Of Doty, killer, imbecile, and thief:
Dirt of my flesh, defeated, underground.

Dave Smith wrote of this poem:

Wright's employment of biographical details which are verifiable, the confessional element, was obvious and demonstrated the poetry of personality. However, the syntactical skill and suppleness, the suspensions and juxtapositions, the rigorous cadence and tight rhymes drove against the poem's spontaneity. Wright created a character in whom we could place trust, a mature and sympathetic and ironic voice. He wrote and published three versions of the poem as he worked it toward the illusion of veracity and away from the dead voices of the past. (xvi)

This "poetry of personality" is, finally, the mark of James Wright's confessional voice "in whom we could place trust." Wright putatively related the following story to a class about "At the Executed Murderer's Grave":

A few years ago I received a letter from a woman who lives in my home town of Martins Ferry, Ohio.... Her words were something like, "I was a young girl then and I remember that Doty case quite well. It was vicious and sadistic. Not only did Doty murder the young woman, but he beat her so badly that her skull was cracked and half her brain was scattered. Still, in your poem, you somehow find sympathy for Doty and question the morality of the society that ordered his death. Well, as far as I'm concerned, George Doty was a disgusting human being who got exactly what he deserved...."
... I must have written four or five separate letters but never mailed any of them.... But in one of those letters...I hit the nail right on the head. I told her that as far as I was concerned there was no doubt that Doty, as she had put it, had gotten "exactly what he deserved." I was not trying to defend or excuse him. What the poem tries to say is simply this: I pray to God that I don't get exactly what I deserve. (Serchuk 88–9)

That no crime is wholly individual was a favorite Wright theme. He ended the poem: "Doty, killer, imbecile, and thief: / Dirt of my flesh, defeated, underground." Human beings are of one flesh, the Wright speaker says in the poem, and as he stands over Doty's grave knowing full well "for whom the bell tolls," he too feels "defeated, underground," where his flesh, like Doty's, has turned to dirt. Therefore an execution of a murderer, even, is an act of suicide, and "where... men's suicides will stop, God knows...." But the public self which Wright defines by the experience related in the poem came to that understanding through the process of examining his guilt over Doty's execution. He begins the poem by stating

the facts of which he is certain: "My name is James A. Wright," etc. In attempting
to define the reasons for his guilt, he examines himself, who he is, where he came
from—a father who taught kindness even though he likely could have become
embittered because he was a "slave to Hazel-Atlas Glass," which is a rather dark
pun. (Ohio was a Free State and Martins Ferry in particular was the destination of
an underground "freedom train" which smuggled slaves to freedom. It is ironic
that after the Civil War, Ohio passed some of the most severe segregation laws.)
Remembering his father's teaching is one reason for his guilt; Wright is "kind"—
enough so to feel remorse.

The voice of the poem gives the "illusion of veracity." Similar to Lowell's realization that he is no better than the other mental patients in "Waking in the
Blue," Wright's compassion leads to his realization that even though he really is
better than Doty, he still does not want what he deserves—he wants mercy. For
both Lowell and Wright, a poem which concludes with a revelation of the speaker
concerning his self—one which helps that speaker define himself more clearly—
becomes an open confessional revealing the (sincere) self's most intimate struggles with personal inquiry. For any poem to be successful in this, the sincerity of
the speaker must be established, even though it may be ambiguous and ironical as
the confessional voices of Lowell and Wright both are. As seen in Lowell's poems
of this mode, one way for the poet to establish the integrity, or sincerity, of the
voice he uses is through craft—the way the poem is constructed.

In "At the Executed Murderer's Grave," Wright disregards Eliot's directive
(which Wright learned at Kenyon College from his first poetry teacher, John
Crowe Ransom) to avoid labeling emotions, to allow instead the poem's images
and objects to evoke them. But Wright, assuming a confessional voice and tone in
this poem, has his speaker state openly: "I burn for my own lies," "I pity myself,"
and so forth. This is one of the aspects of Wright's craft that makes his confessional speaker believable, sincere, as Serchuk has remarked: "For me, Wright's
work was the embodiment of all that poetry could and should be. Simple. Direct.
Understated. Visionary but shy. As formal as the imagination dictated without
ever sacrificing cleanness or the natural rhythms of speech. Wright's poetry never
bored me, and, more importantly, *I believed him.* Casting aside every professional
dictum concerning the separation of the artist from his specific creation, I believed Wright completely, unashamedly. For me, his poems were not merely convincing. As MacLeish's 'Ars Poetica' demanded, they were" (85–6). It is difficult
indeed to find Wright unbelievable (that is, not sincere) when he opens with: "My
name is James A. Wright, and I was born…in Martins Ferry, Ohio," and continues
to add enough factual details (place names like Hazel-Atlas Glass, Belmont

County, and circumstances of the Doty case) which give credence to everything else, true or not. That is, the voice remains sincere even though the speaker may be like that of Whitman's when using factual details, such as saying he was with John Paul Jones. We have the sense, however, that we are getting the *real* James Wright—to paraphrase Lowell—not only because he suggests his is the authentic voice of the poem (by opening with "My name is James A. Wright"), but his use of the "natural rhythms of speech" and the seeming veracity of experience convinces us throughout that his voice is one of candor.

The "personal dead end" that Wright mentioned in the *Paris Review* interview is reflected by the speaker of "At the Executed Murderer's Grave." The struggling to justify an execution, and the resulting suffering over moral and ethical concerns, perhaps completed for Wright all that could be properly expressed in poetry. Consequently, following that book, he remarked in his essay "From A Letter": "[T]he words themselves had gone dead" for him. And regarding the artistic malaise he mentioned, the story Wright told about the poem's meaning clearly has more impact than the poem itself, written in what he later called "the rhymed iambics which no fashionable poet would be caught dead writing these days" (287). But when Robert Bly reminded him that "poetry is a possibility," as Wright told Stitt, "that although all poetry is formal, there are many forms, just as there are many forms of feeling," he found that open forms helped him to express "something," he says, "that I think I wanted to say from the beginning. And that, unfortunately, being damned as I consider myself, I felt I had to say or I would die. I think that most of the people who are alive in the world right now are very unhappy. I don't want people to be unhappy, and I'm sorry that they are. I wish there were something I could do to help. I'm coming to face the fact that there isn't much I can do to help. And I think I've been trying to say that ever since I've started to write books. That's what my books are about" (50). This is one theme of "At the Executed Murderer's Grave," and the sense of personal unhappiness in that poem resonates to include all men and women, all their suffering. So Wright's conception of himself ("being damned as I consider myself") shaped his vision of everyone ("I think that most of the people who are alive in the world right now are very unhappy," he said). It is an individual conception originating from self-exploration, which he makes universal by imposing it on "most of the people who are alive in the world." That Wright's personal anguish extended to his personal poetry is important to remember as we continue discussion of his confessional voice.

He remarked: "I loved *Saint Judas* best because I came to terms with my own pain then." But, if that is clear in the poetry of that collection, he achieves it mostly by allowing a third person voice, a persona, or a historical or mythological character (as used in the title poem, "Saint Judas") to speak for him. In his books following, however, he increasingly relied on a confessional voice, the presence of his public self in the poem. Since Wright regarded himself—including, of course, his own fears and unhappiness—as representative of "most people," his personal poetry, then, is an exploration of the self which depicts a universal consciousness as defined by his own vision. Two poems from *The Branch Will Not Break* will illustrate this: "Autumn Begins in Martins Ferry, Ohio" and "Lying in a Hammock at William Duffy's Farm in Pine Island, Minnesota." The Wright speaker acts as an observer in "Autumn," as the Lowell speaker did in "The Mouth of the Hudson." Unlike Lowell's poem, however, which focused on specific individuals, Wright makes general assertions and then applies them to the people of his poem *en masse*:

> In the Shreve High football stadium,
> I think of Polacks nursing long beers in Tiltonsville...
>
> All the proud fathers are ashamed to go home.
> Their women...
> Dying for love.
>
> Therefore,
> Their sons grow suicidally beautiful...
> And gallop terribly against each other's bodies.

The voice of this poem is personal in that—like "The Mouth of the Hudson"—the thought process of the observer is revealed. The poem represents the speaker's thoughts. And, as this (confessional) speaker sits watching a high school football game, his observations move from the more specific, the regional, to the general: from "Polacks nursing long beers in Tiltonsville" and the "night watchman of Wheeling Steel" to the universal assessments that "all proud fathers are ashamed to go home" and "their women cluck," "their sons grow suicidally beautiful." The poem allows us to witness this progression, and the final assertion, prefaced by the conclusive "therefore," returns the speaker back to the football game at Shreve High where the poem began.

The speaker thinks first about the men who work at the steel mills in the area, then assumes that since they are in the stadium watching the game, they are the fathers of the boys playing. Regardless whether the men are or not, the people in the stadium initiate the speaker's thoughts of first the "Polacks," then the "Negroes in the blast furnace at Benwood" which in turn leads him to theorize that they are "ashamed to go home," that "their women cluck like starved pullets, dying for love," and that, therefore, the men "dreaming of heroes," watch their sons "gallop terribly against each other's bodies." It is a personal voice which depicts a scene as the narrator observes it and, in doing so, gives us his psychoanalytic interpretation of the men he sits among in the stadium, their sons, and wives. The voice is not self-therapeutic as was Lowell's, but interpretive of the society and the people of which he is a part.

In "Lying in a Hammock at William Duffy's Farm in Pine Island, Minnesota," the voice is more self-centered, concerned with the place of the speaker among nature:

> Over my head, I see the bronze butterfly,
> Asleep on the black trunk,
> Blowing like a leaf in green shadow....
> The droppings of last year's horses
> Blaze up into golden stones.
> I lean back, as the evening darkens and comes on.
> A chicken hawk floats over, looking for home.
> I have wasted my life.

Recall Wright's statements: "I don't want people to be unhappy, and I'm sorry that they are. I wish there were something I could do to help.... [T]here isn't much I can do... That's what my books are about." According to Wright's view, the speaker's personal realization in "Lying in a Hammock," that "I have wasted my life," could be declared by most people since most are "very unhappy." For anyone who has failed, like himself, to find solace in the solitude of a pasture, to be appreciative of nature, life has been wasted. Viewing the "bronze butterfly," the "golden stones," and the floating chicken hawk, the speaker feels he should have spent more of his life learning to share in this natural world. Wright said to Stitt: "Human beings are unhappily part of nature, perhaps nature become conscious of itself. Oh, how I would love to be a chickadee! But I can't be a chickadee, all I can be is what I am. I love the natural world and I'm conscious of the pain in it. So I'm a nature poet who writes about human beings in nature. I love Nietzsche, who called man 'the sick animal'" (47). Wright's statement is inclusive; he refers to "human beings" rather than to himself solely, and he emphasizes that Nietzsche saw every man as "sick."

"Lying in a Hammock" illustrates the shortcomings of human beings, their "sickness" which is that of wasting their time away from nature, and in so doing, the poem identifies a principal reason for man's suffering. So the poem can serve as a method to introduce people to another, natural side of themselves even if only transmuted to the printed page. It is one way Wright could help alleviate the human suffering, the sickness he regarded as universal. *The Branch Will Not Break*, then, is "about" both his speaker's realization that he could not help much and the failed attempts in trying.

In specific reference to the last line of "Lying in a Hammock," Wright said, in an interview with Dave Smith, that Americans (again, the implied "all") have a tendency to waste, and that he has tried to teach his students otherwise:

> American critics think that last line is a moral, that it is a comment which says I have wasted my life by lying in a hammock. Actually, behind everything in my general thoughts and feelings was the idea that one of the worst things in American life is waste. I think that our tendency to waste is a truly dreadful one. I have told my students that one of the most horrifing things to me is to stand, being my age, and look at a class of nineteen and twenty-year-old people who are trying to read a passage of say, Milton or Shakespeare and to see their faces saying it is a waste of time. They don't see how precious their lives are. (29)

In "Lying in a Hammock" the personal voice, as an observer, begins by describing the outside world with seeming objectivity, then finishes introspectively. The speaker of "Autumn Begins in Martins Ferry, Ohio" expands his thoughts to make universal judgments. Since Wright believed that his own despair was a condition shared by most people, his personal poems assume a broad significance. Wright wanted to be a shaman of sorts, to help people. He therefore wrote of his own experience of suffering and his methods of coping with it perhaps to suggest by implication that anyone's unhappiness could be dealt with similarly. And, as the loss—the waste—described in "Lying in a Hammock" indicates, man must become closer to nature, commune with it in order to heal.

One example of how the Wright speaker heals his sickness through nature is manifested in the comic poem "Depressed by a Book of Bad Poetry, I Walk Toward an Unused Pasture and Invite the Insects to Join Me":

> Relieved, I let the book fall behind a stone....
> I close my eyes for a moment, and listen.
> The old grasshoppers
> Are tired, they leap heavily now,
> Their thighs are burdened.
> I want to hear them, they have clear sounds to make.
> Then lovely, far off, a dark cricket begins
> In the maple trees.

The confessional voice—immediately recognizable as such by the veracity of experience it describes, its sincerity, syntax, and use of the personal pronoun "I" as subject in a majority of the phrases—states that certain human sounds of speech are depressing, a feeling which can be relieved by listening to the sounds of "the old grasshoppers" and "a dark cricket."

I do not mean to suggest that these poems ("Lying in a Hammock" and "Depressed by a Book of Bad Poetry") are not personal in the sense that they express Wright's concern of self—they are. They relate to Wright's private circumstance (the speaker Wright's), but not exclusively as Lowell's confessional poetry often did. Rather, because Wright considered himself a representative man and saw his unhappiness as a microcosm of everyone's, his personal poems are representative "confessionals," revealing what he believed to be diffuse themes, applicable to both himself and others. Some of his personal poetic meditations are, in effect, public pronouncements.

"A Blessing," near the end of *The Branch Will Not Break*, shows how the speaker finds a joy in the company of horses, how nature—as in "Depressed by a Book of Bad Poetry"—can rejuvenate the speaker. The poem also betrays the speaker's assumption that his anguish, his lonesomeness, are conditions that extend not only to other humans but to the horses as well. "A Blessing," then, combines the two elements characteristic of Wright's personal poetry of this collection: that the personal voice speaks of conditions germane to the many, and that nature offers the best way to alleviate the common anguish. In this poem, two ponies welcome the intrusion of the speaker and a friend into their field. The ponies

> ...have come gladly out of the willows
> To welcome my friend and me.
> We step over the barbed wire into the pasture
> Where they have been grazing all day, alone.
> They ripple tensely, they can hardly contain their happiness
> That we have come.
> They bow shyly as wet swans. They love each other.
> There is no loneliness like theirs....
> I would like to hold the slenderer one in my arms...
> And the light breeze moves to me to caress her long ear
> That is delicate as the skin over a girl's wrist.
> Suddenly I realize
> That if I stepped out of my body I would break
> Into blossom.

The speaker interpolates the ponies' actions in human terms: their eyes "darken with kindness," "they have come gladly out of the willows to welcome my friend and me," "they can hardly contain their happiness that we have come," "they bow shyly." The ponies are viewed as such by the speaker, but the voice is so assured that the scene described is credible. Even though the ponies may have come to the speaker and his friend thinking they brought something for them to eat, say, the speaker sees it as an indication of their welcoming him. And the ponies' movements—the Wright speaker having assigned human characteristics to them—are seen as shy bows.

Further, the speaker attributes to the ponies what may be his own feelings; in doing so, he has again assumed that his feelings are universal, and he has imposed them even on the ponies. They are, he says, lonely, and glad for company. So overcome at giving affection to one of the shy, lonely ponies, the speaker feels he has reached a momentary nirvana. Yet, more likely, it is the speaker who is lonely and therefore comforted by the pony rather than acting to comfort her. Either way, Wright demonstrates in this poem that the common bond we all share—human or animal—is loneliness, which brings the pony and the speaker together, and that nature (at least for human beings) can ease the pains of this particular sickness. Wright, then, in *The Branch Will Not Break* began with his speaker's personal realization that he has wasted his life in "Lying in a Hammock" and finished with a life-fulfilling experience so completely satisfying that he could die at that moment and "break into blossom."

Although Wright may have assumed that his confessional voice spoke for most people, who are "very unhappy," no reader would deny that the poems of *The Branch Will Not Break*—regardless of any all-embracing intentions—concern specific places, circumstances, and people, which make them resoundingly personal of the Wright self acting as the speaker of these poems. If any poem seems less so, more common to all, as does "Autumn Begins in Martins Ferry, Ohio," it is due to the authoritative stance the voice assumes, using inclusive phrases like "the proud fathers," "their women." Yet, though it may seem to relate information impartially, it is still the vision of one only: the confessional speaker rendering his judgment of the people of the Ohio Valley. Wright may have thought his personal consciousness represented a universal one, but his poems remain essentially private because his speaker turns first to himself for answers—just as he began with personal facts to begin his reasoning in "At the Executed Murderer's Grave."

Wright said to Stitt that his poems of *The Branch Will Not Break* came from his life, from his artistic and personal labors of self-understanding:

At the center of that book is my rediscovery of the abounding delight of the body that I had forgotten about. Every Friday afternoon I used to go out to Bly's farm, and there were so many animals out there. There was Simon, who was an Airedale, but about the size of a Great Dane. There was David, the horse, my beautiful, beloved David, the sway-backed Palomino. Simon and David used to go out by Bly's barn. David would stand there looking out over the corn fields that lead onto the prairies of South Dakota, and Simon would sit down beside him, and they would stand there for hours....They allowed me to join them. They liked me. I can't get over it—they liked me. Simon didn't bite me, David didn't kick me; they just stayed there as they were....One afternoon, a gopher came up out of a hole and looked at us. Simon didn't leap for him, David didn't kick him, and I didn't shoot him. There we were, all four of us together. All I was thinking was, I can be happy sometimes. (49–50)

The poems in that book reflect Wright's self-rediscovery, much in the same way as the poems in *Life Studies* reflect Lowell's. Peter Stitt has written of Wright's book in his essay "James Wright: The Quest Motif in *The Branch Will Not Break*": "The basic strategy Wright employs in [the book] is that of a quest. In his search for happiness, for comfort, for consolation, and for sustenance, the poet turns from the city to the country, from society to nature, from human beings to animals, and from a fear of the finality of death to a trust in immortality. The struggle has the stamp of authenticity; the speaker of the poems is the poet himself—not some persona he has created—and the poems are based on his own life" (66), as evidenced in part by Wright's retrospection concerning his stay at the Bly farm. Yet Stitt in this passage misperceives the nature of Wright's poetic voice. The voice is not himself, not authentic. That the poet represents himself and that his poems are based on his own life are two different perceptions and conceptions, as I have tried to show.

In Wright's next book, *Shall We Gather at the River*, the stark confessional voice dominates. That voice can be categorized as either one that speaks of the self directly, or one that speaks to another person, "Jenny." Three poems from that book, "Gambling in Stateline, Nevada," "Outside Fargo, North Dakota," and "Lifting Illegal Nets by Flashlight," will serve to illustrate Wright's methods of using the confessional mode of voice as a means of self-examination. Then two other poems, "To the Muse" and "The Idea of the Good," written to Jenny will show how Wright uses the confessional voice in his "private" communications with a loved one.

The voice and subject of "Gambling in Stateline, Nevada" create the semblance of credibility. They make the poem as seemingly autobiographical as any of those in the "Life Studies" section of Lowell's book. The poem follows a vague narrative line, and employs the same syntax identifiable in other confessional poems:

> a girl named Rachel
> …died of bad luck.
>
> Here, across from the keno board,
> An old woman
> Has been beating a strange machine
> In its face all day.
>
> Dusk limps past in the street.
> I step outside.
> It's gone.
> I finger a worthless agate
> In my pocket.

As was important in Lowell's "Waking in the Blue," the people chosen by the first person narrator to occupy this poem reflect his own, sad mood. In reality, there are other people. The "confession" is an assemblage that is phenomenological, then. The intent of this poem is to convey emotion, and that is achieved because the personal, the confessional, voice elicits pathos from the reader. There is a sadness in the voice of the speaker watching the personified dusk limp, then fade, in knowing that a young girl, Rachel, died of bad luck, that an old woman has been, like the speaker, unlucky in gambling.

Leonard Nathan has explicated "Gambling in Stateline, Nevada" in his essay "The Private 'I' In Contemporary Poetry": "It seems perfectly clear that the poet in this poem is attempting to speak in his own voice"; that is, the poet is the speaker—James Wright speaking in his public voice. Nathan qualifies his assertion by rightly arguing that:

> …the James Wright who wrote this poem is not the same James Wright who is speaking in the poem….The real James Wright is not wholly alone and friendless, even if his only friend were the publisher of his poem. James Wright, the poet, has created James Wright, the wandering unfortunate, out of a large field of possibilities: for instance, traditional poetic models for melancholy, as well as the actual melancholy he himself has no doubt experienced. The James Wright in the poem is a fiction, an artful and persuasive illusion of reality, and we accept him partly because we know he is a work of

art, as well as part of reality. If he were too much art we would cry insincere and dismiss him. (95)

The content of the poem, then, does not need to be based on verifiable autobiography in order for the poem to be of the confessional mode—which employs a speaker who is seemingly the poet himself, whether that speaker is actually the poet or a rejection of that self, an altered version of the poet as is Wright's and Lowell's (where the poet has "lied a bit and invented" as Lowell remarked). In either case, pathos—as shown in the poems by both Lowell and Wright—can be evoked.

"Outside Fargo, North Dakota" brings together the confessional voice and the poet, who could be a created "narrator" of the poem, not necessarily Wright. Here is the poem's final stanza:

> Suddenly the freight car lurches.
> The door slams back, a man with a flashlight
> Calls me good evening.
> I nod good evening, lonely
> And sick for home.

Although the "I" in this poem is used, particularly in the last two lines, to indicate the composer of the poem (who confesses that the narrator is himself), it should not be assumed that that composer is Wright. Robert Hass argues against such an assumption. Of the last lines of "Outside Fargo, North Dakota," he writes:

> They were not written by the poet who is lonely and sick for home, they were written by the man who noticed that the poet, sitting in his room alone, recalling a scene outside Fargo, North Dakota, nods when he writes down the greeting of his imagined yardman, and catches in that moment not the poet's loneliness but a gesture that reveals the aboriginal loneliness of being—of the being of the freight cars, silos, horses, shadows, matches, poets, flashlights. (27)

Hass supports my argument that the autobiography, or supposed autobiography, need not be verified in order to establish the poem's voice as confessional. The voice, whether that of Wright or Wright's imagined poet, sounds sincere and gives the illusion of veracity which is vital if the poem is to elicit pathos from the reader. Like the voice of "Gambling in Stateline, Nevada," the voice of "Outside Fargo, North Dakota" sincerely confesses a personal feeling: feeling unlucky, worthless in "Gambling"; feeling lonely in "Fargo."

The difference in the voice of each poem is that a reader of "Gambling" is left to assume, because of the poem's sincerity, that the narrator is an altered James Wright, whereas a reader of "Fargo," like Hass, because the poem ends with the poet—actual or imagined—in the act of writing it, knows that the narrator is the poet. The reader does not have to assume so as Nathan does in "Gambling." The only question left, then, concerning the narrator of "Fargo" is whether Wright had his actual self in mind or an imagined self, as Hass has implied. The voice of each poem is self-scrutinizing: The poet's loneliness is reflected in the scene he is composing in "Fargo"; in "Gambling" the narrator's worthlessness is parallel to the other characters'.

"Lifting Illegal Nets by Flashlight" is based on an experience that can be proven to be autobiographical, unlike either "Gambling" or "Fargo." Like those poems, the narrator openly admits his emotional state—anguish:

> The carp are secrets
> Of the creation: I do not
> Know if they are lonely....
> What does my anguish
> Matter?...
> This is the firmest
> Net I ever saw, and yet something
> Is gone lonely
> Into the headwaters of the Minnesota.

As with most of Wright's personal poetry, the speaker is not afraid to label his emotions, and this, as has been true of each poem we have seen, adds to the illusion of the speaker's integrity. In this poem, the voice is not assumptive as it was in "A Blessing"; the speaker does not impose his emotional state on the fish and claim that they are feeling the way he is. Now the speaker is more humble: "I do not know if they are lonely," he truthfully admits, and he relegates his own feeling: "What does my anguish matter?" The act of poaching makes the speaker forget his anguish, which is the "something" that goes "lonely into the headwaters of the Minnesota." So nature again relieves the speaker's suffering, but the experience does little for the carp trapped in the nets. In "A Blessing" both the pony, presumably, and the man (the poem's speaker) were joyous because of the shared experience. The focus of "Lifting Illegal Nets by Flashlight" is not the act of communing with nature (as it was in "A Blessing"), but the speaker's emotional state which moves from anxiety ("the poachers drift with an almost frightening care under the bridge") and anguish to satisfaction. And it is the confessional voice which allows us to witness this change as the speaker experiences it.

Although the voice of this poem sounds no more or less sincere, more or less believable, than the voice of "Gambling in Stateline, Nevada" or that of "Outside Fargo, North Dakota," it is based on fact. Annie Wright, James's wife, remembers her first trip to the Bly farm:

> [Bly] thought and acted on impulse. Out of nowhere came the joking compliment to James. "If you keep publishing poems about illegal fishing nets, James Wright, I'm going to have the game warden after me."…as we passed the open door of a storeroom on the second floor, Robert pointed to a big fishing net on the floor. "That's the very net, Annie. That's the illegal fishing net." (79)

Knowing that the event depicted in the poem by a confessional speaker is based on an autobiographical experience of the poet, however, does not necessarily mean that the emotions of the speaker—the anguish, the joy—were those of Wright when he and Bly went poaching carp. Wright told Bruce Henricksen that his poetry "may be autobiographical in the sense that I suppose anybody's poetry is autobiographical, but I don't think it's confessional" (299). This suggestion, then, illuminates Nathan's argument about the speaker of "Gambling," that the melancholy of that poem's speaker is "a combination of traditional poetic models for melancholy, as well as the actual melancholy he himself has no doubt experienced"; so too can be assumed of "Lifting Illegal Nets by Flashlight," which attests to the credibility of the confessional voice. The voice must create an illusion of the veracity of the world of the poem in order for it to be credible, to elicit pathos, regardless whether or not the emotions of the speaker or the situation described can be verified as fact. And the three poems we have just seen do emit, through the power of each poem's voice, a truthfulness, a believability of the scenes and emotions they depict. In response to Dave Smith's question whether the speaker of his poems was an artificial, or created, speaker, or the "actual James Wright," Wright replied: "Sometimes it is an artificial voice and sometimes it is a direct voice" (35). But the confessional voice can be used in whichever way Wright chooses. Like the autobiographical poems of Lowell, diction, syntax, and the credibility of the narrator work in establishing the voice as confessional; an admission of verification by the poet is not necessary.

In the poems "To the Muse" and "The Idea of the Good" (the first poem of the "New Poems" section which follows *Shall We Gather at the River* in his *Collected Poems*), Wright's speaker uses the forum of the poem as an open confessional. The voice of "To the Muse" speaks directly to "Jenny," who has drowned herself in the Ohio River. The following is from the final stanzas of that poem:

> Oh Jenny,
> I wish to God I had made this world, this scurvy
> And disastrous place. I
> Didn't, I can't bear it
> Either, I don't blame you, sleeping down there
> Face down in the unbelievable silk of spring,
> Muse of black sand,
> Alone.
>
> I don't blame you, I know
> The place where you lie.
> I admit everything. But look at me.
> How can I live without you?
> Come up to me, love,
> Out of the river, or I will
> Come down to you.

Here, the speaker does not need to concern himself with his credibility; the poem is a direct communication of the narrator to his dead lover, and the reader is privy to this confessional. He reveals such intimate thoughts as: "I admit everything," "How can I live without you?" and the most intimate admission, "I will come down to you." Jenny is the muse of the poet who is the speaker of the poem.

In "The Idea of the Good," the speaker-poet, again addressing Jenny, states his disregard for the readers of his poems. His sole concern is to speak to Jenny, as this last part of the poem indicates:

> Jenny, I gave you that unhappy
> Book that nobody knows but you
> And me, so give me
> A little life back.
> Or at least send me the owl's feather
> Again, and I promise I will give it
> To no one. How could I?
> Nobody else will follow
> This poem but you,
> But I don't care.
> My precious secret, how
> Could they know
> You or me?
> Patience.

"That unhappy book" refers to *Shall We Gather at the River*, a collection of poems about which Wright said to Stitt:

> I was trying to move from death to resurrection and death again, and challenge death finally. Well, if I must tell you, I was trying to write about a girl I was in love with who has been dead for a long time. I tried to sing with her in that book. Not to recreate her; you can't recreate anybody, at least I can't. But thought maybe I could come to terms with that feeling which has hung on in my heart for so long. The book has been damned because it is so carefully dreamed. (52)

To accomplish his scheme, Wright used the confessional voice as a means of self-exploration which revealed his personal speaker's emotions, and to convey personal thoughts to a deceased loved one.

Another way Wright uses the confessional voice is to bring two characters into a poem—that is, one besides the narrator—and allow the voice to reveal to the reader the narrator's thoughts regarding the other character. Whereas the more private confessional voice, such as in "The Idea of the Good," excludes the reader's concerns, this voice shields his thoughts from the other character but lets the reader know them. An example is "Hook" from *To a Blossoming Pear Tree* (1977):

> I was only a young man
> In those days.
> …I was in trouble
> With a woman, and there was nothing
> There but me and dead snow….
>
> Then the young Sioux
> Loomed beside me, his scars
> Were just my age.
>
> Ain't got no bus here
> A long time, he said.
> You got enough money
> To get home on?
>
> What did they do
> To your hand? I answered.
> He raised up his hook into the terrible starlight
> And slashed the wind.

Oh, that? he said.
I had a bad time with a woman. Here,
You take this....

I took it.
It wasn't the money I needed.
But I took it.

The similarities of the narrator and the young Sioux are clearly drawn: both have had trouble with women and are now alone, and both show compassion for one another. Wright commented in "From A Letter" of such a structure: "If any principle of structure can be disentangled from the poems that I have written in free verse, it is, I suppose, the principle of parallelism, a term which of course need not be limited to a strictly grammatical application" (287). Parallel as the narrator and the Sioux are, their major difference is that the Sioux only speaks to the narrator, while the narrator speaks both to the Sioux and to the reader. The first three stanzas address the reader; the narrator is setting the opening of his story. The two men talk; then the poem closes with the narrator speaking directly to the reader: "Did you ever feel a man hold / Sixty-five cents / In a hook, / And place it / Gently / In your freezing hand?" And following that rhetorical question, the voice assumes an ironical tone, confiding in us: "I took it. / It wasn't the money I needed. / But I took it." This is not confessional but ironical in that he does not tell us what he did need, if not the money.

In reviewing Wright's aesthetic, then, we have seen how he used the confessional voice to speak for his readers (in "Lying in a Hammock"), to speak for his public self (in "Lifting Illegal Nets by Flashlight"), to another person ("The Idea of the Good"), and now to the reader in "Hook." In Anne Sexton's personal poetry, the confessional voice often will speak of the poet herself while speaking to another person—a use of that voice which Wright did not choose to employ.

ANNE SEXTON

"UNTIL I WAS TWENTY-EIGHT I had a kind of buried self," Anne Sexton remarked in her *Paris Review* interview, a self capable of writing poetry about her life as a New England mother and wife who experienced repeated psychotic breakdowns often resulting in suicide attempts. This self, the conscious self, that is, subsequently became obsessively dependent on psychotherapy and therapists, as recounted in *Anne Sexton: A Self-Portrait in Letters* (1977) and Diane Wood Middlebrook's *Anne Sexton: A Biography* (1991). Sexton felt such sessions provided the impetus for her life-affirming desires, and they proved to be the genesis of her first creative efforts, which at once became for her visible manifestation of self-value and so reinforced the therapeutic aim of preserving her sense of life's worth. The first therapist to have spent extended time with her helped her overcome believing that she "was a victim of the American dream, the bourgeois, middle-class dream." And he (soon to be fictionalized in her poetry as "Dr. Martin") firmly confuted her self-deprecatory pronouncements—"I'm no good; I can't do anything; I'm dumb"—as destructive, and advised her to begin educating herself. One night she watched I. A. Richards explicate a sonnet on Boston's educational television and thought she might try writing one, aided as she was by her therapist's encouragement. Sexton's therapy, then, led her to writing, if somewhat indirectly, not strictly in the way Lowell's doctor told him to try autobiographical prose. Consequently, her first poems resemble strongly the exploration of her consciousness as conducted in her therapeutic sessions.

Later she became aware of the copula between her therapy and writing, as she told the *Paris Review*:

> Sometimes, my doctors tell me I understand something in a poem that I haven't integrated into my life. In fact, I may be concealing it from myself, while I was revealing it to the readers. The poetry is often more advanced, in terms of my unconscious, than I am. Poetry, after all, milks the unconscious. The unconscious is there to feed it little images, little symbols, the answers, the insights I know not of. In therapy, one seeks to hide sometimes. (162)

Sexton's often coyly wrought responses such as this—made while in her favorite guise of the "inspired" artist, not knowing where her material came from or what it immediately meant—led her early commentators to call her confessional: what she hid from her therapist, she told her readers. But this is contradictory. Sexton implies here that her unconscious is selective, that it can choose either to conceal itself, thus preventing her from being wholly candid with her therapist, or choose to reveal itself while in Sexton's (conscious) act of writing poetry. Her unconscious "feeds" her poetry the answers and insights of which Sexton the poet is not conscious. Although we cannot presume to know Sexton's means of poetic convocation, we can be certain that it was not an act of confession—in the sense of a conscious and complete revelation—for she admits to a deliberate "hiding" from her analyst, while she unconsciously reveals in her poetry that which she would not in therapy. If we accept her theory of composition (her unconsciously being directed to revealing images which provide answers regarding her conscious self), then we cannot accept her as authentically confessional. She has used the method of the creative process to exhibit a self-consciousness, one formulated by the restrictive conventions of poetry. Further, she was quite aware of the difference between whom she regarded as her conscious self and that self portrayed in her poetry, as her remark in the previous chapter about her father indicates. ("I haven't forgiven my father. I just wrote that I did.") And yet she regarded herself as the only truly confessional poet.

Sexton felt that she was authentically confessional—when in fact she was not—in those poems which exposed her hidden self, the unconscious Anne Sexton who understood the cause of the other Anne's anxiety. Confessional poetry for her must transcend mere reportage of one's selected personal history; it must act to force an articulation of one's repressed answers and insights. This explains her conviction that her creative and therapeutic acts were inextricable, that one augmented the other, but still she remains just "sincere" because of her conscious choices of that which is retained and deleted in her constructing the poem. Whereas Lowell, too, made these decisions, he reached an understanding of his mental condition—his "answers and insights"—before choosing which images, which symbols, to represent it, as indicated by his "Waking in the Blue" of which the final image of the locked razor is descriptive, but revealing to Lowell neither intuition nor solution to his illness. Both poets are confessional in that their "I" speaker remains consistently sincere in presenting autobiographically based accounts as poetry, but Lowell approached his subject as a poet *after* his hospitalization and so could be more objective—rather than receptive—towards seemingly surprising revelations of his own poetic images and symbols. Sexton, however, combined therapy with her writing, as her daughter Linda Gray Sexton (in *A Self-Portrait in Letters*) recounts for us:

> As if to compensate for all her earlier years of scholastic laziness, she worked hard to learn about both poetic form and herself. She found that emotions she couldn't deal with in therapy appeared increasingly in her poetry worksheets. Spending hours listening to the tape recordings of her psychiatric sessions, and days rewriting her worksheets, she slowly pulled poetry from the dark cores of her sickness. (29)

Although she may have regarded the poetry/therapy nexus as the reason for her candor in poetry on subjects she was reticent about in therapy, she knew from her earliest creative attempts that for poetry to be distinguishable as art, it could not be only an authentic confession of one's self-perception. And this, finally, is why Sexton's "I" is not an authentic one in her personal poetry: her willingness to craft a voice distinct from her conscious voice—even the one used in session with the therapist—one that is sincere, but one belonging entirely to the poem as its speaker rather than belonging to the authentic Anne Sexton who speaks as the "I" of her poems. While discussing her long poem, "The Double Image," from her first book, she remarked in a letter to W. D. Snodgrass: "...give me a one word statement about this 'voice' I've got here for two-hundred odd lines of confession and art. (Art I hope?) The difference between confession and poetry? is after all, art" (44). This poem provides us a useful starting point in analyzing Sexton's method of employing the confessional mode of voice.

She reported to Snodgrass that her "The Double Image" had apparently affected one of its first readers in the same way, she believed, that his "Heart's Needle" had affected her. Snodgrass's poem and Sexton's are similar. Both use a parent's addressing his/her child to structure the poem; each recounts a brief, but chronological, history of the emotional instances which parallel the development of the parent-child relationship. Snodgrass's personal poem is constructed as the confessional "I" speaking directly to his daughter, the "you" of the poem; Sexton's speaker is also a confessional "I" who addresses her daughter in the poem by name (Joyce) as well as the seemingly intimate "you." Referring to "Heart's Needle" in her letter to Snodgrass of February 24, 1959, Sexton wrote:

> ...how unusual, how much genius and the fine grip of talent, is in such a poem that reaches down and touches the inmost part of the reader. A writer, showing himself, in his true light, and doing it so well, has indeed done something so great that one might be afraid. Afraid of the writer's truth and their own truth...[her ellipsis] That's what I think you did. That's the great thing you did. And who would expect it from a [sic] "just a poem"...[her ellipsis] I don't mean to imply that I have written anything as good. I have not. (63)

Sexton felt that Snodgrass's decision to engage the confessional voice had allowed the personal subject of "Heart's Needle" to operate intimately with its audience, to touch "the inmost part of the reader." Here Sexton views the personal poem as capable of having a diffuse application, even if the poem's voice addresses a single "you," a person identified in the poem as one of close relationship with the speaker. Yet the "you" functions not exclusively as the lone intended receiver of an intimate communication; it embraces the notion of the more inclusive second person plural use, the all. In this way, the personal poem becomes an open letter, a communique addressing at once the single and the many, so extends beyond the constraints of the limiting poem of personal anguish, by which many poems of this mode mistakenly have become identified.

Sexton knew that even a poem arising from her therapy sessions, such as "The Double Image," which explores the speaker-mother's ambivalent feelings toward her daughter, must be crafted into art, as she remarked to Snodgrass; otherwise it would be mere confession, an introspective, diarylike entry of the quotidian. Sexton found the confessional use of voice to be the balance between the confessional discussions in therapy and the absorption of certain aspects of her life as material for poetry. ("The difference between confession and poetry is art.") This type of poem had to affect emotionally the reader as if the reader were privy to someone's anguish—a safely distanced someone—so Sexton incorporated as an integral part of her aesthetic a contemporary *hamartia*, a flaw of which the speaker is aware and so can reveal it simultaneously to her reading audience and the "you" addressed in the poem. This type of speaker in a Sexton confessional poem begins already having come to her *anagnorisis*; it is in the foreground of the poem. The speaker acts to confess openly that revelation and perhaps the details of what she has come to know of her tragically flawed character.

Sexton responded to Snodgrass's display of *hamartia* in "Heart's Needle" and told Snodgrass (in the previously cited letter) that her "The Double Image" had the same effect on its readers:

> Rose Morgan [wife of the *Hudson Review* editor who first published the poem] said to me, about "The Double Image" "Thank you, Anne, for writing that poem"...[her ellipsis] it meant something quite real to her tho [sic] I don't actually know what. Something about being a woman and a mother. (63)

She felt successful in having presented a sincere voice; the poem "meant something quite real" to a reader. This was proof for her that her poem transcended authentic confession and became art. That a poet, by using the confessional voice, could create a speaker sincerely admitting her *hamartia* in a way to affect emotionally or otherwise personally her audience beyond whom the poem is addressed—the plural "you"—marks for her the distinction between confession and art, or between authenticity and sincerity in Trilling's terms. Sexton had an audience in mind as she wrote, one that could view her poetry as seeming to be authentic confession—as she thought of Snodgrass's poem—and she was obviously pleased when a poem such as "The Double Image" was well received, knowing she made someone, through the medium of her art, relate to her speaker's anguish in the guise of her personal, authentic anguish. And so, perhaps, her readers might empathize with the condition of Sexton the person, for *Letters* shows her insistent need to tell others about her neuroses in whatever means available: long letters to friends and even casual acquaintances filled with intimacies of her sex life with her husband, for instance; long and demanding sessions with psychotherapists, including hysterical midnight telephone calls, ultimately causing each therapist to drop her as a patient; and, of course, the poems.

"The Double Image" uses the first person speaker as a means of portraying the intimacy of a mother (the "I") finally offering to her four-year-old daughter rational explanations of her erratic behavior. The child comprehends neither her mother's behavior nor her words, which is detrimental to the speaker's recovery. She needs the child's understanding, if not her absolution, to help in redefining herself, as suggested in the poem's final sequence of lines: "I, who was never quite sure / about being a girl, needed another / life, another image to remind me. / And this was my worst guilt; you could not cure / nor soothe it. I made you to find me." The confession, here revealed in the last phrase, is the speaker's admission of a wholly selfish motive for bearing the child whom she now contritely addresses. Especially contributory to her guilt, the speaker emphasizes, is her neglect of the child during the important first years of life: her failure to bond properly with the child because of their separation (following her multiple suicide attempts) resulted from her inability to love—including love for her daughter—enough to overcome her desire for death.

The importance of this poem is that it shows Sexton's concern for the sincere voice, the "I" as persona, from the beginning of her writing poetry. She wrote, before "The Double Image," a poem about a child's separation from her mother; this earlier poem was crafted in the first person, the speaker of the poem addressing her illegitimate child whom she gave up at birth. In an interview a year before her death, Sexton again remarked how reading "Heart's Needle" validated for her the writing of personal poetry; prior to her discovery of Snodgrass, she tried to conform her most individual subjects to more conventional modes of expression, such as what she had done to the subject of her separation from her child in the poem "Unknown Girl in the Maternity Ward," in many ways the precursor to "The Double Image." She told William Heyen of this poem:

> ...at that moment my daughter was not living at home—she was living with my mother-in-law because it was felt I was not well enough to take care of her...but I ran up and got my daughter.... And I wrote at that time "Unknown Girl in the Maternity Ward," which is a mask—in other words...is about having an illegitimate child and giving it away, in other words about the loss of a daughter. And as a matter of fact I had met a girl in a mental hospital who had done just this and I was projecting, I was fictionalizing, but of course, I mean, so-called confessing.... I kind of nosed around and found out that Snodgrass would be at a writers conference...and he *definitely* encouraged me, and read that poem about the loss of a daughter, that kind of fictionalized

poem, and he said, "Why don't you tell the real story?" You know, he drew me out about my life. And so I spent the next seven months writing "The Double Image." (311–12)

"Unknown Girl in the Maternity Ward" appeared in the first section of *To Bedlam and Part Way Back* (1960), a book arranged fairly chronologically as the poems were written. That is, a "fictionalized" poem, as she later called it, one about somebody else—created from both fact and mythology—but expressive of her own emotions, was the kind of personal poetry Sexton chose to write in her initial development as a poet. Before finishing that first volume, however, she learned (from studying Snodgrass's technique) to control her personal subject, as she did in "The Double Image," by using the confessional mode of voice rather than deflecting a personal subject by "fictionalizing" its account, as she had done in "Unknown Girl in the Maternity Ward." The confessional "I" could allow Sexton the freedom to sound as personal, anguished, as her subject matter dictated, and yet it gave her the means for using a persona—which satisfied her critical dictum inclining her towards "fiction," away from a more direct expression of material arising from her personal history.

The "unknown girl," referring to both the speaker of the poem and her newly born child, serves as the emblem for a kind of penance the mother must endure: "You break from me. I choose / your only way, my small inheritor / and hand you off, trembling the selves we lose. / Go child, who is my sin and nothing more." Nameless, the child is given to the doctors, and this causes some regret for the speaker: "It is you my silence harms. / I should have known; I should have told / them something to write down." The speaker here regrets her having failed to provide her child with at least a tentative identity, that which the speaker of "The Double Image" admonishes herself in the final line for having failed to do: "I made you to find me." To find *me* is the speaker's emphasis, not to become *you*. So each poem uses as its dramatic conflict the speaker-mother's act of recognition, or *anagnorisis*: that she is to blame for their physical separation as well as their estrangement in terms of knowing one another as parent and child. In each poem the mother's knowing burden of having failed to provide her daughter with a name, an identity of the child's own, becomes the essential doubt, the reason, the speaker believes, for their actual/personal separateness.

These two poems show Sexton's care in preserving the integrity of poetic art while simultaneously treating a personal subject, something which she had been taught from the outset to exclude from poetry. ("I was told over and over: 'You can't write personal poems; you can't write about madness; you can't do this.'

Everybody I consulted said 'Nix. You don't write about that, that's not a theme,'"
she told Heyen [310].) "Unknown Girl in the Maternity Ward" was as much about
Sexton's "giving up" her daughter to her mother-in-law during a long period of
her mental illness as it was about the unwed mother and her illegitimate child.
The "fiction" which Sexton refers to regarding this poem is that of using the unwed mother as her mask to explore a personal theme she had thought improper
to the realm of art. "The Double Image," however, was bold enough to venture a
sincere treatment of a similar personal theme. The difference for Sexton had been
her use of the confessional voice, which she learned from Snodgrass. Now she
could take as her subjects any personal aspect of her life and yet retain her integrity as a poet—and keep the poem as art—by employing a persona as a speaker,
even if that persona appeared to be the authentic Anne Sexton (but actually the
sincere one) revealing the most private intimacies of her troubled life. The "I" of
"Unknown Girl in the Maternity Ward" can proclaim "There is nothing more /
that I can say or lose," with sincerity, with emotion, because readers know she is
fictional, a character in the world of a poem used to elicit such an emotional response from them. The "I" of "The Double Image," though, apparently is not a
fiction, if only the speaker of a particular poem, and so can also evoke an emotional response in the reader. It, too, is sincere, and this is why it too is a persona,
the confessional speaker revealing an instance from the poet's life, but fully aware
that this revelation is confined to the medium of poetry.

    That Sexton was interested in crafting her autobiographical material into
poems is demonstrated by her obsessive work habits: the "hours listening to the
tape recordings of her psychiatric sessions, and days rewriting her worksheets," as
her daughter reports, her insistence on writing the compulsory one poem a day,
her neglect of family responsibilities, health, relationship with her husband. All
was of secondary importance to her art; seemingly, her shaping poetry from her
life was more interesting to her than her life. She would have been a diarist, rather
than poet, if she desired merely to record her personal history. That she selected
to write of her life in the form of poetry would indicate her dedication to the
making of art. Even though we can be reasonably certain that the impetus for her
starting to write resulted from her sessions in therapy, the two always remained
distinct for Sexton. Therapy could provide material for her poetry and her poetry
could prove therapeutic, yet poetry was never therapy alone.

    If her finished poems sometimes resembled drafts, or polished journal en-
tries, it was not due to her authentic self's genuine emergence from the shackles
of a crafted voice, but to her lapse in skill as a poet. Alicia Ostriker has noted:

...I must say immediately and with regret that she is not a *fine* artist. At her best she is coarse. Musically her instrument is the kazoo. If Plath, say, is porcelain and Robert Lowell bronze, Sexton is brightly painted earthenware. Reading every book of hers but *Transformations*, I burn with the desire to edit. She repeats herself without noticing. Her early poems before she hits her stride tend to be too stiff, her late ones tend to be shapeless. Her phrasing is sometimes sentimental, her endings sometimes flat. (11)

But one must remember Sexton's lack of any formal preparatory training. She considered her poems primitive, she said, "because I didn't know a damn thing about poetry. Nothing! I had never gone to college, I absolutely was a flunk-out in any schooling I had, I laughed my way through exams.... And until I started [writing poems] at twenty-seven, hadn't done much reading," she admitted to Heyen (315). And Louis Simpson wrote in his review of her first book: "From the jacket I learn that she has been writing poems for only three years. This then is a phenomenon, like Rimbaud, to remind us, when we have forgotten in the weariness of literature, that poetry can happen" (64).

It seems that Sexton's work had been enhanced by her rather inchoate aesthetic since shoddy craftsmanship tends to make a personal poem all the more sincere—the poet, after all, had not the time to shape more artfully the verse; the importance of transferring the emotion, the incident, to the page was primary, not the sound or look of the poem. Yet given Sexton's conscious use of the confessional "I" (even if we grant her "unconscious" rendering of material to her readers, that which she may be concealing from herself, as she suggested), the apparently spontaneous images—coarsely constructed or not—help provide the veracity of a sincerely intended confession. Regardless whether Sexton played her "kazoo" to evoke the sincerity of her speaker, one result of her aesthetic was that she succeeded in this; her confessional voice does indeed sound sincere.

And sincerity had been the intention of many of her personal poems. She once echoed Lowell's remark about *Life Studies*, that "if a poem is autobiographical you want the reader...to believe he was getting the *real* Robert Lowell," when in truth the reader was getting Lowell's confessional voice, successful in portraying its sincerity and so convincing many readers it was the "real" Robert Lowell. Sexton similarly said to the *Paris Review*:

> I don't adhere to literal facts all the time; I make them up whenever needed. Concrete examples give a verisimilitude. I want the reader to feel, "Yes, yes, that's the way it is." I want them to feel as if they were touching me. I would alter any word, attitude, image or persona for the sake of the poem. (182)

She begins her remarks in a slightly marked difference from Lowell's emphasis. She would alter the facts of an autobiographical experience in her poem's account of it in order to allow the reader to relate better to the experience. But she makes clear her desire for her readers to say they felt as though they were "touching" the authentic Anne Sexton, not the Sexton persona of the poem, the confessional voice in the first person. Craft, specifically voice, is the most viable method a poem can use to generate such verisimilitude, to make a reader believe he or she is "getting the *real* Anne Sexton."

"The Double Image," as we have seen, is Sexton's admitted attempt to unmask herself, covered as she was in an earlier poem as the "unknown girl." But she did not reveal all of her private—authentic—self in that poem either. The use of the confessional mode allowed her to appear sincere enough for her readers "to feel as if they touched" her and still retain some of the persona guise she employed in "Unknown Girl in the Maternity Ward," as she told the *Paris Review*:

> In "The Double Image" . . . I don't mention that I had another child. Each poem has its own truth. Furthermore, in that poem, I only say that I was hospitalized twice, when in fact, I was hospitalized five times in that span of time. But then, poetic truth is not necessarily autobiographical. It is truth that goes beyond the immediate self, another life. (182)

If poetic truth, as Sexton terms it, is not necessarily autobiographical, it is often in her early poetry—such as "The Double Image"—at least autobiographically based to a large extent. The altering of certain details, however, preserves the distinction between "poetic truth," which also could be known as the sincere self speaking (or the confessional voice), and that which is "autobiographical," in Sexton's sense of the term, or wholly authentic—the details of the poem remaining true to fact.

Yet Sexton insisted she was perhaps the only truly confessional poet because she wrote about "what my parents were really like, the whole Gothic New England story," about her childhood, suicide attempts, which all takes the courage to be prepared for "the appalling horror that awaits you in the answer," she said to the *Paris Review* (163). If, then, Sexton could separate poetic truth from her autobiography, she could not help but regard herself as "an actress in my own autobiographical play." The poem easily could be seen as a type of "play" for Sexton because she adopted the confessional voice over her (authentic) own voice for use as the speaker. She said later in that interview that her poetry readings "take so much out of you, because they are a reliving of the experience, that is, they are happening all over again. I am an actress in my own autobiographical play" (189).

The initial experience of composing the poem dictated another self as speaker, an "actress"; so, too, does the reliving of the experience via reading her poems to an audience: Another self must be created to tell of the self depicted in the poem. Her reading persona, although possibly very different from her poems' speaker, is as much an actress as the sincere "I" of the personal poems involving poetic truth rather than autobiography. Sexton could not reveal her authentic self in verse any more than she would be able to in reading the poems—written, of course, by her private self—which are in the confessional mode. She is an actress, a self that is sincere, presenting sometimes distorted scenes from her history. The reading of her poetry was as if it were "happening all over again" in the sincere form of voice.

Although this matter of distinguishing the poet from the poem seems readily understandable, the issues again become unclear when the poet depends so greatly on her autobiography for material: When does the poet cease being her authentic self and become instead an artificial device, the speaker of her poem? This is the question that has confused Sexton's commentators from the outset, and still does today. Diana Hume George bases her psychoanalytic study of Sexton on the predication that Sexton's confessional speaker—and George is careful to refer to a poem's voice as such—is representative of the authentic Anne Sexton, and so uses Sexton's personal poetry as evidence for her analysis, failing to recognize that the sincere "I" persona (of these poems of poetic truth) is but one type of speaker, one persona for the actress, not wholly reflective of the Anne Sexton authoring her poetry. Perhaps Sexton's intention of having her poems make their readers feel as though they were actually "touching" her was too successful; too many of her readers and critics feel they are "getting the real Anne Sexton" when in fact they are reading the work of a poet who created—as one of the many facets of her technique—another self as speaker.

Two critics of her time, Louis Simpson and James Dickey, both praised her first book, claiming in turn that it was emotive, that Sexton was courageous for undertaking such openness in revealing her life's nightmarish story in verse. Dickey wrote of *To Bedlam and Part Way Back* that the craft is undisciplined even though "the experiences she recounts are among the most harrowing that human beings can undergo: those of madness and near-madness, of the pathetic, well-meaning, necessarily tentative and perilous attempts at cure, and of the patient's slow coming back…" (318). Simpson, as noted, remarked that Sexton's first book proved that poetry still can "happen." Even though Dickey was her harshest critic, he seemed pleased nonetheless that Sexton wrote of madness, about which he said: "In addition to being an extremely painful subject, this is perhaps a major one for poetry, with a sickeningly frightening appropriateness to our time" (318).

As long as she wrote about "the experience of madness," as she said of her first book, the reviewers seemed content to relegate her rather primitive (she later called it) artistic constructions as less important than her content. But when she undertook an exploration of "the causes of madness," which she believed was the aim of her second book, the critics questioned her taste in poetic matter; that is, once more they deemed her subject inappropriate to poetry. Dickey, in the *New York Times Book Review*, called "her attitude" in *All My Pretty Ones* (1962) "a curious compound of self-deprecatory cynicism and sentimentality-congratulating-itself-on-not-being-caught, as when Miss [sic] Sexton sees her stomach, after surgery, as being 'laced up like a football / for the game' (as though footballs were laced up for games) or when she says to 'K. Owyne': 'I washed lobster and stale gin / off your shirt. We lived in sin / in too many rooms'" (50). Sexton sees? *She* says to "K. Owyne"? Obviously Dickey did not know that Sexton had adopted the confessional mode of voice, distinct from herself as poet. He was content with Sexton's treatment of her experience with madness in her first book because that for him seemed appropriate for what he considered to be the authentic Anne Sexton speaker, yet when her subject shifted in her second book to her reasoning as to the causes of madness, Dickey no longer could accept what he thought authentic, the private Sexton as voice of her poetry, and so condemned it for faulty technique.

Comparably, Louis Simpson, in reviewing her 1966 book *Live or Die* (a book, she said, in which she decided whether to live or die, having resolved—at least in poetry—the experiences and causes of her madness), criticized her work: "A poem titled 'Menstruation at Forty' was the straw that broke this camel's back," he said after praising her first book as "great." After Sexton succeeded in using herself as her principal poetic subject—thus overcoming the objections of her very first tutors and readers—and having been lauded for these early efforts, she again encountered the criticism she heard at the outset: Her personal history was not suited for poetry. These objectors, however, failed to understand her personal subjects as poetry, as artistic creations utilizing a type of persona for voice.

Two poems will help determine where this distinction can be made between the authentic and the sincere (but authentic sounding) Sexton voice, and show more fully her method in creating such a voice. Her much anthologized "You, Doctor Martin" combines autobiographical details with Sexton's poetic truth—her images, parallels, metaphors—in order to craft her style of personal poetry, her kind of confessional verse. The first matter to clear about this poem is that a "Dr. Martin" was never her therapist; a Dr. Martin Orne, her second analyst, treated her for seven years (from 1956 to 1963), as Maxine Kumin writes in her introduction to Sexton's *Complete Poems* (1981), and whose treatment is well recounted in Diane Wood Middlebrook's *Anne Sexton*. But even this documented (and small) fact is overlooked by those critics anxious to correlate with Sexton herself every detail related by her first person speaker, as Manju Jaidka does when she says: "Her psychiatrist, Dr. Martin, advised her to write poetry as a way to exorcise her terrors..." (45), which statement itself is not wholly accurate, as we know from Sexton's telling of how she came to write.

Similar to Lowell's construction of "Waking in the Blue," Sexton's "You, Doctor Martin" adheres to a rhyme scheme. Unlike Lowell's poem, though, Sexton's is formed by a rather tight stanza pattern throughout, each following her original scheme of abcabcb, but the line meter is not regular. Lowell scattered couplets throughout "Waking in the Blue" without regard to any particular form, stanza pattern, or meter regularity. The two poems offer themselves for comparison since both—besides using the confessional mode—concern the speaker's experience of recovery in a mental ward following a breakdown. Both poems' speakers move toward self-realization as one consequence of their hospital stay, and both attempt a relaxed manner of diction, a conversational style—a technique Dickey objected to in his review of *To Bedlam and Part Way Back*, saying: "[It] is a kind of writing I dislike to such an extent that I feel, perhaps irrationally, that everyone else including Mrs. Sexton ought to dislike it, too, for its easy, A-student, superficially exact 'differentness' and its straining to make contrivance and artificiality appear natural" (318). Dickey is accurate about her "contrived" diction, and it is this very point which suggests Sexton's conscious effort to sound "confessional," as if she were speaking of her direct experience in an offhanded, more honest and real, rather than poetic, way. Her "artificiality," the striving to make her speaker sound as if it were the real Anne, was her artistic method to affect a "differentness," which was her means of convincing readers of her sincerity. She told William Packard that: "I'm too rhythmic. You fight what you've got. I can't bear to be too rhythmical if I'm going to be confessional" (46)—confessional, that is, in the sense of creating a sincere voice that is speaking poetic truth only. A specific and regular meter count in "You, Doctor Martin" might have impeded her crafting a poem that was to make its readers believe they were touching actually the poet.

The opening stanza is exemplary of many aspects of Sexton's aesthetic in this regard:

> You, Doctor Martin, walk
> from breakfast to madness. Late August,
> I speed through the antiseptic tunnel

> where the moving dead still talk
> of pushing their bones against the thrust
> of cure. And I am queen of this summer hotel
> or the laughing bee on a stalk

This stanza, as does much of the poem, relies on completely grammatical sentences, each using the simple-sentence formation of subject-verb-object syntax; many sentence subjects are personal pronouns, often "I." Lowell frequently used in his "Life Studies" sequence the simple-sentence construction with "I" as subject in order to validate his speaker's sincerity; Sexton, too, accomplishes the same with her use of prose in verse. It is one way she "fights" her being "too rhythmic," and it serves to create a more believable speaker, one whose sincerity makes it seem that the reader could be touching the authentic poet. The credibility of the speaker is what ultimately determines the artistic success of a Sexton confessional poem, and (judging from her critics' responses) she mastered the making of a sincere poetic voice to appear as authentically real as she.

The poem's speaker, although more focused on the psychiatrist of its title, attempts to explore her self-identity, and finally comes to a momentary understanding of her present self—again, similar to Lowell's "Waking in the Blue," whose speaker declares in the final line: "each of us holds a locked razor." Both poems concentrate on the theme of self-discovery, of comprehending the sense of beginning the long recovery which must include an awareness of one's present self. The poem lures the reader away from Dr. Martin to one of his patients, the speaker of the poem who implies that she is not very representative of the group confined to psychiatric care in that institution—she "speeds" among the "moving dead," for example, and says of herself: "I am queen…or the laughing bee," considering herself as either reigning over the other patients or mocking her (and their) certain "death" of a more normal life, free of psychotherapy. Such a life is Dr. Martin's, one of normalcy. He casually views his patients' mental illnesses as his business to which he must attend: "You…walk / from breakfast to madness," while "we," the speaker thus implies, do not leave it behind at five until the next working day, but must endure it always, and so the poem's emphasis becomes the issue of how the speaker sees her doctor treating her own mental condition.

He is in her view "an oracular / eye in our nest," but nevertheless incapable of answering for her: "Am I still lost?" Patients are "the foxy children who fall // like floods of life in frost," pulling at their doctor in their helplessness. Deftly he twists away, leaving to answer the page of the intercom. If the speaker's attitude toward her psychiatrist in this poem is ambivalent (he is alternately described as "oracular" and as a cagey businessman), her self-realization seems resolute, yet tentative: "Am I still lost? / Once I was beautiful. Now I am myself, / counting this row and that row of moccasins"—made by the mental patients as an aspect of their therapy—alludes to Sexton's speaker's "waiting" either for a more full recovery or to suffer yet another breakdown. Like the moccasins, too, the speaker at this point may see herself as having been packaged, made to be silent (that is, momentarily free of hysterics, psycho-illness), made to conform, perhaps, to the therapy offered her by Dr. Martin. He sees his patients (given this last reading), then, as tasks which are terminal and fairly easily completed—like banal and daily functions of business. This represents the darkest side of the speaker's indeterminate view of her therapist; seen at his brightest, his methods are compared to the classic oracle's.

The speaker's view of self changes as she oscillates between her perceptions of Dr. Martin. Whereas Lowell's speaker is absolute about his self-attitude by the end of "Waking in the Blue," "You, Doctor Martin," with its dual focus—the psychiatrist and the speaker—eventually elicits a theme reflective of the speaker's uncertainty regarding her self-identity. The speaker's equivocal definition of herself parallels the poem's aesthetic. The principal attention of both voice and structure remains blurred—as does the speaker's conception of her present self.

If the sincere voice appears seemingly indecisive about her mental condition, her future, the authentic Sexton—composer of the poem—is of course quite in control of her craft. Sexton carefully designed her poem's voice and structure to reflect the final focus of the poem. Further, she used a stanza scheme she invented to formalize her speaker's rather protean attitudes—by this, Sexton the poet can contain the disparate mind of the Sexton voice of the poem. Something like Dylan Thomas, who often couched violent images in the beauty of his lyrics and in tight forms, Sexton followed her formal stanza ordering when presenting her autobiographically based account of the breakdown of pattern, the disillusionment of form—madness. The subject matter of the poem is confessional (like Lowell's) because it is derived from her personal history, and it was this history she was compelled to write of in verse. Yet the self presented in the poem as having experienced confinement in a mental ward is not the authentic Sexton as we know. Inasmuch as certain details were altered in the presentation of her autobiography in verse—details such as her therapist's name, the ordering of her thoughts to conform to a particular rhyme scheme and image sequence, of parallelism in the thought process of the speaker—Sexton the poet, the person who in fact suffered the mental breakdown and subsequent treatment by a Dr. Martin Orne, absents herself from the poem carved from her life. The poem, although taken from her life's experience, is not a history of a part of her life. It is, rather, intended as art, a rendering of a Sexton artifice as speaker.

Another confessional poem a bit later in *Bedlam*, "Said the Poet to the Analyst," further called into question in the minds of many commentators Sexton's rather thinly disguised line between the voice of her poem and herself. Here, seemingly, Sexton did not bother to attempt a distinction between Sexton the creator of the poem and Sexton the artistic creation as character and voice of it. Her title would make it nearly impossible to discuss the two as separate—after all, the "poet" now acts as both the poem's composer and its voice, something critics had assumed of all the poems in the volume. The poem is structured simply as two stanzas, each apparently confined to a single topic—the first about the poet, the second about the analyst—but both finally revolving around the poet, the voice of the poem. Here the nine-line stanzas are not as regularly end-rhymed as in "You, Doctor Martin," but Sexton does show her inventive style of stanza pattern: xxa-babcxc (the rhymes beginning with the third line), albeit without consistent meter or syllable count. This should be taken as our first hint that the poet-voice of the poem is crafted sincerely, made up by the Sexton who might have said such things to her analyst. But, that Sexton wanted to formalize her poem based on autobiography through the means of rhyme and stanza regularity would suggest her willingness to mask her authentic self and create another in its place. As we have seen in "You, Doctor Martin," Sexton's crafting art from her experience led to her developing a persona. Her rhymes demonstrate her control in the presentation of her subject, indicating a conscious restraint that inevitably precludes any poet's revealing of his or her authentic self in poetry.

"My business," the poet says in the opening line, "is words." (The poet will counter that statement with the initial line of the following stanza addressed to the analyst: "Your business is watching my words.") The poet in the first stanza compares her business to "swarming bees," that is, to the many working in tandem to create the illusion of a unified force moving toward a single goal. She says ("I confess") that: "I am only broken by the source of things," a phrase that would suggest her poetic spirit's disengagement when remembering her source of inspiration, that when the poet uncovers—possibly for the first time—her impetus for writing, her subject, and motivation for her words, she is broken, remindful of her sorrowful state, her mental collapse which led her to her work of words. If, then, there is any confession to make, the poet says, it is her self-delusion in thinking her "words are like labels, / or coins, or better, like swarming bees." And when "broken by the sources of things," the words then seem as if they "were counted like dead bees in the attic," individual, no longer in death able to swarm and focus. Single words, too, are powerless unless properly placed—if they work in conjunction purposefully—toward the comprising of the poem. Her confession here is one of fear of the failure of her business, that she may produce a swarm of words but it may be just as dead and useless as the easily counted bees in the attic.

This rather ill-chosen allusion to bees aside (an example of what Sexton might have seen as primitive—called unrestrained and coarse by critics), it does reveal the poet-voice's admitting to covering (not illuminating) the emotional or physical source of the poem—in this case, her mental illness. So to keep this guise, to continue to believe her poems are less than honest with respect to her not risking exposing words individually (but rather hiding each in a mass, as does the swarm for the individual bee), she says: "I must always forget how one word is able to pick / out another, to manner another, until I have got / something I might have said... / but did not." The one word seen in relation to the rest might divulge the poet's stimulus in writing it, or it might disclose the authentic poet herself. If so, writing becomes too daring a practice unless the poet can forget that any one word can be seen to influence the reading of others so that a particular interpretation of "something I might have said... / but did not" is gleaned from the poem. The poet actually is confessing to the intentional obscuring of her private self in the poem. If the poet somehow "remembers" that any one word can betray her, she will not write—therefore she "must always forget" the possibility that even her best efforts at "swarming" can be subverted by an unconscious placing of words, acting in such capacity as they can do to declare some private aspect of the poet's self.

It is this kind of revealing of one's private self that most interests the analyst, as the poet informs us in the second stanza. We have already read how in sessions with her psychiatrist Sexton at times concealed those images or ideas she wished to use in her poetry; here she gives us a poem in which a poet (her persona) declares the same. "I admit nothing," the poet says to her analyst. However, that the actual poet Sexton has written a poem in which her poet-voice tells her therapist that her poems are not consciously revealing of her authentic self attests to Sexton's assiduity in preserving the mode's integrity: by presenting a voice—here a poet—which adumbrates only that self whose mental condition generates the poem she writes. "I work best," the poet continues, "when I can write my praise for a nickel machine, / that one night in Nevada." This refers not only to her claiming that she considers her best poetry that which is about inanimate objects, anything deflective of personal matter, but to her metaphoric use of "coins" in stanza one, that her poetic words are like them. In writing her "praise" for a slot machine, the poet reveals her writing about herself: The machine produces nickles and she produces words. And this is the closest the poet will admit to writing about herself, an obfuscated version of the self as gambling machine, one able to make words into poems that at once wish to take the chance of disclosing and concealing the poet's self. And if the analyst should find the poem about the slot machine more revealing of the poet's self, "then," the poet says, "I grow weak, re-membering how my hands felt funny / and ridiculous and crowded with all / the believing money." This is to say that after the analyst points out to the poet-pa-tient where in the poem she has betrayed her private self, the poet will succumb to his reading, "remembering" how certain images and details do indeed suggest a more intimate conception of her private self than she first realized or intended.

This interpretation of "Said the Poet to the Analyst" would argue for the speaker-poet's unconscious desire to present to her analyst through the medium of the poem that which she is reticent about with him in a therapeutic session. The poem acts as a barrier, the poet believes, but as an instrument of discourse as well: It allows the poet to write of the most haunting images relevant to an under-standing of the self and the horrors of mental collapse, and it can mask them as art. Unknowingly to the poet, the poem serves though not as a barrier but an en-lightenment for the analyst—as much as dreams or journal entries can be for his analysis. This poem seems to make clear how always conscious Sexton was of her aesthetic. Her creation of a poet who is craft-conscious in the hopes of not expos-ing her private self suggests that Sexton was aware of how her poems could be used in analysis, and how untrustworthy—to a certain extent—an instrument of analysis a poem could prove since her speaker is as much an artistic device as the symbolic material making up the poem: the slot machine, the bees. Sexton could create a poem in which a poet reveals a part of herself—if not deliberately—through the words she chooses and the way she places them in configuration with one another, through the images and symbols she decides upon in expressing her poem's themes, but Sexton the poet declared that "in therapy, one seeks to hide sometimes"—maybe an image about remembering her parents, one she felt could be used best in a poem and would not be immediately helpful in a therapeutic session. She told the *Paris Review*:

> …my analyst asked me what I thought of my parents having intercourse when I was young. I couldn't talk. I knew there was suddenly a poem there, and I selfishly guarded it from him. Two days later, I had a poem…. (162)

She then showed the poem to her analyst, no longer afraid her poetic material might be lost by discussing it in analysis. Yet still an image in that poem—the

"royal strapping" the father gave to the speaker's mother— was seen by the analyst as Sexton's subconscious association with a childhood whipping her father
once gave her. Until the analyst pointed it out, Sexton had not seen the connection. It could be, then, that the poet can reveal bits of her most private self by a
certain choice of words, but Sexton was not fearful of this (her first regard was to
keep the incident from her therapist only long enough to write the poem—which
she later showed him), even if the poet-voice of her poem was.

The two cannot be equated accurately; we must be mindful of Trilling's argument concerning the sincere voice, the one that can "lie and invent a bit" about
what really happened (as Lowell said of his confessional voice). The prevailing
thought suggesting that Sexton used an authentic voice in her poetry may result
from believing that a persona—even one that is called "I"—will detract from the
dramatic and emotional impact of the poem. However, any successful poem of
this mode, such as many of Sexton's, will accomplish the same emotive impact of
which an authentic voice presumably is capable since it will have used a persona
which directs readers into feeling they actually were touching the poet. They will
have been touching in a Sexton confessional only the poet represented as the
speaker in the poem, not of it.

MARK STRAND'S "SHOOTING WHALES" and John Berryman's "The Ball Poem"
use many aspects of the confessional voice we have been identifying. "Shooting
Whales," from the "New Poems" section of Strand's *Selected Poems* (1980), is
structured by its narrative. The Strand persona, an "I" speaker, recalls an incident
from his childhood in this poem and, in the manner of Lowell's "Dunbarton," the
voice attempts to simulate that of Strand speaking as a child—that is, from the
child's perspective. Consequently, the tone is one of a child's fright, insecurity. So
whereas "Dunbarton" ends with the child Lowell persona proclaiming his feeling
of warmth and security: "I cuddled like a paramour in my Grandfather's bed,"
Strand's poem ends with the child alone in his bed, afraid and unable to sleep:

> But the plankton kept coming in
> and the whales would not go.
>
> That's when the shooting began.
> The fishermen got in their boats
> and went after the whales,
> and my father and uncle
> and we children went, too....

When we cut our engine and waited
for the whales to surface again,
the sun was setting,
turning the rock-strewn barrens a gaudy salmon.
A cold wind flailed at our skin.
When finally the sun went down
and it seemed like the whales had gone,
my uncle, no longer afraid,
shot aimlessly into the sky....

At midnight
when I went to bed
I imagined the whales
moving beneath me,
sliding over the weed-covered hills of the deep;
they knew where I was;
they were luring me
downward and downward
into the murmurous
waters of sleep.

The poem follows a linear narrative and contains complete, lyrical sentences, often one to a stanza. The sincerity of the first person speaker, the plausibility of the poem's dramatic situation, and the syntax are indicative of the confessional voice. "Shooting Whales" marks a distinction from Strand's earlier work, which is characterized by wit, unrealistic plot circumstances, and an impersonal, detached narrator. (Those poems will represent the uses of voice in personal poetry of the self-effacing mode analyzed in chapter 4.)

John Berryman's "The Ball Poem," from *The Dispossessed* (1948), is a personal poem in which the voice projects individual concerns on the subject. In this way, it is like Wright's "A Blessing" where the speaker attributes his own emotions to the ponies. The voice of "The Ball Poem," in which the first person speaker addresses himself, weighs the loss of a boy's ball against his own losses and desolation. The boy is never actually addressed by the speaker and therefore cannot be consoled by the speaker's reasoning. The speaker who seemingly intends his remarks for the boy betrays his self-pity, but attempts to hide his personal emotions in words of consolation for another person. The speaker of the poem, upon witnessing the boy lose his ball, reveals his private fears while describing the boy's supposed emotional reaction to his loss:

What is the boy now, who has lost his ball,
What, what is he to do?...
No use to say 'O there are other balls'...
            Now
He senses first responsibility
In a world of possessions. People will take balls,
Balls will be lost always, little boy,
And no one buys a ball back. Money is external....
            I am everywhere,
I suffer and move, my mind and my heart move
With all that move me, under the water
Or whistling, I am not a little boy.

Although the first person speaker understands that the boy "senses first responsibility" and learns "how to stand up" to the loss, the speaker cannot bear his own
loss; he is not a little boy. This passage from John Haffenden's biography of Berryman suggests that Berryman's personal self-pity at the time was reflected in the
poems of *The Dispossessed*:

> At the end of February 1944, [Berryman's] appointment at Princeton ended,
> the cue to a more intense phase of despondency at unemployment. "Each
> year," he wrote,

>> I hope that next year will find me dead, and so far I have been disap-
>> pointed, but I do not lose that hope, which is almost my only one. I de-
>> spair, placed as I am, of making anyone very happy, my own griefs are
>> deep, ineradicable, and my hope of writing something of value, while it
>> has not vanished, dwindles. In the lake of the heart, storm, the frag-
>> ments of the houses of my youth.

> He became so accustomed to self-pity that the fatalism of such statements
> took on a disinterested air, as if spoken of a third person. It was characteristic
> of his attitude that he should have espoused the poetry of Aragon...where a
> bitter sentimentality and personal defeatism vis-à-vis the war in Europe har-
> monized with Berryman's own sense of affairs. Many of the poems that Ber-
> ryman was to write for a while—later included in *The Dispossessed*—followed
> Aragon's example and tone. He intended to see the conflicts of his own soul
> mirrored in the European holocaust. (152)

Given Berryman's despair during the time he wrote "The Ball Poem," the loss of
the boy's ball can be read as inciting the Berryman speaker's fear of impotence.
"Another ball is worthless," he would tell the boy, "People will take balls, / Balls

will be lost always, little boy, / And no one buys a ball back." But the Berryman speaker is not a little boy, as he says in the last line, and now when his "ball" is lost, it is of adult consequence. Another entry in Berryman's notebooks at about the time "The Ball Poem" was composed offers some corroboration to this reading:

> Extreme gloom. The end of my 30th year. I may do something hereafter, or later something something [sic] already done may show as worth while, but it does not appear so. My talent lost, like my hair, sex crumbling like my scalp. Disappointment & horror. And the collapse of will: self-distrust, contempt, sloth, & paralysis. Everything begun…everything abandoned. Every day I wish to die. (Qtd. in Haffenden 156)

The voice of "The Ball Poem" is confessional, focused on the "I" speaker—a personal one—rather than the boy. The voice masks its own concerns with the boy's circumstance (just as Berryman's fatalistic "statements took on a disinterested air, as if spoken of a third person"), yet as the poem's final lines indicate, the personal, "self-pitying fatalism" of the speaker emerges as the dominant theme of the poem.

This poem, although using the confessional voice, serves as a rather fitting prelude—in that the speaker shields his concern by the narrative of the boy's incident—to the ensuing discussion of the persona mode in the next chapter, a mode exemplified by Berryman's work.

Three

჻

The Persona Mode

JOHN BERRYMAN IS THE OBVIOUS representative poet of the persona mode because of his sustained work in using his persona "Henry" as the speaker of his long book of verse, *The Dream Songs* (1969), and because of the amount of biographical evidence available that can be used to suggest some meaningful parallels between Berryman and his persona. Two full-length biographies have been published: John Haffenden's *The Life of John Berryman* (1982) and Paul Mariani's more recent *Dream Song: The Life of John Berryman* (1990). This biographical evidence informs us, too, of the differences separating Berryman's actual life experiences from how he chose Henry to represent them. Berryman's use of the persona mode allows the poet to reveal his emotions and to express his most personal desires—all through the voice of a persona who is the poet's alter ego and is nearly, though not entirely, indistinguishable from the poet himself. The persona voice, though, gives Berryman the freedom to say in his verse anything he likes, show any emotion, muse over any subject, and escape the accusation of having written inferior verse—a charge often aimed at those writing in the confessional mode—for it is "Henry," albeit a weakly disguised Berryman, and not "John Berryman with a social security number" (as he used to say), who is sentimental, nostalgic, introspective—reconditely so.

Yet this single voice of "Henry" accounts for differing perspectives. In *The Dream Songs*, Henry refers to himself sometimes in the first person, sometimes in the third, and in each the tone of voice is different and used for varying purposes as we shall see.

Other poets experimented in slightly different ways with the persona mode. Weldon Kees has a more subtle persona in "Robinson" in that we cannot be certain whether Robinson's experiences correlate directly to Kees's own life. Given the sparse biographical information on Kees, we cannot assume any parallels between him and his persona as readily as we can with Berryman and Henry. However, Kees regarded his Robinson as a representative man, an archetype of modern man confronted with the fears of imminent extinction. This use of the persona voice presents another method of self-examination: The behavior of the one, who is typical of the many (including of course the poet), is explored in the poetry through the voice of the persona.

Different in his thematic concerns as well as his aesthetic approach to the persona voice, Galway Kinnell explores the possibilities of changing not merely into another mask, but altogether from the human form into animal form. From this persona, with its shifting perspective, Kinnell attempts to augment his self-knowledge, particularly in order to overcome his speaker's fear of dying.

All three poets found, through the persona mode, a means to express ideas about the self: Kees and Kinnell use the persona to voice their concerns about an individual's worth, the value of his life, in a modern world that seems to them to be growing more alien daily; and Berryman discovered that he could write about himself, about his personal feelings, under the guise of a persona voice, something he could not do for much of his writing career in his own personal voice.

JOHN BERRYMAN

JOHN BERRYMAN'S FIRST WIFE, Eileen Simpson, remembers that Berryman did not like talking about himself, even in conversations with close friends. In the following passage, she writes of his and Delmore Schwartz's contrasting behavior in this regard:

> ... John often wondered aloud how it was that he, who with other people was so articulate, was so silent with Delmore.... If the four of us were together, or there were guests at the Schwartzes', the talk was literary and John did almost as much talking as Delmore. It was when it was just the three of us, and Delmore's conversation was autobiographical rather than bookish, that John (though keenly interested in what Delmore had to say) was likely to be silent. The natural thing would have been for him to talk about his family too, but it

was a subject about which he was reticent in the beginning, even with me. He rarely mentioned his father. His mother, who was so actively involved in his life that he couldn't have left her out of his conversation had he wanted to, he talked about in the present tense....

So Delmore's candor about the flaws in Harry Schwartz's character... astonished John. Once, pushed beyond endurance by something his mother had done, Delmore said he hated her. John, who had learned his catechism well, was shocked. One must honor one's father and mother. (36–7)

That Berryman was reticent in discussing the "flaws" of his parents' characters and that he chose to "honor" them perhaps out of religious obligation even, does not, however, satisfactorily explain why he, unlike Schwartz, was not disposed towards talking about his own autobiography.

Certainly Berryman "talked" freely of his personal life in his creative work. A striking example of this can be found in an early prose work. First I will quote Simpson's account of a particular experience of Berryman's, then show how Berryman portrayed the same experience in fiction. Simpson recounts the incident, which Berryman told her about, as follows:

One night, on his way home to Lexington Avenue, he cut across Union Square and stopped by a cluster of men to listen to a dispute. Before he knew what was happening, he was caught up in an argument about the entrance of the United States into the war. When he tried to inject reason into the "savage" argument, the ringleader told him to shut up, and called him a Jew. John's objection that he wasn't a Jew but a Catholic enraged the leader, who shouted at him, "You look like a Jew, you talk like a Jew, you are a Jew," and challenged John to disprove the charges by reciting the Apostles' Creed. Partly because by now John, too, was angry, partly because he hadn't said the Creed in years, he could recall from his days as an altar boy only phrases of the Latin—proof, the leader told the crowd, that John *was* a Jew. The crowd, which was convinced by the leader's reasoning and thought there was nothing further to be said, lost interest and drifted off to join other groups. (7)

This, now, is from the last part of Berryman's story "The Imaginary Jew," published in 1945:

Looking around I saw sitting on a bench near me a tall, heavy, serious-looking man of thirty, well dressed, whom I had noticed earlier, and appealed to him, "Tell me, do I look Jewish?"

But he only stared up and waved his head vaguely. I saw with horror that something was wrong with him.

"You look like a Jew. You talk like a Jew. You *are* a Jew," I heard the

Irishman say....
    "Now listen, you Jew. I'm a Catholic."
    "So am I, or I was born one, I'm not now. I was born a Catholic...."
    "Yeah?" said the Irishman. "Say the Apostles' Creed."
    Memory went swirling back, I could hear the little bell die as I hushed
it and set it on the felt, Father Boniface looked at me tall from the top of the
steps and smiled greeting me in the darkness before dawn as I came to serve,
the men pressed around me under the lamps, and I could remember nothing
but *visibilum omnium... et invisibilium?*
    "I don't remember it."
    The Irishman laughed with his certainty.

Even allowing for the likelihood of Simpson's remembering the "fictional" story
better than Berryman's telling her of his encounter (which probably accounts for
the similar dialogue in the two), it is clear that Berryman found a medium which
allowed him to overcome his reticence of discussing his autobiography. The first
person narrator of "The Imaginary Jew," when attempting the Apostles' Creed,
thinks of his days serving Mass for Father Boniface. So, too, did Berryman serve
for the same priest. In an interview with Peter Stitt, he said: "I had a strict Catholic training. I went to a Catholic school and I adored my priest, Father Boniface. I
began serving Mass under him at the age of five, and I used to serve six days a
week. Often there would be nobody in the church except him and me" (319).

    Berryman in fact seemingly had a penchant for recording his memorable
experiences directly into his prose fiction. In his novel, *Recovery* (posthumously
published in 1973), the first person narrator, Dr. Alan Severance, tells a fellow patient about the time he was distraught at not being allowed to leave the hospital in
order to lecture his university class:

    "...class met at one-fifteen, it wasn't even clear that I could get my secretary
    on the phone in time, much less the Director, and besides what could they
    do? *I sweated.* Meanwhile the tone of the Group had metamorphosed.... They
    were all consolation, advice, sympathy, even praise.... I simply did not know
    what to do, in my opinion nothing *could* be done.... You see the lecture was
    on the Fourth Gospel.... Somebody suddenly said, 'Vin's trained in divinity!'
    and there was Vin looking hot-faced at me saying, 'I'll give your lecture for
    you.' I felt stunned. I said, 'You're not serious.' 'Oh yes I am,' he said.... I had
    hit him very hard two times that morning. 'You're not kidding me?' I
    said... 'No, no, I'll do it—if necessary, I'll teach it in Greek!' I saw he meant it,
    Mary-Jane, God Almighty. I said, 'I could kiss you!' He said—he's a maniac—
    'Well, do,' and so help me I leaned across Keg (who, it vaguely and irritably

even in that moment came to me, was *laughing*) and Vin and I embraced and kissed cheeks." (47–8)

In speaking of an experience from his life that was for him a manifestation of "the idea of a God of rescue," Berryman recounted for Stitt the following scene, which took place while he was in group therapy:

> Then I was in real despair. I couldn't just ring up the secretary and have her dismiss my class—it would be grotesque. Here it was, eleven-thirty, and class met at one-fifteen. I didn't even know if I could get my chairman on the phone to find somebody to meet them. And even if I could, who could he have found that would have been qualified? We have no divinity school here. Well, all kinds of consolations and suggestions came from the group, and suddenly my counselor said, "Well, I'm trained in divinity. I'll give your lecture for you."
>
> And I said, "You're kidding!" He and I had had some very sharp exchanges. I had called him sarcastic, arrogant, tyrannical, incompetent, theatrical, judgmental, and so on.
>
> He said, "Yes, I'll teach it if I have to teach it in Greek!"
>
> I said, "I can't believe it. Are you serious?"
>
> He said, "Yes, I'm serious."
>
> And I said, "I could kiss you."
>
> He said, "Do." There was only one man between us, so I leaned over and we embraced. (318–19)

Berryman recorded in his fiction even the details of this experience: the time the class met, the dialogue, the expression of joy and relief. It was obviously memorable to Berryman, but the incident carried a spiritual significance for him also. He continued: "Well, when I thought it over in the afternoon, I suddenly recalled what has been for many years one of my favorite conceptions. I got it from Augustine and Pascal. It's found in many other people, too, but especially in those heroes of mine. Namely, the idea of a God of rescue. He saves men from their situations, off and on during life's pilgrimage, and in the end" (319). This was precisely the epiphany that Berryman's fictional protagonist Severance was trying to explain to Mary-Jane in *Recovery*.

Apparently Berryman felt that his critical work could serve as a means of expressing his personal concerns as well as his fiction could. Eileen Simpson believes that Berryman saw himself reflected in the life of Stephan Crane, whose biography Berryman was writing in 1949. She reports of that time:

Freud had the answer, John told me, trembling with excitement after reading the paper called "A Special Type of Choice of Object Made by Men."

The danger was that if Freud explained Crane's behavior, he also threatened to explain John's. For, more and more, John saw similarities between Crane's life and his own. Crane had lost his father early, had been raised by a strong-minded mother who had favored him in a way that undermined his adult relationships with other women. He had been an apostate whose strong conscience tortured him over his sexual behavior. He had felt a need, as Mark Van Doren had written, "to live, at least as an artist, in the midst of all but unbearable excitement." He, too, had been pulled toward suicide. When John wrote such sentences as "His force the boy got from his mother," he wondered if he was writing biography or autobiography. (186)

So the critical studies as well as the fiction reflected his personal experience. The former perhaps even unconsciously became a vehicle for self-expression, and certainly was much more subtle than the self-representation in his fiction, but still acted as an outlet. Yet Berryman only gradually came to use his verse as such. He began to inject himself consciously into his poetry when composing *Homage to Mistress Bradstreet* (1956) in the form of a character in the poem whom Berryman simply called "the poet." Although some of his earlier work made use of the confessional mode of voice (as seen in "The Ball Poem" discussed in chapter 2), *Homage* was the first poem in which Berryman purposefully incorporated himself in his verse as a character in the guise of "the poet." Similar to the reported self-interest he found in the Crane biography, Berryman was obsessed with *Homage* to the point where, Simpson recalls, "Mistress Bradstreet was vividly present in the apartment at all hours of the day and night (John's working schedule). Her life was so intertwined with ours it was sometimes difficult for him to distinguish between her and himself, between her and me. After years of childlessness... [Bradstreet] becomes pregnant. It had been to remove the one possible physical impediment to my conceiving that I had just undergone elective surgery, and returned from the hospital full of optimism... an optimism which, in the face of John's ambivalence, was highly unrealistic" (224). It is fair to suggest, then, that Berryman chose subjects for study which mirrored his personal situation—at least as suggested by Simpson in regards to the Crane and Bradstreet projects. Or it could have been that Berryman's intense involvement with his work made them seem to him self-reflective. Simpson reports further that as Berryman progressed with *Homage*, Anne Bradstreet began sounding more like Simpson herself, and "the poet," more like Berryman:

Parts of the dialogue between the poet and Anne had a familiar ring. How many times had John awakened in a fright, saying something not far from:

> I trundle the bodies, on the iron bars,
> over the fire backward & forth, they burn;
> bits fall. I wonder if
> *I* killed them.

And I, attempting to reassure him, had said, at greater length and unpoetically:

> —Dreams! You are good.—

> How many times had we taken opposite sides on the question: Does God exist? Would Anne, with her greater knowledge of Scripture, be more successful at convincing him, as he yearned to be convinced, than I had been? (227)

Yet in the poem, the "I" must still be regarded as "the poet"—and not Berryman—who is a speaker that appears first, to open *Homage*, and remains to the poem's ending. That is, "the poet" is as much a character, a fiction, as the Bradstreet character who has an affair with the twentieth century poet. It is not necessary to assume, however, that Berryman is "the poet" in order to suggest that *Homage* marked the appearance of a character as a speaker used to voice Berryman's own concerns and to reveal something of his personal life.

Even in a poem that is principally about someone else—about Anne Bradstreet—Berryman could not merely create a separate voice exclusively his subject's. In *Homage* he brought in "the poet" and fused his voice with Bradstreet's, as William Martz has argued:

> As a poem of personal caring, with consequent emphasis on personal identity, *Homage* also immediately defines itself as a poem distinctly and appealingly modern in subject and in theme. But the personal identity is the combined identity of the poet and Anne, the union, if you will, of past and present. Although the voice of the poet opens the poem and thus provides a framing point of view for what follows, the two voices blend, modulate from one to the other, and, though often distinct, are finally one voice, a voice of passion and caring, which is the final identity sought, and an emblem of our common humanity. (27)

Berryman was mostly in agreement with this perspective, for as he said in an interview with Richard Kostelanetz: "The 'I' of the twentieth-century poet modulates into her voice" (345). The poet as character, intended as a persona by Berryman to narrate *Homage*, may be more inclusive, however, of the actual poet John Berryman.

He explains his use of the pronoun "I" in the passage below taken from his essay "One Answer to a Question: Changes." Although he was referring to "The Ball Poem," his remarks are applicable to his use of pronouns in all his verse. (He once told *Life* magazine [July 21, 1967] that "if I were sitting around praising myself...I would claim to understand the pronoun better than any other living writer.")

> ...a commitment of identity can be "reserved," so to speak, with an ambiguous pronoun. The poet himself is both left out and put in; the boy does and does not become him and we are confronted with a process which is at once a process of life and a process of art. A pronoun may seem a small matter, but she matters, he matters, it matters, they matter. Without this invention...I could not have written either of the two long poems that constitute the bulk of my work so far. If I were making a grandiose claim, I might pretend to know more about the administration of pronouns than any other living poet writing in English or American. (326–27)

The "poet himself"—in reference to "The Ball Poem"—means Berryman himself, unlike *Homage* where a character who is a poet is part of the poem, its movement and dramatic situation. In either case, however, Berryman has suggested that the "I" is ambiguous, a pronoun that "matters" because it could refer to both subjects of a poem: both the boy and the "I" speaker in "The Ball Poem," and both the poet and Anne Bradstreet in *Homage*. It is evident that Berryman, whether or not in the guise of a persona as "the poet," could not keep from blending the "I" with his subjects and therefore modulating them into a single voice. As similar to his work on the Crane biography, where at times he putatively "wondered if he was writing biography or autobiography," and his work on *Homage*, which led to Bradstreet's life becoming "intertwined" with his own to the point where reportedly "it was sometimes difficult for him to distinguish between her and himself," Berryman projected himself on his subjects. The work, consequently, lost its separate "identity," becoming instead—to borrow from Martz's phrase—a personal identity which is the combined identity of the poet and subject. Berryman simply could not leave himself, his "personal identity," out of his work.

What he wrote in his essay "'Song of Myself': Intention and Substance" about Whitman's use of "I" reveals his conception of that pronoun, how it operates in verse, and his intentions for it in his own work:

For Whitman the poet is *voice*. Not solely his own—let us settle this problem quickly: a poet's first personal pronoun is nearly always ambiguous, but we have the plain declaration from Whitman that "the trunk and centre whence the answer was to radiate ... must be an identical soul and body, a personality—which personality, after many considerings and ponderings I deliberately settled should be myself—indeed could not be any other." I would sorrow over the credulity of anyone who took this account-of-the-decision-as-conscious to be historical; but I am convinced of the reality of the decision. A voice, then, for himself and others; for others *as himself*—this is the intention clearly (an underlying exhibitionism and narcissism we take for granted). What others?—Americans, man. A voice—that is, expressing (not creating)—expressing things already in existence. (230)

Berryman's "I," functioning the way he sees Whitman's operating, is not wholly personal but something like "the poet" of *Homage*, a persona—a voice "for himself and others; for others *as himself*." But he does not exclude entirely the personal side of the "I." Rather, it, like the "I" of Whitman which Berryman emphasizes, is a pronoun both universal (for others) and individual (as himself). That he intended his remarks concerning Whitman's "I" to include the personal is evident in the following passage taken from the same essay:

"'Leaves of Grass' ..." [Whitman] says, "has mainly been the outcroppings of my own emotional and personal nature—an attempt, from first to last, to put *a Person*, a human being (myself, in the latter part of the Nineteenth Century, in America) freely, fully and truly on record." I call your attention to an incongruity of this formulation with Eliot's amusing theory of the impersonality of the artist, and a contrast between the mere *putting-on-record* and the well-nigh universal current notion of *creation*, or making things up. (230)

Berryman's "Henry" of *The Dream Songs*, perhaps similar to Whitman's "voice" in that it is one expression of the consciousness of the age, can be viewed as the voice of his—Henry's—and Berryman's age as well, a voice expressive of the Zeitgeist. John Haffenden, in his introduction to Berryman's posthumous *Henry's Fate & Other Poems, 1967–1972* (1977), suggests this comparison of Henry with Fitzgerald's characters: "F. Scott Fitzgerald claimed that all his characters, filtered through his own mind and personality, belonged to the consciousness of the race, and that he could not keep the truth out of his work. The same might be said of Berryman vis-à-vis Henry's role in *The Dream Songs*, pausing only to exclude the conceit of Fitzgerald's remark" (xv-xvi). This seems much the same observation that Berryman made of Whitman: a voice for oneself and others, and because it originates from the individual, it is necessarily a voice for others—a universal expression of Zeitgeist—that is, personal, one point of view.

And this is how Berryman conceived of art. A poet begins with a personal subject, a concern for the self, in order to serve the creation of poetry. Louis Simpson's ideas about an author's personal voice may further clarify this point. Even though he was speaking of writers in general, Simpson's remarks in *A Revolution in Taste* seem relevant to Berryman:

> …what I have called the personal voice is an expression of character. And character is something made. The self that appears in the novel or poem has been constructed according to certain aesthetic principles. This version of the self is not intended to direct attention upon the author but to serve the work of art. The purpose is to create a symbolic life, a portrait of the artist that will have meaning for others and so create a feeling of community, if only among a few thousand. (169–70)

To this end—so that "a symbolic life, a portrait of the artist… [could] have meaning for others"—Berryman created a persona in his verse character, Henry, who could represent the universal consciousness.

The personal voice in his poetry is "the soul," Berryman told Kostelanetz, separate from himself:

> All the way through my work is a tendency to regard the individual soul under stress. The soul is not oneself, for the personal "I," me with a social security number and a bank account, never gets into the poem; they are all about a third person. I'm a follower of Pascal in the sense that I don't know what the issue is, or how it is to be resolved—the issue of our common human life, yours, mine, your lady's, everybody's; but I do not think that one way in which we can approach it, by the means of art, coming out of Homer and Virgil and down through Yeats and Eliot, is by investigating the individual human soul, or human mind, whichever you prefer—I couldn't care less. I have tried, therefore, to study two souls in my long poems. (345)

For Berryman, who feels that the study of the individual soul or mind will not resolve "the issue of our common human life," an investigation of a more "objective" soul or mind—insofar as all his work is "about a third person" because he considers his "I" as such—is the best means of expressing more universal concerns. Given his rationale, then, the voice of Berryman's work is always of the persona mode, whether in the guise of Henry, or another "third person" by which he means his use of "I." And the "souls" in his long poems, of course, refer to the

Bradstreet of *Homage* (where the poet's voice "modulates" into hers) and to Henry of *The Dream Songs*.

This distinction—between the "I" as the poet, the author of the verse, and the "I" as a persona, a third person—is one that Berryman insisted on making. Henry, a "third person" in the truest sense, is a persona, a voice through which Berryman speaks, and he, Henry, is thus representative of a universal soul or mind. Nevertheless, in the course of a single interview (with Stitt for *Paris Review*) Berryman made the following contradictory statements about Henry:

> I think the model in *The Dream Songs* was the other greatest American poem—I am very ambitious—"Song of Myself"—a very long poem, about sixty pages. It also has a hero, a personality, himself. Henry is accused of being me and I am accused of being Henry and I deny it and nobody believes me. (307)

Then he modified his stance:

> Suppose I take this business of the relation of Henry to me, which has interested so many people, and which is categorically denied by me in one of the forewords. Henry both is and is not me, obviously. We touch at certain points. But I am an actual human being; he is nothing but a series of conceptions—my conceptions. I brush my teeth; unless I say so somewhere in the poem—I forget whether I do or not—he doesn't brush his teeth. He only does what I make him do. If I have succeeded in making him believable, he performs all kinds of actions besides those named in the poem, but the reader has to make them up. That's the world. But it's not a religious or philosophical system. (309)

Still later in the interview, the following exchange took place while discussing *Homage*:

> The great exception was this; it did not occur to me to have a dialogue between them—to insert bodily Henry into the poem…*Me*, to insert me, in my own person, John Berryman, *I*, into the poem…
>
> Interviewer: Was that a Freudian slip?
> Berryman: I don't know. Probably. (311)

So in 1970, fourteen years after the publication of *Homage*, Berryman—who was careful to note the "I" character of that poem as "the poet," distinct from himself—not only admits that his "character" was actually himself, but also confuses himself with Henry, which was the very idea he had adamantly denied. One may take into consideration Berryman's mental health problems induced by his alcoholism which he endured around the time of this interview, but this complex matter of who Henry represents was not clear, it seems, even to the author in good health. The confusion is due mostly to Berryman's desire to create a universal voice—the way he believed Whitman had done—speaking for others, but about his personal experiences, which nevertheless he regarded as representative of his time.

Yet for an analysis of the persona mode of voice, it will not be necessary to determine conclusively whether or not Henry is in fact Berryman, whether or not Henry is no more than the poet's pseudonym. For our purposes it will be most useful to regard Henry as Berryman's persona. That is, Berryman recounts his selected autobiography through Henry, and, because it is in the form of a third person speaker (Henry), Henry as persona achieves for Berryman the voice of a universal soul or mind. Henry can claim as much authority in this role as can Whitman's "I," according to Berryman, because one person's history is at least a component of the consciousness, or the soul, of the age. As Jascha Kessler has written, Henry is "someone who has to take the praise and blame merely because he is there, in that body. Berryman calls him Henry, as if to imply that he himself is not Henry, though he may be carried along with him" (34), just as, at times, Berryman's personal history is recorded through Henry.

Those critics who disclaim Berryman's prefatory note to *His Toy, His Dream, His Rest* (1968), the second volume of *The Dream Songs*, which says that Henry is "an imaginary character (not the poet, not me)," are not quite convinced that Berryman could remove himself from his poem simply by giving the central character a name other than his own. Jo R. Porterfield writes of that preface that "Berryman is evasive. We detect a certain nervousness in the vehemence of that 'not the poet, not me.' Reading the poetry we become increasingly skeptical of the trustworthiness of our guide in the preface" (33). Christopher Ricks, in his review of *The Dream Songs*, wrote: "'An imaginary character (not the poet, not me) named Henry': anybody credulous enough to take Berryman's word for it would be incapacitated from taking Berryman's words. But at least his egomaniacal hilarities, glooms, puzzlements are not drawling vanity or sober-sided grandiosity" (314). But while Ricks suggests at the end of this remark that the creation of Henry has succeeded in providing some measure of objectivity to Berryman's personal and "egomaniacal hilarities," Robert Lowell, writing in *New York Review of Books*, makes it clear that he feels Henry *is* Berryman without question, and that Berryman intended it that way: "Anything he has seen, overheard, or imagined can go in [*The Dream Songs*]. The poems are about Berryman, or rather they are about a person he calls *Henry*. Henry is Berryman seen as himself, as *poète maudit*, child and puppet. He is tossed about with a mixture of tenderness and absurdity, pathos and hilarity that would have been impossible if the author had spoken in the first person" (31). So Lowell states an alternate reason for Berryman's use of Henry: Aside from the poet's intention for a third person, a universal voice, Berryman could mix "tenderness and absurdity, pathos and hilarity" all in the guise of a persona. And if any part of the poem is too tender, pathetic, etc., it is not a shortcoming of Berryman's poetic skills, but evidence of artistic intentions which have Henry behaving in certain ways.

The critic Charles Molesworth lends credence to Lowell's observation with these following remarks:

> In the ironic balance between display and evasion, Berryman's Henry appears a master. Here, in a late *Dream Song*, he talks to himself about himself, an occupation the confessional poet is often at pains, though unsuccessfully to avoid:
>
> > —Oh, I suffer from a strike
> > & a strike and three balls: I stand up for much
> > Wordsworth and that sort of thing.
> > The pitcher dreamed. He threw a hazy curve,
> > I took it in my stride & out I struck,
> > lonesome Henry.
> >
> > These songs are not meant to be understood you understand.
> > They are only meant to terrify and comfort.
> > Lilac was found in his hand.
>
> Here Berryman is simultaneously Casey at the bat and the poet laureate; self-parody and self-glorification jostle each other with knowing wit. The offhanded irony of "and that sort of thing" occurs often in the *Dream Songs* and is the extension of the mixing of modes that becomes the work's characteristic signature. (68)

With Henry as the speaker of the poem, Berryman can "glorify" himself; poems using the confessional voice would appear too self-indulgent if such a glorification were attempted, and the self-effacing poems (which we will examine in the next chapter) would not consider it.

Henry, then, was an outlet for Berryman, one which allowed him to say anything, express any emotion in his poetry and label it a poetic device, an aesthetic intention. When Kostelanetz asked him, after the publication of *The Dream Songs*, whether he was now finished with Henry, Berryman replied: "Well, mostly

I'm through with Henry, but the minute I say that, pains course through me. I can't bear to be rid of that admirable outlet, that marvelous way of making your mind known to many other people" (341). And as it turned out, Berryman continued to use Henry as a voice in his work throughout his life; some of these poems have been posthumously published in *Henry's Fate & Other Poems* (1977) for example, and *Delusions Etc.*, the book he was working on just before his suicide in 1972. Many others are yet uncollected.

The persona mode of voice for Berryman was his way of speaking his mind, showing his emotions—something he was so reticent to do either in conversation when a young adult or in the first person voice of the confessional mode in his poetry, excluding the poems of *Love & Fame* (1970). And Berryman was aware that his use of the third person—at least in *Recovery*—acted as the medium for himself. Haffenden, quoting from Berryman's journals, suggests that "his novel *Recovery*, a strictly autobiographical work, is in large part a redaction of his own hospital diary. Speedily drafting that work, he became aware at an early stage that Severance, the hero, 'often *unconsciously* thinks of himself in the 3rd person, as I do. Let this stand, when it happens. Maybe even *use* it.' (The same consciousness of himself as a third person had informed the technique of *The Dream Songs*)" (402). Berryman once confided, reports the poet Michael Dennis Browne, that, "There is a fiendish resemblance between Henry & me." And Browne suggests that "the creating of a persona is for the conscious mind both unwelcome, in some sense, and a necessary extension of it. In the case of Henry, all kinds of material previously inaccessible was released and swarmed into the poems, much of it fearful, all of it *vital*. So much that previously was inexpressible could now find a voice as the whole range of invention and language widened" (79).

To illustrate how the persona can function as an extension, or representation, of the poet's voice, I will concentrate on a particular type of poem recurrent throughout *The Dream Songs*: the elegy. The elegies are significant to the work, as A. Alvarez noted in his review of it: "[Berryman] has written an elegy on his brilliant generation, and in the process, he has also written an elegy on himself." But before showing how Berryman used the persona mode of voice to grieve in verse for those of his generation who died young—and often violently or tragically— some biographical background is necessary.

In February 1942, Berryman and his close friend and Harvard colleague, Delmore Schwartz, went to New York to visit Eileen Simpson, Berryman's fiancée at the time. She recalls the genuine, brotherly concern Schwartz showed for his friend, though often displayed in an affected manner:

Without a trace of the shyness I thought I had seen at first, [Schwartz] continued in a bantering manner to play the role with John of a worldly-wise advisor to a naïf who didn't know how to look after himself. Sancho Panza and Don Quixote was the way they characterized this part of their relationship. John jaywalking, John being undiplomatic with his publisher, John being stand-offish with his colleagues, John moving from Cambridge to Boston (as he had done following our summer together in New York). This last had isolated him from the academic community, Delmore said to me, and had been bad for his career.

"It's not good for John to be so much alone. He's a recluse, you know."

(10)

Although Schwartz attempted to mask his concern with his manner of expression, he obviously felt that Simpson should be apprised of his friend's situation. His insinuation was clear that, as Berryman's future wife, she should help him pursue his "career."

One year later, when Berryman (now married) was at Princeton, a more solemn Schwartz betrayed his deep affection for his friend. He felt Berryman had changed, and accused him, together with R. P. Blackmur, of acting strangely, as Simpson recalls:

What may have been strange to Delmore was the relationship that had developed between Richard and John, a relationship Delmore knew about through the two men's letters but experienced for the first time when they appeared together. He felt that his two old friends had become close in a way that excluded him. Richard and John read and criticized each other's writing in the way Delmore and John had done at Harvard. ("Slow? There never was a man as slow as Richard," John said, "but my God, what a reader!") And although, because of the difference in generation and Richard's natural reticence, they never developed the kind of intimacy Delmore and John had shared, they saw each other far more often, and were, at the time of this meeting, as close intellectually as two men could be. What had begun on John's side as awe had changed into admiration and affection.

Delmore also claimed that John had changed. "You're wearing a new suit," he said accusingly. (88–9)

Schwartz's reference to the new suit was his implication that Berryman, under Blackmur's influence, had turned into a "proper Princetonian." Schwartz, jealous that he apparently had been supplanted by Blackmur as Berryman's best friend and personal advisor, felt even more protective of Berryman than before, but now his approach was that of an equal, a close friend, rather than an older and wiser brother.

Berryman accepted Schwartz's show of friendship and responded similarly. When Schwartz needed help later on in their relationship when both men's lives were more turbulent, Berryman provided it. Haffenden, in his biography of Berryman, records the following 1962 incident. Berryman remained a steady friend even though Schwartz—showing signs of the mental breakdown that was imminent—was extremely abusive of him:

> Word had come during the party that Delmore Schwartz had been arrested for drunkenness and was in jail. When Berryman and Wilbur went to investigate, it turned out that Schwartz had gone berserk in his room, had torn the telephone from the wall, and had hurled an ashtray through the window. The police thought he was only drunk and kept him six hours, but he was more mad than drunk. Discharged at last, he was not at all grateful for being rescued: for one thing, his belt had been taken away from him. He abused Berryman violently and was heard with perfect patience…. Schwartz, sloppily dressed but carrying his umbrella, arrived in a state of bedraggled ferment back at the hotel. Victoria, who loved him, was forbidden to enter the room. "Go and sleep with Berryman!" he screamed at her. In any event, Berryman stayed in Wilbur's room, and Victoria with Kate…. Throughout the incident, as Richard Wilbur recalls, Berryman was a solicitous and loyal friend. Dream Song 149, one of Berryman's elegies for Schwartz, records that: "I got him out of a police-station once, in Washington, the world is *tref* / and grief too astray for tears." (312)

These soap-operatic accounts illustrate that throughout their adult lives Berryman and Schwartz were close and cared for one another, more so than ordinary friends commonly do. So when Schwartz died, as Haffenden has noted, one way Berryman expressed his grief was to write elegies, collected in *His Toy, His Dream, His Rest* (which later became the last two-thirds of *The Dream Songs*), which he dedicated, in part, "to the sacred memory of Delmore Schwartz."

Part VI of *The Dream Songs*, then, begins with a long elegy for Schwartz in the form of several, separate, poems. However, Dream Song 157, near the end of the sequence, states in its opening line that they represent "Ten Songs, one solid block of agony…" which shows that Berryman clearly intended that grouping as a single verse unit. (Actually, it was thirteen, not ten, songs by the time he finished his lamentation: Dream Songs 146–158.) It is an elegy that is useful in demonstrating the ways Berryman employed the persona mode of voice.

In Dream Song 146, the first of the sequence, the first person speaker explains that the subject of deceased acquaintances provides the necessary drama in order for "Henry," not the poem's "I" speaker, to lament Schwartz's passing:

> These lovely motions of the air, the breeze,
> tell me I'm not in hell, though round me the dead
> lie in their limp postures
> dramatizing the dreadful word *instead*
> for lively Henry, fit for debaucheries
> and bird-of-paradise vestures
>
> only his heart is elsewhere, down with them
> & down with Delmore specially, the new ghost
> haunting Henry most:
> though fierce the claims of others, coimedela crime
> came the Hebrew spectre, on a note of woe
> and Join me o.

Henry's thoughts and the thoughts of the "I" speaker seem to merge in the first stanza, making them a single, unified voice whereby the speaker refers to himself in the third person by the name of Henry. This is what Berryman would want us to believe, as indicated in his introductory remarks to *The Dream Songs*: "The poem... is essentially about an imaginary character (not the poet, not me) named Henry... who has suffered an irreversible loss and talks about himself sometimes in the first person, sometimes in the third, sometimes even in the second...." However, in the elegy for Schwartz the first person speaker is distinct from Henry. In the opening of the poem, the first person speaker is listless, as though dead. He knows he is alive, however, because the "lovely motions of the air, the breeze" tell him he is "not in hell" even though he is surrounded by the dead who "lie in their limp postures." So as the first person speaker languishes, Henry is said to be "lively."

And there is another distinction marking the two as separate. Henry grieves for "Delmore specially, the new ghost" while the first person speaker is preoccupied with thoughts of his own death. This is the poem's last stanza:

> 'Down with them all!' Henry suddenly cried.
> Their deaths were theirs. I wait on for my own,
> I dare say it won't be long.
> I have tried to be them, god knows I have tried,
> but they are past it all, I have not done,
> which brings me to the end of this song.

The fact that the first person speaker knows he is not in hell, as he reveals to us in stanza one, is the catalyst which brings Henry into existence in this poem; the two have similar thoughts because Henry is created by the poem's speaker. Henry's thoughts are revealed to us by the "I," the poem's speaker, and told to us as though from Henry's point of view. In the final stanza, Henry, in an angered tone, cries that he is finished, for the time, thinking of others' deaths, especially Schwartz's. It is time now for the first person speaker to contemplate his own. But it was Henry who acted as the vehicle which brought the first person speaker from a listlessness while regarding "the dead in their limp postures" to a more active involvement with himself, as manifest by his preoccupation with his own death. Even having accepted Berryman's insistent claim that the "I" in *The Dream Songs* is always Henry, "not the poet, not me" (yet many critics, as previously noted, have contended that he protests too much; but Helen Vendler, in her *Part of Nature, Part of Us*, seems to have struck a compromise with her suitable line: "Henry is not Berryman, but neither is Henry not-Berryman"), the two voices—that is, the two points of view, the first person speaker's and Henry's—are distinct, each a separate persona able to express what the other cannot. Henry is lively when the first person speaker is not; Henry cries, "Down with them all!" without motive seemingly, but which however allows for the first person speaker to repress his thoughts about others in order to concentrate on himself. Whereas in the first stanza, his thoughts were on the dead "round" him (confused as to whether they were actually with him or merely in his head, he wondered if he were in hell, but finally concluded otherwise), in the last stanza his concern is solely personal. Henry, in stanza two, tried unsuccessfully to think of the *instead*, his own death, and his "heart . . . elsewhere, down with them / & down with Delmore specially, the new ghost / haunting Henry most. . . ." Henry, then, was "down with them" in "hell," thinking of them, but the first person speaker adopts Henry's cry, "Down with them all!" which the speaker now interprets as a call for the repression of haunting ghosts in favor of self-concern, his personal death wish.

When confronted with the news of a friend's death, Berryman, like the "I" of the final stanza, often grew introspective and turned towards notions of his own death, or his father's suicide. Perhaps this was his means of deflecting his sorrow; more likely, rather, it suggests his preoccupation with himself. Haffenden records that "when Saul Bellow's father died Berryman had told Bellow with apparent impersonality:

> 'My father died for me all over again last week, in a terrible dream which when I analyzed it turned out to be about him not dying at once, as I was told

he did (he shot himself, on an island in Florida where we lived, when I was twelve), but living a while unable to move or call out for help, but then in the dream he said "saved"—as of his soul, I mean. His father's death is one of the few main things that happens to a man, I think, and it matters greatly to the life when it happens. I can't help feeling that you are lucky to have had your father for so long, and then just to have seen him again as A says you did. The trouble with a father's dying very early (not to speak of his killing himself) is not so much just his loss as the disproportionate & crippling role the mother then assumes for one.'" (274)

Although there is a fleeting attempt at consolation, Berryman keeps the focus of his remarks on how, through adulthood, he had been affected by his father's suicide. When Theodore Roethke died, Berryman wrote to Ralph Ross:

> I was slugged...and for the first time I revise the 2nd of the Songs for him I'd been reluctantly & despairingly working at. *That is the last "free" Dream Song.* I send it to you. I don't know what its fate will be. But I imagine it will be around a while. I sent it to Beatrice, his widow, with a letter pseudo-consoling.... I haven't decided who to give it to yet; I'm tempted by *Kenyon....* (Qtd. in Haffenden 331)

He indeed may have been "slugged" by Roethke's passing, but apparently it was difficult for him to console Beatrice, just as he neglected to console Bellow. He was instead more concerned about where to publish the poem he wrote in commemoration of Roethke. And when he learned of Robert Frost's death, Berryman's initial reaction was: "...it's *scarey.* Who's number one? Who's number one? Cal is number one, isn't he?" (Haffenden 319), which of course betrayed his intense competitiveness rather than any remorse for a fellow poet's passing on. When Randall Jarrell died, Berryman wrote to William Meredith that "Randall's death hurt me—shock and sorrow to Mackey, please. Everybody is dying—I personally am dying of diarrhoea & nerve-ends."

Yet, Haffenden offers a reasonable explanation for Berryman's seeming callousness. He writes:

> On the other hand, Berryman may have chosen to avoid any show of sentimentalism by such a brisk, if unfortunate, transition. In the early part of 1966, Yale University organised a memorial for Jarrell, with about a dozen speakers; Richard Eberhart remembers emphatically: "Berryman was pretty far gone when I saw him last at the Yale Jarrell memorial. He was pathetic. I felt sorry for him but also felt that he should not have appeared in public." Robert Penn Warren recalls, in contrast, that "Berryman's witty, funny, and moving

remarks made a profound impression.... [H]e was coherent, amusing, and effective—in spite of, or because of, his favorite beverage." (332)

Obviously Berryman was confused any time he learned of a death—particularly a close friend's death—and his inconsistent, and often inappropriate, reactions to these deaths were spawned by conflicting emotions relating to his father's suicide, thoughts of his own suicide, and ambivalent feelings towards his deceased friends. Haffenden continues:

> In one respect, he enshrined his friends as ... "the sacred dead," who offered him no further competition and unquestionably received his jealous identification. But he could express himself with a seemingly equal emotion for those who were not his friends, especially if their deaths were violent, or suicidal like Sylvia Plath's, and triggered both an old manner of grief for his father and his theory about the dispensation of his own life. He could arrogate the dear dead to himself as emblems, and sometimes expressed a grief in excess of familiarity. There is no reason at all to doubt the reality and intensity of his mourning, however, since it was proper only to himself. Yet there is an ambivalence evident in the degree to which those deaths readily served Berryman as copy for his verses. (331)

He did not know Ernest Hemingway, but Berryman wept when he learned of the death. Berryman associated Hemingway's suicide with his father's—which perhaps explains the reason he could "express himself with a seemingly equal emotion for those who were not his friends"—and this, in turn, became the subject of Dream Song 235:

> Tears Henry shed for poor old Hemingway...
>
> Save us from shotguns & fathers' suicides.
> It all depends on who you're the father *of*
> if you want to kill yourself—
> a bad example, murder of oneself...
>
> Mercy! my father; do not pull the trigger
> or all my life I'll suffer from your anger
> killing what you began.

So Henry's expression of grief in verse for Hemingway—for someone Berryman did not really know—could be as sorrowful, as mournful as for someone Berryman knew intimately because both kinds could engender grief, the reality of which and "intensity of his mourning... [were] proper only to himself." And both the deaths of close friends and of others could be suitable as material for verse because Berryman associated all suicidal or otherwise tragic deaths with his personal history. Berryman, through Henry then, can shed tears for Hemingway because both he and Papa were sons of fathers who committed suicide.

In real life, conversely, Berryman sometimes chose "to avoid any show of sentimentalism" for those he knew well. This attitude of course carried into his verse. When he used the first person voice in the elegies of *The Dream Songs*, it was often a voice attempting to sound personally untouched by the death, the subject of the poem—and to this end, it seems at times a playful voice, bringing wit and irony to the elegiac reminiscences. At the Jarrell memorial referred to earlier, for example, Berryman ended his remarks (which Warren found "witty, funny, and moving") by reading Dream Song 121, of which the first two stanzas follow:

> Grief is fatiguing. He is out of it,
> the whole humiliating Human round,
> out of this & that.
> He made a-many hearts go pit-a-pat
> who now need never mind his nostril-hair
> nor a critical error laid bare.
>
> He endured fifty years. He was Randall Jarrell
> and wrote a-many books & he wrote well.
> Peace to the bearded corpse.
> His last book was his best. His wives loved him.
> He saw in the forest something coming, grim,
> but did not change his purpose.

"Grief is fatiguing" for the poem's speaker, which means that it is bothersome as well as difficult and emotionally tiring to mourn the death of a friend. The opening line of the elegy, then, establishes a curious tone of a seriousness—indicative of heart-felt grief—combined with an irony which perhaps is intended as a means to remain in emotional control, to suppress the speaker's true agony. All forms of grief and all causes of grief are fatiguing, at any rate, so at least now in death Jarrell is "out of it, / the whole humiliating Human round"—grief-causing human round. So even though this expression of grief may be fatiguing for the speaker, the initial sentiment expressed in the poem—that Jarrell is free of grief—is devoid of irony. Yet the following sequence of lines seems ill chosen, filled as they are with details inappropriate in content and diction of a traditional elegy. "He made a-many hearts go pit-a-pat" is a line that end-rhymes with the one previous, but surely "pit-a-pat" was not chosen merely to conform with the rhyme scheme. It sets the nearly irreverent tone of the rest of the stanza, lines which suggest Jarrell was vain about his appearance and prideful of his literary acumen—his worrying over the chance of making a "critical error." These "griefs"—minding his nostril hair, having an error exposed—are those for which, the speaker ironically informs us, we can be thankful Jarrell is spared in death.

In the second stanza the irony is more subtle, but still prevalent. There is little mention of Jarrell's personal life during his "fifty, endured, years" other than that "his wives loved him." Instead, the speaker concentrates on Jarrell's professional life, the fact he "wrote a-many books & he wrote well." The elegy at this point, if the language and tone are discounted, reads more like a literary commemorative found in a little magazine (ending as it does with "his last book was his best") rather than a public memorial in verse. This could be attributed in part to the speaker's willful detachment "to avoid any show of sentimentalism." But a more likely reason for the seemingly mundane content of this stanza is the speaker's clever phrasing, which is purposely ambiguous. It is likely that the "many books" Jarrell wrote refers literally to his work and figuratively to episodes in his life, suggesting each was another "book" marking an event in his fifty years—many of which, such as his wives who loved him, he "wrote well." In accordance with this reading, then, the book he last wrote, the best one, alludes to his accidental death / probable suicide. (Jarrell, having been recently released from psychiatric care, was strolling one late night when fatally struck by a car; many people closest to him, including Berryman, believed he threw himself in the car's path.) That it was suicide rather than an accidental death would appeal more to Berryman, as we have seen, and that it was regarded by him as Jarrell's finest act, his last and best book, if we are to follow this interpretation, may have been self-projection. As with all the elegies, as Haffenden has informed us, "there is no reason to doubt the reality and intensity of [Berryman's] mourning... since it was proper only to himself."

Berryman's elegy for one of his closest friends (recall Eberhart's observation that he was "pretty far gone... he was pathetic" at Jarrell's memorial) is, however, suspiciously free of Berryman himself and his own emotional effusion; in its place we find mildly disturbing jingles and pathetic ironies. Yet we also know from Robert Penn Warren that Berryman apparently masked fairly successfully his suffering over Jarrell's passing. Berryman, as evident from the many examples of his ostensible callousness in times of friends' deaths, doubtlessly could not publicly mourn very well—he may not have had the capacity to do so—which perhaps accounts for the inconsistency of emotions he displayed.

In his verse elegies, however, he commonly incorporated both types of behavior. His self-concern, which initially reads as an uncaring detachment, is manifest in his use of irony, and his emotional involvement, in which his unrestrained
grief overrides his concern for poetic conventions, is much devoid of that irony.
The elegy sequence for Delmore Schwartz uses both; the first person speaker is,
usually, the more detached and ironic expression, and Henry's point of view is
employed as the voice of grieving. The two are brought together in the first of that
sequence, Dream Song 146, as we have already seen.

Let us now return to the Schwartz elegy with this background knowledge of
Berryman's complex reactions to friends' or others' violent deaths. Dream Song
146 ends with the "I" awaiting his own death. His thoughts of his deceased
friends, "Delmore specially," are not of mourning but of begrudging their being
"past it all": "I have tried to be them, god knows I have tried, / but they are past it
all, I have not done, / which brings me to the end of this song." The line "drama-
tizing the dreadful word *instead* / for lively Henry" in stanza 1 acts to bring self-
pity to the first person speaker in the final stanza. Yet the next Dream Song (147) is
spoken entirely from Henry's perspective, and consequently the focus of the
poem shifts back to grieving Schwartz's death:

> Henry's mind grew blacker the more he thought.
> He looked onto the world like the act of an aged whore.
> Delmore, Delmore.
> He flung to pieces and they hit the floor....
>
> He lookt on the world like the leavings of a hog.
> Almost his love died from him, any more.
> His mother & William
> were vivid in the same mail Delmore died.
> The world is lunatic. This is the last ride.
> Delmore, Delmore.

Like the elegy for Jarrell, this poem has several end-rhymed couplets, but their
content suggests a profoundly mournful tone rather than one of black humor.
Henry's more serious tone can be attributed to Berryman's close friendship with
Schwartz and, perhaps, to the unusually tragic circumstances surrounding his
death—of which Eileen Simpson provides a graphic portrait:

> Delmore, a recluse, who had once been "flagrant" with "young male beauty"
> and so gifted that it was thought he would be the star of his generation, had
> fallen dead in a hallway outside his squalid room in a fleabag hotel in Times
> Square. The heart attack that took him was neither easy nor quick. He had

been "tearing his sorry clothes" for over an hour before the noises of struggle attracted attention.... At the morgue, because "there were no readers of modern poetry" around, as Saul [Bellow] wrote of his character Humboldt, Delmore's body lay unclaimed for two days. (244)

As "Henry" thinks of all this, he considers how unjust the world is, a world he now regards as "an act of an aged whore," "the leavings of a hog," and he uses a line of Shakespeare to express further that a world that could take Schwartz in such a manner is one which is, as "Marcus Aurelius taught, / 'All that is foul smell & blood in a bag.'" Unlike the Jarrell elegy where the world was viewed merely as "humiliating," Henry, his mind "blacker the more he thought," believes in this poem that the world is disgusting and debased for leading Schwartz to his awful death.

In the second stanza, Henry recalls how he learned of Schwartz's dying. Berryman, in fact, had been working on his study of Shakespeare when he received a letter from his mother and the news about Schwartz. Consequently, "His mother & William" were "vivid" to Henry "in the same mail Delmore died." That "this is the last ride," the latest by people of his generation, including Roethke, R. P. Blackmur, Jarrell, and "in between" Sylvia Plath (Dream Song 153), results in Henry's apparently unrestrained grieving: "The world is lunatic. This is the last ride. / Delmore, Delmore." (Eileen Simpson amends "Henry's" list, however, mentioning that Berryman "was so cross he named Richard [Blackmur], who was not of their generation, and forgot Dylan [Thomas], who was.")

Henry then recalls the more pleasant times of Schwartz's youth in the final stanza, which is the first of the ensuing remembrances of scenes from earlier days of "heights where Delmore & Gertrude sprang / so long ago, in the goodness of which [his poetry] was composed." As Simpson saw it:

> John grieved and grieved for Delmore, and was haunted by the way in which his old friend had died. If there was no one to claim Delmore's body, and only a handful of people to follow it to the cemetery, there are the Dream Songs to mourn his death—"Ten Songs, one solid block of agony,"—in which John cried out his anguish. The years of estrangement faded. The scenes of their youth became vivid again. It was the Delmore of the Cambridge days whom John tried to put in the place of the anonymous man who had been taken to the morgue. It was the fellow poet who had been his chief support during his own years of failure and obscurity. The one solace John offered himself was the belief that as long as poetry was read, Delmore would not be forgotten. (245)

It is true that in this one solid block of agony Henry forgets the trying times the two men had later in their relationship, their "years of estrangement," and concentrates, rather, on "the Delmore of the Cambridge days," the one trying to orchestrate Berryman's career, the one demonstrating an uncommon closeness to his friend. Yet the first person speaker, who, as we have seen, drifts in and out of the sequence, remembers Schwartz going berserk and Schwartz's unwarranted accusations as well as the more pleasant Harvard years. The middle part of Dream Song 149, from the "I's" point of view, provides an example:

> In the brightness of his promise,
>
> unstained, I saw him thro' the mist of the actual
> blazing with insight, warm with gossip
> thro' all our Harvard years
> when both of us were just becoming known
> I got him out of a police-station once, in
>   Washington, the world is *tref*
> and grief too astray for tears....
>
> in New York: he sang me a song
> 'I am the Brooklyn poet Delmore Schwartz
> Harms & the child I sing, two parents' torts'
> when he was young & gift-strong.

The first person speaker of the opening elegy related Schwartz's death to his own misery; so, too, does the "I" in Dream Song 149 keep bringing himself in: "when both of us were just becoming known." Unlike the reminiscences from Henry's point of view of the early days at Harvard (which was Berryman's choice for personal reflection according to Simpson), the "I" recounts Schwartz's more troubled times: his arrest for drunkenness in 1962 while attending the National Poetry Festival in Washington, and his subsequent false indictment of his girlfriend for sleeping with Berryman. Nor can this first person speaker resist implying, in the poem's final line, that Schwartz's poetic gift vanished with age. Berryman may have "cried out his anguish" in the elegy, as Simpson suggested, but he did so as Henry; the "I" remained concerned principally with himself.

The final stanza of 150 returns again to the quality of Schwartz's later work: "I'd bleed to say his lovely work improved / but it is not so." Henry, in 147, avoids mention of whether or not Schwartz's poetry diminished: "High in the summer branches the poet sang. / His throat ached, and he could sing no more." The emphasis is on the beauty of his singing "in the summer branches"; that his "throat

ached," which prevented him from singing, does not necessarily suggest a later de-
cline in the quality of his verse. But the first person speaker clearly distinguishes
the early work as superior poetry. The "I," then, may be more closely aligned with
the competitive Berryman, the one afraid that Lowell, rather than himself, was
"number one" after Frost's death. In his elegies, Berryman portrayed several sides
of his complex personality. He was able to capture his mixed reactions to his
friends' deaths by using a bifurcated voice: Stated simply, Berryman, through
Henry, found a persona who "grieved and grieved for Delmore"; as the "I," Berryman could articulate his other, self-centered thoughts surrounding a tragic death.

Andrew Hudgins has argued that "one of the major structural devices of
The Dream Songs...is the dialectic of opposites which do not synthesize or resolve, but rather exist in conflict, in ebb and flow, in cyclical movement. One
quality will be predominant at one moment, the other the next. When the opposites, be they body and mind or the drive-to-life and the drive-to-death, are
present in Henry's psyche, they do not cancel out one another; they clash fero-
ciously, and Henry can barely contain them" (93). Hudgins then adds a qualifier:
"Keeping ever in mind Henry's protean nature, I am reluctant to divide up Henry
neatly into body and mind, though those do seem to be two discrete and uninte-
grated aspects of Henry's psyche" (95).

Hudgins's argument extends my reasoning even though he neglected to distinguish the separate voices within Henry. As we have seen, the "I" is clearly different in thought and expression from those of Henry's point of view. Although
Henry is revealed to us through—to use a term common to prose—an "omniscient narrator," it does not seem likely that that narrator is the "I," even though
Berryman insists it is. Their perspectives are too dissimilar; their reactions to
Schwartz's death too unidentical. The voices in the elegies represent sound examples of Berryman's structural device of "the dialectic of opposites which do not
synthesize." Consequently they are not different aspects of a single voice, but two
voices. We can even accept that Henry sometimes refers to himself in the first person, sometimes in the third, yet as he does so, he adopts a separate voice for each.
It is clear that Berryman's personality, his varied reactions to his friends' deaths,
required different voices for expression in verse. The "I" in the Schwartz elegy,
then, is as much part of Berryman's persona as the voice speaking from Henry's
point of view; Berryman uses this bifurcated scheme for his persona in order to
express the differing sides he found within himself. What he often could not do in
real life—stop thinking of himself in times of mourning—he could have Henry
do in *The Dream Songs*; and he still found a way, through his use of a first person
speaker, to use those times for self-reflection. Berryman was not solely one or the

other, but more like Hudgins's description of the dialectic in *The Dream Songs*: He
existed "in conflict, in ebb and flow, in cyclical movement."

An illustration of this, the "ebb and flow" of the conflicting voices together
in movement, is Dream Song 151 in which the first person speaker calls attention
to his own lack of sensitivity regarding Schwartz's death. In this poem, the "I"
hurries the elegy along before he "forgets" Schwartz, but Henry comes into the
end of the poem "sick and heartbroken." Dream Song 151 clearly demonstrates the
division of voice and the conflicts operative within them:

> Bitter & Bleary over Delmore's dying:
> his death stopped clocks, let no activity
> mar our hurrah of mourning,
> let's all be Jews bereft, for he was one . . .
>
> I need to hurry this out before I forget
> which I will never—He fell on the floor
> outside a cheap hotel-room . . .
>
> He was tortured, beyond what man might be
> Sick & heartbroken Henry sank to his knees
> Delmore is dead. . . .

Like the "I" of Dream Song 121 (the elegy for Jarrell), the first person speaker of
this poem uses playful rhymes, such as "mar our hurrah," and is nearly mocking
in certain lines, "let's all be Jews bereft, for he was one." The "I" needs "to hurry
this out before I forget / which I will never," lines indicative of the first person
speaker's tone and level of grief. Although the "I" may be truly grieving, he expresses it through irony, black humor, and flippant or otherwise disrespectful remarks and diction. Yet as Schwartz's death is recounted, the voice gradually
transforms to one more serious; this is the voice speaking from Henry's point of
view, as seen in such lines as: "Sick & heartbroken Henry sank to his knees / Delmore is dead." This display of mourning is in marked contrast from the earlier
lines, the first person speaker's, such as "let no activity / mar our hurrah of
mourning" and "I need to hurry this out before I forget."

The first person speaker can be serious—as we have seen in the first poem
of the elegy sequence—but only when he relates the subject to his personal concerns. When the subject of the elegy is mourning a deceased friend, the "I" does
so mockingly, ironically; yet when the "I" diverts the focus of the elegy on himself,
he is more solemn and devoid of irony. Just as Berryman used the occasion of
Roethke's death as material for a new Dream Song—one he regarded highly ("I

imagine it will be around a while," he wrote to Ralph Ross)—the first person speaker in 157, near the end of the sequence, indicates that his grieving over Schwartz ends when it has been exhausted as material for his verse: "Ten Songs, one solid block of agony, / I wrote for him, and then I wrote no more. / His sad ghost must aspire / free of my love to its own post...." This sounds as though it could have been spoken from Henry's point of view. The seriousness, the sentiment is close to that of Henry's, but it is so because the "I" is speaking now of his most serious subject—himself, his own verse, his own love which he is seemingly capable of dispensing at will. Although there are no biographical accounts recording Berryman's behavior upon learning of Schwartz's death, it is reasonable to suspect that his reactions were as varied as those he showed over any violent or tragic death. He might have—as he did with Bellow—made insensitive comments, or he might have directed the conversations of Schwartz's tragedy toward talk of himself. It is probable, too, that privately and publicly Berryman, like Henry, "sank to his knees" sick and heartbroken. By having Henry address himself in the first person and sometimes in the third in *The Dream Songs*, Berryman, through Henry, was able to "cry out his anguish," as Eileen Simpson remarked, in a way that incorporated many of these probable emotional responses to Schwartz's death.

Berryman's persona mode of voice is one solution to the problem of a Romantic kind of weeping in verse identified by Leonard Nathan in his article "The Private 'I' in Contemporary Poetry," which is that an unabashed show of sentimentalism (that can occur rather often in a poem of the confessional mode of voice) obscures the poetry, the art of the piece. Berryman felt that suffering was essential to good poetry. Howard Munford remembered that once, in India, Berryman rose from his sickbed and:

> proceeded to give a lecture different from anything he had done previously, a stunning discourse on the springs and nature of poetry. For weeks, he said, the Indians had been telling us that America had never produced any poetry, that the Indians were the most poetic people in the world, but that what he had seen of Indian poetry led him to believe that what passed for poetry with them was a loose kind of spiritual sentimentality. "Now," he said, "I'm going to tell you something about what poetry really is." He quoted from Rilke and Lorca and then gave some English paraphrases. One of these was from "The Song of the Blind Man" and his paraphrase went something like this: "My eyes were two sacred fonts in which the Devil has stirred his finger." His point was that much of the greatest poetry sprang from the pain and anguish of human experience—which he went on to illustrate from a wide range of Western

poetry. The audience was enthralled and would have held John in excited
conversation indefinitely had his weakness not forced him to stagger out of
the room and back to bed. (Qtd. in Haffenden 266)

And Berryman, even though he suffered much anguish in his lifetime, wanted
even to suffer more, so that he too could continue to create "what poetry really is."
In the last interview before his death, Berryman told Stitt:

> My idea is this: The artist is extremely lucky who is presented with the worst
> possible ordeal which will not actually kill him. At that point, he's in busi-
> ness.... And I think that what happens in my poetic work in the future will
> probably largely depend... on being knocked in the face, and thrown flat, and
> given cancer, and all kinds of other things short of senile dementia. At that
> point, I'm out, but short of that, I don't know. I hope to be crucified. (322)

Henry became Berryman's outlet for expressing such anguish. It is Henry, "an
imaginary character... a white American in early middle age sometimes in black-
face, who has suffered an irreversible loss," as Berryman indicated in his prefatory
note to The Dream Songs, who has been "knocked in the face, and thrown flat,"
and whom Berryman spoke through. His use of the persona in this way allowed
Berryman to employ his grief as an aspect of his craft in a more objective way
than he could have in the confessional mode of voice. Donald Justice has written
of the difference, and how Berryman achieved this objective stance:

> His subject was the self, often enough the self involved with history. But his
> personal exposures have a different feel about them than those of his contem-
> poraries. No matter how painful and honest they seem, they have first been
> subjected to the pressures of his art. Events, however catastrophic, are valued
> not so much for themselves as for what they can be made into, in words and
> music. The impersonality of the art remains, therefore, as important as the
> personality of the poet. (Qtd. in Browne 83–4)

Berryman's suffering over his many friends' premature deaths led him into the elegies—which comprise one, unifying, theme of The Dream Songs—but he was
able to subject his emotions, his memories, "to the pressures of his art" by invent-
ing Henry as his speaker, a persona mode of voice which ensured that "the impersonality of the art" remained as important to the poetry as the personality of the
poet.

WELDON KEES

ALTHOUGH WELDON KEES WAS born in the same year, 1914, as Berryman, the two men were not·contemporaries in the sense that, say, Lowell (1917–1977) and Berryman were. But in approach to voice, they were far closer than Lowell and Berryman, who shared a friendship, but not an approach to poetry. Whereas Lowell and Berryman knew each other, had actually begun their friendship early in their literary careers, shared similar tastes in poetry and a love for Shakespeare, and reviewed—always favorably—one another's books, among other things, Kees probably only knew of Berryman, if at all, as a frequent contributor to the same literary magazines in which his own verse was beginning to appear. Kees's poem "The Lives," which was included in his last book, *Poems 1947–1954* (1954), was initially published in the August 1948 number of *Partisan Review*, for example, a magazine Berryman had been reviewing for; the previous month's issue carried Berryman's "A Peine Ma Piste," a review of *T. S. Eliot: A Selected Critique* edited by Leonard Unger. If, therefore, the two men never met—which is likely considering that Kees, disgusted with New York (where, besides a poet, he had several one-man shows of his abstract-expressionist paintings, and played the jazz piano at a few fashionable clubs) and its literati, moved to San Francisco in 1951—nor exchanged theories about poetry and favorite writers and recommendations of whom to read, as Berryman and Lowell had done, it is interesting that Kees and Berryman developed artistically more closely than Berryman and Lowell. The poetry of Kees and Berryman in the persona mode binds them as "contemporaries," then, more so than merely their chronology. Both show Eliot's influence on their work (Eliot's "Prufrock" was the model for Kees's "Robinson," as we shall see, and in type for Berryman's "Henry," although Berryman eschewed Eliot's theory of impersonality in art [in the *Partisan Review* article just mentioned] and made Henry very personal), and both were concerned with voice—more so than Lowell who, as mentioned in the last chapter, straightforwardly announced: "the first person is me, not an imaginary me"—as bordering on the personal-autobiographical and the impersonal-fictional.

Kees almost immediately learned to control the tone of his poems, and it is because of this that his voice seems to move effortlessly between the personal anguish, or confessionalism, of Berryman's "Henry" and the more cynical voice of Berryman's "I" of the elegies who seemed detached from the mourning. As an example of Kees's choosing an apparently personal subject to be narrated in an impersonal tone of voice, let us look at an early poem, "For My Daughter," from his first collection, *The Last Man* (1943):

Looking into my daughter's eyes I read
Beneath the innocence of morning flesh
Concealed, hintings of death she does not heed....
Or, fed on hate, she relishes the sting
Of others' agony; perhaps the cruel
Bride of a syphilitic or a fool.
These speculations sour in the sun.
I have no daughter. I desire none.

The consistent tone of voice throughout the poem—before we learn that the speaker actually has no daughter as well as the final lines—is characteristic of Kees's work. As the speaker quietly muses over the tragic possibilities that await his daughter who must live in this civilization, he carefully avoids betraying any emotional outrage he might easily feel in remembering his own "parched years." And the revelation of his last remarks is similarly devoid of emotional display. Kees has therefore combined a personal subject matter with an impersonal voice—that is, one that is consistent in its tone, evenly recording the speaker's thoughts without showing any emotional intensity which might lie behind those thoughts.

The speaker does not desire to have a daughter because the world is presently terrible, and it will be the same when she grows into an adult, if not get worse: "foul, lingering / Death in certain war." But these thoughts of the speaker remain "speculations," nothing more, even if they "sour in the sun." His thoughts of horror, of his daughter, "fed on hate," relishing "the sting / Of others' agony; perhaps the cruel / Bride of a syphilitic or a fool," are spoken in the same, quiet voice—evocative of a scene depicting the speaker lazily musing over his random thoughts as he sits in the sun—as those, more serene, speculations about his imaginary daughter's eyes, and the "innocence of [her] morning flesh." Of Kees's voice in "For My Daughter"—in much of the poet's work—Donald Justice has written:

> Kees is original in one of the few ways that matter: he speaks to us in a voice or, rather, in a particular tone of voice which we have never heard before. In the early poems, it is true, there are echoes of other poets. But almost immediately he found his proper tone. Already in his first book it can be heard in such a poem as "For My Daughter," with the terrible but quiet shock of its last line. And almost always his is a quiet voice. That will not seem very surprising until one pauses to consider how very bitter are the things this quiet voice has to say. (ix)

This quiet tone that Justice has described, which does not change as the speaker moves from line to line in "For My Daughter," is remarkably the same for most of his poetry. It derives from Kees's control over his subjects, no matter how they might change within a poem, like "For My Daughter," or from poem to poem. He achieves such control because he adopts the same attitude—or his speaker adopts the same attitude—towards each subject: a bitterness of the world that is reflected in anything encompassed in Kees's poetic vision. Justice continues:

> For Kees is one of the bitterest poets in history. "Others," wrote Kenneth Rexroth, "have called themselves Apocalyptics, Kees lived in a permanent and hopeless apocalypse." Yet he appears to accept whatever is, however terrifying or ridiculous it may seem, with the serenity of a saint. The wall cracks; the stain spreads; he does not budge from his chair. This calm in the face of a certain doom, the most characteristic attitude of his poetry, is the ultimate expression of the bitterness at the center of his work; it is also a curious anticipation of the atomic despair so familiar now, though arrived at by Kees some years before the bomb. (ix)

The theme of "For My Daughter," a resentment of the modern life where unexpected horrors await, and a bitterness towards life itself, growing old and dying, will recur through Kees's later work.

Rexroth's remark that Kees had "lived in a permanent and hopeless apocalypse" suggests, somewhat, a parallel with Yeats's "The Second Coming," although Yeats certainly did not believe in a permanent extinction as Rexroth apparently thought Kees did. Rather, as Yeats explained in *A Vision* (1925), the dissolution of civilization—the apocalypse—marks the end of one cycle in history and the subsequent beginning of another. He wrote: "What if the irrational return? What if the circle begin again?" If so, the surviving humans "may be about to accept the most implacable authority the world has known," and that irrational, implacable authority takes the figure of a "rough beast, its hour come round at last" in "The Second Coming."

Even though Yeats believed that civilization is regenerative and Kees suggested that it is probably not, "For My Daughter" alludes to a kind of rough beast as one factor in his daughter's future years: "foul, lingering / Death in certain war, the slim legs green." Yeats's beast was shaped "with lion body and the head of a man"; Kees's, with "slim legs green." Yeats's influence on Kees's poem is more pronounced when we examine Yeats's "A Prayer for My Daughter," which followed "The Second Coming" in *Michael Robartes and the Dancer* (1921). Yeats's speaker of that poem is caring for his newly born daughter, who is sleeping while it storms outside. Here is the second stanza of "A Prayer for My Daughter":

> I have walked and prayed for this young child an hour
> And heard the sea-wind scream upon the tower,
> And under the arches of the bridge, and scream
> In the elms above the flooded stream;
> Imagining in excited reverie
> That the future years had come,
> Dancing to a frenzied drum,
> Out of the murderous innocence of the sea.

Her future years arising from "murderous innocence" follows Yeats's visions of the future depicted in "The Second Coming."

Yet the central difference between this poem and Kees's is voice. Yeats, whose daughter, Anne Butler, was born on February 26, 1919, first published this poem in June 1919. Its voice is of the confessional mode because of the many allusions to this personal life—including a line in reference to Maud Gonne: "Have I not seen the loveliest woman born"—and because of the tone of the "I" speaker, which is, like Lowell's confessional voice, pathetically evocative. Kees's "I," however, only alludes to his personal life to the extent that the poem reflects; that is, Kees did not have a daughter, as the "I" informs us in the last line. And the poem does not intend to evoke pathos in the reader; the finality of the last statement is too certain, too assured, to induce pathos, as perhaps Yeats's stanza functions in "A Prayer for My Daughter." Rather, Kees's last line is cold, "bitter," yet consistent with the tone of the rest of the poem. The voice of Kees in "For My Daughter," therefore, is not confessional in the manner Yeats's is, but it is not entirely impersonal. The "I" reveals a personal fact of Kees's existence: He had no daughter.

He was also pessimistic about our civilization's future. A review by Kees appeared in the July 18, 1955, issue of *New Republic* entitled "How to Be Happy: Installment 1053" in which he wrote: "In our present atmosphere of distrust, violence, and irrationality, with so many human beings murdering themselves—either literally or symbolically..." and so forth. On that day Kees's car was found abandoned on the Golden Gate Bridge where, presumptively, he leapt to his death. That is to say, he was very capable of having such thoughts as those recorded by the speaker of "For My Daughter." The voice, finally, not personal, not of the persona mode—in the sense of Whitman's "I" that Berryman was fond of citing—is one that eliminates any possibility of pathos (except our possible pathos for such a bitter man) by its "quiet" tone, which, we have seen, is a result of his restrained emotional expression, his calmness and evenness of tone.

"Kees's 'I' is certainly not always to be taken autobiographically—it is far more frequently the voice of a detached observer or poet-figure," writes the critic William Ross, author of the first book-length study of Kees's work. He continues:

> ...because it is the world that is absurd and not just a single individual or group, Kees is able to become part of a tendency that M. A. Rosenthal notes is common among several poets of Kees's generation. He can become a confessional poet without becoming intimately autobiographical. That is, he can speak with deep passion and anguish about his doubts concerning the value of existence, without rooting those doubts in personal experiences. The sources of his pessimism, Kees is convinced, lie in the objective universe, not in some hypothetical psychological damage done to him in the past. It is part of Kees's cosmopolitanism, in other words, to assume that he is talking about problems we all face and therefore to see no need to parade idiosyncratic experiences in front of us, or, by and large, to assume that a Freudian psychoanalytical explanation of his or his characters' behavior is in order. (43–4)

Ross's remarks can be applied to our discussion of "For My Daughter," a poem in which Kees certainly does not display any personal, "intimately autobiographical" emotions nor openly parade "idiosyncratic experiences in front of us" since the poem's theme, one expressive of the speaker's malaise in its most mild interpretation, or of his "profound hatred for a botched civilization," as Donald Justice wrote of Kees's work in general—"Whitman's America come to a dead end on the shores of the Pacific"—derives from Kees's vision of the world, his pessimism, rather than isolated autobiographical experiences. He differs from the "confessional poet" who is "intimately autobiographical" in that his attitude is imposed on any of his personal life. The poet of the confessional mode rather attempts to understand life, develop an attitude towards it, even, by using his autobiographical experiences as a means of interpretation. Such is the case with Lowell's asking: "Ought I to regret my seedtime?" Kees, in "For My Daughter" or most of his poetry, assumes, as Ross says, "that he is talking about problems we all face," and therefore avoids the personal, idiosyncratic concerns and experiences.

Kees's quiet tone, then, results from both his restraint in emotional display—or a consistency in the level of emotional rhetoric, tone, etc. in the poem—and his impersonal detachment from the poem's subject. This impersonality that moves between the fictional and autobiographical, the quiet pessimism and perhaps the "profound hatred," is achieved because Kees acts as a spokesperson for what he considers to be general, universal concerns and attitudes, those which happen to be his, but not exclusively, wholly personal.

Kees's first book of poems also showed his propensity for his special kind of satire. Often we cannot enjoy the cutting humor of it because it is used as another way to express his hopelessness for an intolerable present and an even more bleak future. But this satire further contributes to Kees's controlling his tone which makes the poem's speaker less of a personal, unique voice, and one that is more representative of the general condition of our "botched civilization." An example is his poem "The Speakers":

> "A equals X," says Mister One.
> "A equals B," says Mister Two.
> "A equals nothing under the sun
> But A," says Mister Three....
> Some linger in the shade to see
> One and Two in neat disguise
> Decapitating Mister Three.
>
> "This age is not entirely bad."
> It's bad enough, God knows, but you
> Should know Elizabethans had
> Sweeneys and Mrs. Porters too.

What begins as a satire of a philosophical debate among three intellectuals, whose names are as seemingly as random as their arguments are vapid, ends in a gruesome murder. "Mister Three" is decapitated by the other two because his conclusion is, in part, obviously verifiable; "A" of course equals itself, if nothing more, although it could stand for something in addition, which "Mister Three" never considers. This action is juxtaposed with the speaker's remarks in the second stanza.

The opening line of dialogue, "This age is not entirely bad," is spoken by an unidentified person, although we learn later in the stanza that it is supposed to have been T. S. Eliot, whose theory about literary tradition is contradicted by the speaker of Kees's poem. Whereas Eliot held the English Renaissance in high esteem, particularly in comparison to the state of literature in his time, Kees's speaker reminds him that the Elizabethans were no less decadent than contemporary man. And he uses Eliot's own examples of modern decadence to suggest the comparison: "Sweeney," who was described by Eliot in terms of an ape and who behaves as an ape might, as manifest by his unrestrained sexual desires, and "Mrs. Porter," who earns her living by operating brothels in which, it is hinted, she puts her own daughters to work. These are the kind of people who inhabit the modern world, suggests Eliot; but they are no different from those to be found among the

Elizabethans, counters Kees (through his speaker). The two are enacting a mock philosophical debate here, just as the three "Misters" did in stanza one. The present age may not be entirely bad according to Eliot because, using his "mythic method," one may infuse contemporary literature with the golden past, even though his mythic method also reveals that contemporary myths and figures pale in comparison to those in the past literary tradition.

That Eliot, Kees assumes, never considered the Elizabethans to have such depraved persons as Sweeney and Mrs. Porter in their culture, one which he believed much superior to his own, makes him as vulnerable as "Mister Three" who, like Eliot, was only partially correct in his theory. What the speaker knows, and tells Eliot, is that: "The past goes down and disappears... / ...and you'll be dead." If the parallel to "Mister Three" is extended to include his manner of death, then the poem presents a most peculiar kind of satire: Eliot, who was of course alive in 1943 when the poem was published, will eventually be decapitated despite his marvelous theories—theories which were obviously shunned by Kees. They offered little optimism for the future of a civilization already too far beyond repair to Kees's mind. Eliot's "The Waste Land," to use another example, proffers some spiritual hope, but Kees would have rejected it, as he did any solution. His severe pessimism of the present—much more pronounced than Eliot's—dominated over any suggestion of a panacea. Kees's bitter vision of the world prevented him from accepting any recourse other than suicide. Yet his dark vision is suppressed in the final stanza of "The Speakers" by Kees's use of satire, which aids in keeping his tone more quiet rather than outraged.

The last four lines are lyrical, but as they comprise the final quatrain of the poem, are also vaguely reminiscent of a nursery rhyme—another characteristic of Kees's odd sense of satire. Still, it is in these lines that the speaker's bleakest thoughts are revealed, quietly so:

> The past goes down and disappears,
> The present stumbles home to bed,
> The future stretches out in years
> That no one knows, and you'll be dead.

The present is ineffective in that it can do nothing more than grope towards the end of its day ("home to bed"); and no one knows anything of the future other than it brings the certainty of death. Kees is bitter, but satire keeps his emotions in control in his verse, and his tone "quiet."

Having seen how Kees's tone is the combined result of his rhetorical control of voice through means such as satire and his imposition of impersonality on his poems, or, more appropriately, his consideration of his speaker as a universal, representative voice whose concerns and outlook are shared commonly by everyone of this civilization, let us now turn to Kees's more specific use of the persona mode of voice as he employs it in his poems about "Robinson," his representative man. Robinson first appeared in Kees's second volume, *The Fall of the Magicians* (1947), in a poem entitled simply, "Robinson." The other three poems pertaining to Robinson, "Aspects of Robinson," "Robinson at Home," and "Relating to Robinson," were included in the last book Kees published before his death, *Poems 1947–1954*. Together, the four poems comprise a continuity of subject and voice uncommon to the rest of Kees's work. Robinson is less an alter ego of Kees than Henry was of Berryman, but is still closely enough a side of Kees, an "outlet" (as Berryman said of Henry), to warrant Donald Justice's remark that Robinson should be considered as Kees's "typical man," which, as we have seen, means "everyman," including the poet himself, for Kees assumed he wrote of "problems we all face," not of individual confessions. And Robinson also reminded Kenneth Rexroth of Kees—to a certain extent; Rexroth wrote:

> Where the narrator of Weldon Kees's poems is in the third person he is sometimes given a name: Robinson—modern man at the end of his rope. Kees is only distinguishable from his hero by his pity. However, he himself, as narrator-hero, is not lost beyond the end of night in a world of shoddy failures and low life. He is Robinson Crusoe, utterly alone on Madison Avenue, a stranger and afraid in the world of high-paying newsweeklies, fashionable galleries, jazz concerts, highbrow movies, sophisticated revues—the world in which Weldon Kees was eminently successful. When he said, in these gripping poems, that it filled him with absolute horror, he meant it. (236–7)

One point of clarification: Rexroth is referring to Robinson, not Kees, when he states that "he ... is not lost beyond the end of night...." The Robinson Crusoe allusion is an openly inviting one to make because of the four poems' theme as well as the name of their narrator-hero, a collective theme that is consistent with Kees's other work: the rejection of all cures for the malady of contemporary life, of which "The Speakers" was an early example. William Ross argues that Kees's "apparent rejection of psychoanalysis is not simply the rejection of an explanatory mode, however; it is also the rejection of a solution or cure. Kees ... knows no cures, rejects all solutions. It is therefore not surprising that Donald Justice can call him 'one of the bitterest poets in history.' This bitterness or anguish, established primarily before the second world war, was to carry over beyond the war years and make Kees one of the chief examples of postwar, postnuclear-bomb angst" (44), which is to paraphrase Justice's remark regarding the nature of Kees's bitterness, that it is an "anticipation of the atomic despair so familiar now, though arrived at by Kees some years before the bomb." Robinson Crusoe, then, is an appropriate analogy in that, to quote Ross, he "was cut off from the rest of humanity by geography. Our modern hero [Kees's Robinson] is cut off from the rest of humanity by his solipsistic perception" (112). Kees believes his "typical man" is the last of his race, "cut off" not merely from humanity because of his perception— he rather believes that his perception is similar to everyone else's—but from the civilization humanity has known since its inception. With such a view of the modern world—that it is the end—the future cannot hold any promises and the past is meaningless. To Robinson, therefore, Eliot's theories relating the present to past traditions and speaking of hope for the future are of course absurd, prone to failure, as is anything Robinson, in his state of "postwar, postnuclear-bomb angst," is likely to encounter in this horrible modern world.

A comparison of Kees's Robinson to Crusoe, as Rexroth and Ross have done, is however less enlightening to our purpose of demonstrating Kees's use of the persona mode of voice than a comparison of Robinson to Berryman's Henry, a comparison about which Sharon Libera has written the following general summary:

> Like Berryman's Henry, of whom one is surely reminded, Robinson is urbane, materialistic, not self-scrutinizing so much as serving as the vehicle for the writer's detached and ironic observation of himself and his world. Kees's suicide as well as his preoccupation with death and personal futility make the parallel with Berryman more than casual. The poems' plain manner sets them apart from the *Dream Songs*, though they are far from conservative since their realism functions only to provoke questions about what is actual. (155)

Robinson is Kees's invention of a character that is used in the persona mode in two principal ways: in a general application in the sense that Robinson, typical man, acts as the persona for everyone living the horrors of civilization, and in a more private sense in that he acts as an outlet for the narrator's personal, even idiosyncratic, concerns. This second use for Robinson is clearly evidenced in the final poem of the sequence, "Relating to Robinson," in which he is shown to be the narrator's Döppelganger. Robinson, therefore, provides an outlet for the narrator of the poetic sequence, the four "Robinson poems," a narrator whom we should not assume is Kees himself. It will become evident in the ensuing discussion of "Relating to Robinson" that the narrator "in the third person" (as Rexroth referred to it), who as the speaker of each of the four poems has been describing Robinson to us, is none other than Robinson, as Rexroth thought: "[W]here the narrator...is in the third person he is sometimes given a name: Robinson."

In "Robinson," the first poem, we encounter Robinson solely through the perspective of the third person narrator because Robinson is actually absent for the entirety of the poem:

> The dog stops barking after Robinson has gone.
> His act is over. The world is a gray world,
> Not without violence, and he licks under the grand piano,
> The nightmare chase well under way.
>
> The mirror from Mexico, stuck to the wall,
> Reflects nothing at all. The glass is black.
> Robinson alone provides the image Robinsonian.

Not only does the dog's barking stop after Robinson leaves, but everything stops: the mirror stops reflecting, the objects in the room cease to exist because nothing can garner their image. "His act is over," refers to the dog's act of barking; he now sleeps under the grand piano—which cannot be reflected in the black mirror—where he has nightmares. Even a dog, Kees seems to be saying, cannot escape the horrors of modern life—the nightmare being symptomatic of such life. That the world is gray suggests both that it is confused, neither black nor white, and that it exists only within the confines of the gray matter of the brain; that is, "Robinson alone provides the image Robinsonian." Robinson believes the world does not exist when not recognized by the mind (when he is not in the room, the mirror reflects nothing at all), which of course accords with one tenet of Berkeley's philosophy and which clarifies Ross's remark that Robinson's is a "solipsistic perception." (Solipsism is used here, I believe, as a collective term meaning that the self, only, is existent. Robinson can know just that which he perceives, just as the self—in Berkeley's theory—can know nothing but its own adaptations.) Consequently, the Robinsonian "image" is "all of the room," the contents of which are enumerated in the following stanzas:

> walls, curtains,
> Shelves, bed, the tinted photograph of Robinson's first wife,
> Rugs, vases, panatellas in a humidor.
> They would fill the room if Robinson came in.

> The pages in the books are blank,
> The books that Robinson has read. That is his favorite chair,
> Or where the chair would be if Robinson were here.
>
> All day the phone rings. It could be Robinson
> Calling. It never rings when he is here.

The objects which fill Robinson's rooms are meaningless—they are nothing; they do not exist for him in his absence. "They fill the room" only when he returns, bringing to them, as Robinson does, his personal and special associations. The glass of his mirror is black until he sees himself in it or remembers the occasion of purchasing it in Mexico; his books are blank until he reads them or remembers having read them. These objects do exist literally when Robinson steps out of the room, yet apart from him and the meaning he brings to each; on their own they fail to produce an image of his personality, his selfhood. Only Robinson can.

The poem ends with the suggestion of the disparity between any object, or thing, of itself and those objects to which Robinson's mind can bring special associations:

> Outside, white buildings yellow in the sun.
> Outside, the birds circle continuously
> Where trees are actual and take no holiday.

Things outside Robinson's room—the buildings, birds, trees—are "actual," just as those inside are, yet they are not part of Robinson, his image, and therefore can take no holiday (that is, cease to exist) from his mind. They do not intrude into Robinson's "solipsistic perception" of the world because they hold no special significance for him, just as the telephone—another possible intrusion from outside—holds none; it only rings when he is not home to answer it.

"Robinson" is a description of a protagonist who does not appear in the poem. It establishes a sense of Robinson by depicting a world from which he is absent. The third person narrator accomplishes this because it speaks from Robinson's point of view and knows how his dog behaves, how his possessions seem to appear, when he is home and when not. In this, that the point of view of the poem's voice is Robinson's, the poem "Robinson," like any Dream Song which had as its voice a third person narrator speaking from Henry's point of view, narrating how he mourned, and so on, is of the persona mode.

"Aspects of Robinson" depicts mainly the public life of Robinson and shows that he is a debonair man who moves easily with the fashionable crowd of the city:

Robinson at cards at the Algonquin; a thin
Blue light comes down once more outside the blinds.
Gray men in overcoats are ghosts blown past the door....

Dressed for the links, describes an old Intourist tour.
—Here's where old Gibbons jumped from, Robinson.

Robinson walking in the Park, admiring the elephant.
Robinson buying the *Tribune*, Robinson buying the *Times*.
    Robinson
Saying, "Hello. Yes, this is Robinson. Sunday
At five? I'd love to. Pretty well. And you?"

He is distinct from the collective mass of "gray men in overcoats" whom he regards as "ghosts blown past the door" of the Algonquin; he is comfortable "above
the Heights," walking about, accepting social invitations. There are many public
"aspects of Robinson," although each seems to demonstrate his appearance of
success. In the first three stanzas, his name is stated ten times, probably not for
rhythmic effect, but to emphasize the many roles of Robinson the public man. A
different side, or aspect, of Robinson is revealed by each situation he encounters;
he is "typical modern man," and as such, has many roles even though so far they
seem to be reflective of only one part of modern life, the apparently successful, the
leisurely, side.

But this representation quickly changes in the next lines where we see that
the private Robinson, though still with some élan, is vulnerable to other aspects:

Robinson alone at Longchamps, staring at the wall.

Robinson afraid, drunk, sobbing Robinson
In bed with a Mrs. Morse. Robinson at home;
Decisions: Toynbee or luminol? Where the sun
Shines, Robinson in flowered trunks, eyes toward
The breakers. Where the night ends, Robinson in East Side bars.

Robinson's success cannot make him less alone, afraid; he gets drunk, commits
adultery (the "Mrs." seems to suggest this), decides between reading Toynbee and
taking luminol to induce sleep as if they were the same. He is representative man
who enacts many roles during the course of a day and night.

There is the implication, too, that these sides of the private Robinson con-
stitute a truer representation of who he is: a product of modern life, this "botched
civilization." In the poem's last stanza, the narrator describes Robinson's public
attire, and states that it is an affectation, a covering, of himself:

> Robinson in Glen plaid jacket, Scotch-grain shoes,
> Black four-in-hand and oxford button-down,
> The jeweled and silent watch that winds itself, the brief-
> Case, covert topcoat, clothes for spring, all covering
> His sad and usual heart, dry as a winter leaf.

Like anyone in modern life, no matter what the possessions, the clothing, Robinson, finally, is alone, unable to love, "his sad and usual heart, dry as a winter leaf." This stanza illuminates Rexroth's remark, that "Kees is only distinguishable from his hero by his pity," for Robinson is a pathetic figure here, the model for which is Eliot's "Prufrock" who was overly concerned about his public appearance:

> With a bald spot in the middle of my hair—
> (They will say: 'How his hair is growing thin!')
> My morning coat, my collar mounting firmly to the chin,
> My necktie rich and modest, but asserted by a simple pin—...
>
> Shall I part my hair behind? Do I dare eat a peach?
> I shall wear white flannel trousers, and walk upon the beach.

Just as Prufrock covers himself, hides his bald spot by parting his hair a certain way, rather than uncover himself—and this is why he is afraid of women, of entering into a relationship—Robinson, when in public, is concerned with how he covers himself. The dress of Prufrock, the necktie and pin or the white flannel trousers, could easily be worn by Robinson when making his way about the city. And both end the day sadly, their hearts dry; they are modern men suffering from the afflictions of modern life. They are similar, further, in that the poets Kees and Eliot regard their respective protagonist with some pity.

"Robinson at Home" complements "Aspects of Robinson" in that it shows him in his private surroundings. In this sense it presents another, solitary, aspect of Robinson, yet because we find him sleeping in the poem, we cannot learn how he acts when around his personal belongings to which, as the poem "Robinson" indicated, he brings his special associations. In each of the three poems discussed so far, then, Kees gives us but very few glimpses of Robinson: In the first, he was absent from the poem, in "Aspects," he was careful to maintain his public exterior, or image, except for the short scene of his drunkenness, and now in "Robinson at Home," he is shown to us by the nightmares he dreams:

> Curtains drawn back, the door ajar.
> All winter long, it seemed, a darkening

began. But now the moonlight and the odors of the street
Conspire and combine toward one community.

These are the rooms of Robinson.
Bleached, wan, and colorless this light, as though
All the blurred daybreaks of the spring
Found an asylum here, perhaps for Robinson alone…

This sleep is from exhaustion, but his old desire
To die like this has known a lessening.
Now there is only this coldness that he has to wear.
But not in sleep.—Observant scholar, traveller,

Or uncouth bearded figure squatting in a cave,
A keen-eyed sniper on the barricades,
A heretic in catacombs, a famed roué,
A beggar on the streets, the confidant of Popes—

All these are Robinson in sleep, who mumbles as he turns,
"There is something in this madhouse that I symbolize—
This city—nightmare—black—"

                              He wakes in sweat
To the terrible moonlight and what might be
Silence. It drones like wires far beyond the roofs,
And the long curtains blow into the room.

The coming of spring offers little promise to the hopeless Robinson. This poem
continues the pathetic depiction of Robinson begun in the closing stanzas of "Aspects." The light of spring, rather than suggestive of vernal images or the renewal
of nature, is "colorless" like "blurred daybreaks," a time when it is neither wholly
dark nor light. This "bleached, wan, and colorless" light finds "asylum" in Robinson's rooms; it is the way he perceives something that should be serene. But to
Robinson, the spring days need asylum because he sees them as either horrific in
themselves and as such in need of confinement, or as needing refuge from the
horrors that exist outside his rooms. Regardless as to which, he closes his mind to
these "daybreaks of the spring" because they do not bring with them a moonlight
or a music which might wake him.

   He is unsure of his identity in his dreams. The nightmares suggest a loss,
rather than confusion, of selfhood, for he is many persons: scholar, hermit, heretic, confidant of Popes, etc.—one self contradictory to the next. None resembles
anything like the Robinson of the other poems. "All these are Robinson in sleep,

who mumbles as he turns, / 'There is something in this madhouse that I symbol-ize— / This city—nightmare—black—.'" What he symbolizes is precisely that which he has dreamed: a nightmare of people who inhabit a city of horror, a loss of self-identity reflected by a night whose moonlight is terrible, not peaceful, and whose silence "drones" disconcertedly rather than soothingly. He "wakes in sweat" knowing that he, alone in his "madhouse" of mind, symbolizes humanity of this time, that he is representative man—in all his various guises—but one, like Crusoe, cut off from the rest of civilization. In the final poem of the sequence, a terrified Robinson walks through the streets trying to inform others of his vision for the future.

Yet "Relating to Robinson" focuses on the narrator, how he relates to Robinson, and in this, that Robinson himself is not highly visible in the poem, it is much like the others. The narrator, though, knows Robinson intimately enough to imply that Robinson is his Döppelganger—and might well have been throughout the sequence. The narrator first encounters Robinson while walking along a deserted street in the evening:

> Somewhere in Chelsea, early summer;
> And, walking in the twilight toward the docks,
> I thought I made out Robinson ahead of me.
>
> From an uncurtained second-story room, a radio
> Was playing *There's a Small Hotel,* a kite
> Twisted above dark rooftops and slow drifting birds.
> We were alone there, he and I,
> Inhabiting the empty street.

But the narrator is not certain whether he sees Robinson, or someone else, for he remembers that Robinson usually spends his summers out of town. When Robinson stops walking to gaze into the window, the narrator almost calls out his name, believing it must be him, but concludes:

> There was no chance. Just as I passed,
> Turning my head to search his face,
> His own head turned with mine
> And fixed me with dilated, terrifying eyes
> That stopped my blood. His voice
> Came at me like an echo in the dark.

The men face one another, their heads turning to meet each other's searching face simultaneously as if each knew how the other would turn his head. The narrator actually is looking at himself, perhaps reflected in the store's window, and he recognizes terror in his Döppelganger's eyes because he already anticipates his words:

> "I thought I saw the whirlpool opening.
> Kicked all night at a bolted door.
> You must have followed me from Astor Place.
> An empty paper floats down at the last.
> *And then a day as huge as yesterday in pairs*
> *Unrolled its horror on my face*
> *Until it blocked—*" Running in sweat
> To reach the docks, I turned back
> For a second glance. I had no certainty,
> There in the dark, that it was Robinson
> Or someone else.
> The block was bare....

The moment the narrator faces his worst fear—Robinson, and what Robinson has to say—it vanishes; this makes the Döppelganger theory a plausible one. But even if in actuality they are two men, Robinson, having experienced the terror of his age, still remains representative man, the persona of all men and women of a modern life which renders them identity-free and insane—feeling at home only in the madhouse of their minds ("Robinson at Home")—and one which promises more terror, "the whirlpool opening." Robinson is the spokesperson for his time.

Although what Robinson says is not that frightening, it is enough to terrify the narrator, to make him sweat and run away. Just as Robinson anticipated the narrator would look at him earlier, the narrator anticipates how Robinson will finish speaking, and quickly leaves before allowing him to. The narrator is able to understand the horror implicit in what Robinson has already said, to read the terror in his eyes. The poem ends with the scared narrator hurrying West, finding no comfort in what should be the peaceful scene of the lights coming on across the bay where "boats moved silently and the low whistles blew"—just as Robinson, in "Robinson at Home," took little recognition in the coming of spring and no comfort in the moonlit night.

In that Kees, bitter with his New York life, "hurried West" to San Francisco, where he found life no better, some parallels could be made between the poet and his "typical man," Robinson. Yet rather than assume any parallels based on incomplete—at best—biographical information, we should regard Robinson, as an everyman figure, functioning as a general persona—for Kees, for the first person narrator of the Robinson sequence (if in fact different from Robinson himself), for anyone, "typical man" or woman. Given Kees's tone and themes of his other work as we have discussed them, it is more than reasonable to view Robinson as such. Kees, therefore, differs in his use of the persona mode of voice from Berryman's use of Henry in that Robinson is an outlet speaking for everybody, not for the poet alone. Kees regarded his private concerns to be common to all; so, too, must his persona be.

Whereas Robinson's final remarks bespeak a hopelessness for a botched civilization, Galway Kinnell's persona will present a possible solution which offers some hope for modern life.

Galway Kinnell

Commenting on Emily Dickinson's poem, "I Heard a Fly Buzz When I Died," Galway Kinnell wrote in his essay "The Poetics of the Physical World":

> Of course, it is repulsive that a fly come to you, if you are dying and if it may be a corpse fly, its thorax the hysterical green color of slime. And yet in the illumination of the dying moment, everything the poet knew on earth is transfigured. The fly appears, alive, physical, voracious, a last sign of the earthly life. It is the most ordinary thing, the most despised, which brings the strange brightening, this last moment of increased life. (135)

Kinnell's interpretation of "I Heard a Fly Buzz" expresses the same themes operative in his own verse as well. That one's awareness of mortality leads to a more fulfilling life, particularly—as suggested in his explication of the Dickinson poem—the experience of "the dying moment" which is a "strange brightening, this last moment of increased life," has been Kinnell's principal thematic concern since as early in his work as *What a Kingdom It Was* (1960). Among other poems about death, that volume included one of Kinnell's most memorable pieces, "Freedom, New Hampshire," an elegy for his brother who died prematurely. The poem, as David Young explains, "gives us three sections in which we watch the two boys encountering birth, death, and the generative energies of nature in the country setting where they grew up. In the fourth section, these experiences are recapitulated as the poem moves on to the experience of human loss and grief..." (242–43). In much of the work succeeding "Freedom, New Hampshire," it is not merely death that is explored, but the subsequent "generative energies of nature" which follow.

The subject of any poem, Kinnell continued in "Poetics," is "the thing which dies. Zeus on Olympus is a theological being; the swan who desires a woman enters the province of poetry. In '*Eloi, Eloi, lama sabacthani,*' so does Jesus. Poetry is the wasted breath" (135). Poetry for Kinnell must represent the loss, "the wasted breath," but in doing so making that loss an illumination of life. Death of this life could mean the beginning of another kind of life, or at the very least, of a new experience. A loss, then, should be celebrated, for it is at the moment it occurs, at the instant of gasping "the wasted breath," that which makes, for Kinnell, the essence of poetry.

Even so, death is not welcomed solely because it provides the thematic core of a poem, or because it is the possible beginning of a new experience awaiting after life. Rather, death calls attention to the last moment of life, making it—as Kinnell wrote of Dickinson's poem—one "last moment of increased life." While indicating, in "Poetics," how he attempts to use the subject of death in his poetry, Kinnell remarked: "That we endure only for a time, that we know this, is the thrilling element in every creature, every relationship, every moment" (136). These are the themes Kinnell works with in his poetry, the most clear example of which is his book-length poem, *The Book of Nightmares* (1971); and because his themes are often the reason for his working in a particular mode of voice, it will be useful to examine how they operate in that book.

The epigraph to *The Book of Nightmares*, which follows, is taken from Rilke:

> But this, though: death,
> the whole of death,—even before life's begun,
> to hold it all so gently, and be good:
> this is beyond description!

In an interview with Wayne Dodd and Stanley Plumly, Kinnell explained the meaning of this passage in relation to *The Book of Nightmares*:

> This passage appears after the dedication to Maud and Fergus [Kinnell's children]. From one point of view, the book is nothing but an effort to face death and live with death. Children have all that effort in their future. They have glimpses of death through fatigue, sleep, cuts and bruises, warnings, etc., and also through their memory of the nonexistence they so recently came from. They seem to understand death surprisingly clearly. But now time passes slowly for them. It hardly exists. They live with death almost as animals do. This natural trust in life's rhythms, infantile as it is, provides the model for the trust they may struggle to learn later on. *The Book of Nightmares* is my own effort to find the trust again. I invoke Maud and Fergus not merely to instruct them, but also to get help from them. (45–6)

Given that the book was intended as both instructional and as a quest to regain the "natural trust in life's rhythms" (the rhythms, that is, of life to death and then,

maybe, to another kind of life, or perhaps not—just the rhythm of life to death if
the regenerative qualities of nature remain unconsidered in this context), *The
Book of Nightmares* remains unbalanced in favor of its didactic side in that whatever Kinnell learns about recapturing this trust, this acceptance of the naturalness
of death, is recorded for his children's use so that they too, when adults, can benefit from his acquired knowledge. For the children will of course increasingly move
away from that understanding as they grow toward adulthood, even though they
presently "seem to understand death" having so recently come from the "nonexistence," which Kinnell compares to the sphere of death. Consequently, at the
end of the first section, "Under the Maud Moon," the Kinnell speaker tells his
daughter that the book can offer some guidance and instruction when she reaches
the age one begins to fear death, to mistrust it, having forgotten any inherent inclination to regard death as a natural rhythm of existence. And that age is, as implied in "Under the Maud Moon," sometime in adulthood when the death of
one's parents, when feeling "orphaned," engenders thoughts of this kind. The
speaker gives his daughter these instructions, which act as the prelude for his own
quest, his "effort to find the trust again":

> And in the days
> when you find yourself orphaned,
> emptied
> of all wind-singing, of light,
> the pieces of cursed bread on your tongue,
>
> may there come back to you
> a voice,
> spectral, calling you
> *sister*!
> from everything that dies.
>
> And then
> you shall open
> this book, even if it is the book of nightmares.

What Kinnell, the poet and father, hopes the book will do for his daughter—and
his son, Fergus, who is addressed late in the poem—is allow them to submit to the
calling, the voice speaking "from everything that dies," and to see it as something
natural and benevolent rather than as a menacing specter.

The book is then mostly concerned with Kinnell's trying to free himself from
his acquired—that is, his adult—behavior in order to understand his primordial
instincts. One such instinct is of his time in the womb, a time of "nonexistence"

that Kinnell believes was an early "glimpse of death" we each had. His use of
Rilke's line, "the whole of death, even before life's begun," is well chosen in cor-
roborating this notion. And poetry, Kinnell feels, can be used as a means of self-
exploration—even a way of recalling primordial instinctive behavior; through it,
a better understanding of the self can result. In his preface to *Walking Down the
Stairs*, he wrote that poetry is "a form of expression in which there is at least the
possibility of finding oneself as one is" (xiv). To that end, *The Book of Nightmares*
presents a method how: shedding the adult dread of dying, and learning to relinquish life. The principal "nightmare" is losing life; the way to end that fear is to
come to an understanding, to trust in it. If one can learn to let go of this human
fear—and in doing so transform, at least in thought, into a more primitive being,
an animal, perhaps—then one entertains the "possibility of finding oneself" in
the most natural form, "as one is." In this sense, Kinnell reiterates one of the basic
tenets of religion—Eastern or Western—which holds that one must retain a
child's perspective in order to comprehend the mysteries: losing oneself to find
oneself.

He begins his quest (the book's second section) with recalling how easily a
hen accepts death, the hen seemingly "longing only to die":

> Sprawled
> on our faces in the spring
> nights, teeth
> biting down on hen feathers, bits of the hen
> still stuck in the crevices—if only
> we could let go
> like her, throw ourselves
> on the mercy of darkness, like the hen...
>
> the breastbone risen up
> out of breast flesh, until the fatted thing
> woozes off, head
> thrown back
> on the chopping block, longing only
> to die.

Kinnell, in remembering his experiences in killing fatted hens, assumes they wel-
come death. The hen easily surrenders her life, "lets go to the mercy of darkness."
And this is the knowledge for which he quests—"if only we could let go like her."
The last verse of this section, then, finishes with an admonishment to himself:

> Listen, Kinnell,
> dumped alive
> and dying into the old sway bed,
> a layer of crushed feathers all that there is
> between you
> and the long shaft of darkness shaped as you,
> let go.
>
> Even this haunted room
> all its materials photographed with tragedy,
> even the tiny crucifix drifting face down at the center of the earth,
> even these feathers freed from their wings forever
> are afraid.

He must "let go" of two fears in order to regain his trust in life's natural order: his fear of dying, and his fear of losing the self he has become, the civilized man who recognizes a crucifix as a religious symbol and who lives among—who cannot live without—"materials photographed with tragedy." Every material possession of mankind is "photographed with tragedy" because it came into being as a result of the decimation of the natural. That is, the "old sway bed," for example, upon which the "Kinnell" of the poem lies in this verse passage, is made of "crushed feathers freed from their wings forever." All that he is used to, the comforts of civilized life, religion, etc., stands between him and "the long shaft of darkness," which is his natural self; it is because of mankind's becoming civilized that he distrusts and fears the natural rhythms of the world.

His rationale is that by overcoming the desire for, and the dependence on, rooms, materials, religion, he will more closely resemble his primordial self, which for Kinnell could be either the fetus of the womb, or something like Neanderthal man—both are primitive states of being, and both now seem of the distant past; mankind for too long has used its "materials" as the sole means of its existence. He begins the actual journey back to this more primitive state in the next section of the book, "The Shoes of Wandering," where he says he is "frightened / I may already have lost / the way: *the first step*, the Crone / who scried the crystal said, *shall be / to lose the way*"—that is, to become more childlike in the sense of learning to trust one's natural inclinations. Kinnell's civilized self tells him to be frightened of his "wandering." He begins to leave behind some aspects of his present self, though, in that he takes the counsel of the Crone who tells him "to lose the way"; she has supplanted his Christianity in providing spiritual guidance. Also, she gave him instruction orally, which is more natural, and "primitive," in the sense that religious or other instruction was, in pre-Gutenberg times, conveyed in this manner. Although Kinnell could have found the same message in the Bible—the basis for his religion as civilized man—the Crone "scried the crystal" for it, an image that evokes the mysticism of pre-Christianity. After journeying for a time, he finds a "path among stones" where he realizes that his wish to become more primitive will end—in the same way that each stone's desire to be a star will end—with a "falling back, knowing / the sadness of the wish / to alight / back among the glitter of bruised ground." Because he does not fully learn how to "lose himself," *The Book of Nightmares* offers little instruction to his children. It remains, as its title suggests, a record of the fears Maud and Fergus can expect to encounter as they grow up, as their knowledge of the "nonexistence" fades while they become older and more civilized. That the speaker did not reconcile his present, civilized self with the primordial being he sought, and that he did not regain his trust in life's rhythms completely—although his fear of death is lessened because of his spiritual quest—accounts for the ambivalence of his words of instruction to his son upon birth, in the final section of the poem, "Lastness":

> A black bear sits alone
> in the twilight...
>   He sniffs the sweat
> in the breeze, he understands
> a creature, a death-creature
> watches from the fringe of the trees,
> finally he understands
> I am no longer here, he himself
> from the fringe of the trees watches
> a black bear
> get up, eat a few flowers, trudge away,
> all his fur glistening
> in the rain.
>
> And what glistening! Sancho Fergus,
> my boychild, had such great shoulders,
> when he was born his head
> came out, the rest of him stuck. And he opened
> his eyes: his head out there all alone
> in the room, he squinted with pained,
> barely unglued eyes at the ninth-month's
> blood splashing beneath him
> on the floor. And almost
> smiled, I thought, almost forgave it all in advance.

This passage begins with a portrait of a solitary black bear, and ends with Sancho Fergus making his way out of the womb, which is his initial experience with existence as civilized man. And the two are related: At the moment the bear understands that he is some kind of "death-creature," watching a black bear, Fergus's head appears from the birth canal. The poem suggests a closeness of man and animal; and particularly, it points to a shared consciousness between Fergus and the bear. The bear senses a "death-creature" which is Fergus about to be born, and who, in this pre-birth state, is capable of reason: "finally he understands / I am no longer here," no longer the black bear he thought he was who sniffed a "death-creature"; this "death-creature," he realizes, is himself. Once a part of the bear, the "nonexistent" being who shortly will be Fergus—recall that Kinnell referred to his children's time in the womb as a time of "nonexistence"—is now separate from it and can only watch as the bear trudges away. The message from Kinnell is that pre-civilized man not merely shares common traits with animals, but actually begins as an animal, as a bear for example, because the animal is not conscious of death as something to fear. Man, when he acquires his life becomes a "death-creature" because he begins to learn life's nightmares, one of which is the fear of dying. Fergus leaves the "nonexistence," which is a bear-like consciousness, for human life.

In the next stanza, Kinnell again makes clear the parallel of his son and the bear:

> When he came wholly forth
> I took him up in my hands and bent
> over and smelled
> the black, glistening fur
> of his head, as empty space
> must have bent
> over the newborn planet
> and smelled the grasslands and the ferns.

Fergus has "black, glistening fur" on his head; the bear was last seen by the "death-creature" trudging away, "all his fur glistening / in the rain."

Although Kinnell may be certain of the relation between the bear and his son, he is not certain that he has resolved all the nightmares of life or whether he has learned any substantive answers from his quest: "Is it true / the earth does not last?" he asks himself while holding Fergus, waiting for him to begin crying and thus start his life. "Stop," he suddenly commands Fergus, "Stop here. / Living brings you to death, there is no other road." But he ends the section, and the poem, undecided what he wants for his son:

> This poem
> if we shall call it that,
> or concert of one
> divided among himself...
>
> Sancho Fergus! Don't cry!
>
> Or else, cry.
>
> On the body,
> on the blued flesh, when it is
> laid out, see if you can find
> the one flea which is laughing.

Even the final four lines are ambiguous. It is not clear whom Kinnell, the poet, is addressing, the "Kinnell" speaker of the poem or the "Fergus" character—both are personas in the poem, of course. These lines' meaning could be that the flea on the dead body is laughing because it is happy—which would suggest that death has finally been accepted as part of life's rhythms, that it is nothing to fear—or that the flea is mocking the seriousness which human beings take in worrying about an unavoidable matter. For Kinnell, however, absolute answers are secondary to the search for them because they remind him of his mortality which, as he said, is the essence of poetry and the means by which life can be more intensely illuminated.

This last section of *The Book of Nightmares* is, in theme, similar to Emily Dickinson's "I Heard a Fly Buzz When I Died" in that it attempts to imagine the "increased life," the heightened feeling, one experiences for the world upon leaving it. And what brings this "strange brightening, this last moment of increased life" (as Kinnell wrote of the Dickinson poem), is the knowledge that it is about to be left behind forever. But it is the transcendence from a pre-birth existence to life, and then to death, that Kinnell is most interested in, and it is this concern that leads him to broaden his conception of selfhood, of which he remarked in an interview with A. Poulin, Jr.:

> In some great poems, like "Song of Myself," a reader is taken through one person into some greater self; there is a continual passing into the "death of the self," to use that phrase. It's one of the things that makes "Song of Myself" glorious. As we read this poem, we have to open ourselves if we are to get anything at all out of it. When we come to the lines "I was the man, I suffered, I

was there," we already understand what it is to disappear into someone else. The final action of the poem, where Whitman dissolves into the air and into the ground, is for me one of the great moments of self-transcendence in poetry. In one way or another, consciously or not, all poems try to pass beyond the self. The best poems are those in which you are not this or that person, but anyone, just a person. If you could go farther, you would no longer be a person but an animal. If you went farther still you would be the grass, eventually a stone. If a stone could speak your poem would be its words. (22–3)

Berryman and Kinnell each take from Whitman's poem the conception that his own use of "I" embraces a larger realm than just his individual self. Berryman saw it as a representative pronoun, a persona in the sense that the "I" means everyone; Kinnell feels that Whitman accomplished his "I" to "pass beyond the self," Whitman having "dissolved" in "one of the greatest moments of self-transcendence in poetry." But whereas Berryman believed Whitman to retain himself in his "I," which is inclusive of all men, Kinnell believes that Whitman was able to finally transcend his own self in favor of becoming "not this or that person, but anyone, just a person." And although it may seem impossible to transcend one's self beyond a person to an animal (nonhuman) state or to that of the grass or a stone, Kinnell, because of his conviction that poetry is a means of self-exploration, that poetry is "a form of expression in which there is at least the possibility of finding oneself as one is," uses the persona mode of voice to attempt a transcendence of the self beyond a person to an animal.

In answer to Mary Jane Fortunato's question on the kind of "nature poetry" Kinnell was writing, he remarked:

> I don't think the distinction between "nature poem" and "urban poem" is useful any longer. The idea that we and our creations don't belong to "nature" comes from the notion that the human is a special being created in God's image to have dominion over all else. We are becoming aware again of our connection with other beings. That's hopeful, since for several centuries our civilization has done all it could to forget it. (17)

In analyzing the last section of *The Book of Nightmares* we have already seen one "connection" between man and animal in Kinnell's poetry—the human consciousness (Fergus's) emerged from the black bear, separating them forever. The purpose, then, of achieving a self-transcendence—at least in the poem—is to attempt a reconciliation between the two, to connect that which "our civilization has done all it could to forget." The poems in *Body Rags* (1968) try to show the many similarities between humans and other animals so that civilized man may recall some of these forgotton ties.

"Lost Loves," appearing early in the first part of that collection, sets the principal theme for many of the poems. The first person speaker lay dreaming "on ashes of old volcanoes" where he remembers experiences and people that had special significance for him in his life: "Mole Street. Quai-aux-Fleurs. Francoise. / Greta. 'After Lunch' by Po Chu-I. / 'The Sunflower' by Blake." And here, in the first stanza, he laments the passing of his life because it will mean the end of these memories (thus, "lost loves"), leaving no opportunity for new ones. In the second stanza, however, as he continues "baking / [his] deathward flesh in the sun," he finds solace in his realization that the end of this life means the passing into another stage of existence:

> And yet I can rejoice
> that everything changes, that
> we go from life
> into life,
>
> and enter ourselves
> quaking
> like the tadpole, his time come, tumbling toward the slime.

In this inverted personification, Kinnell attributes animal development to humans. The tadpole, "his time come," gropes his way "toward the slime," toward becoming a frog. (The tadpole slowly sheds its outer, protective covering—which is slimy, mucous—freeing the developing frog: First the back legs penetrate the mucous covering, then the front, the head, and last, the tadpole's tail dissolves.) The "slime" in the stanza also refers to the pond, the new life the frog has been born into, and which the "quaking" tadpole is hesitant to begin. Humans, too, will have their time come when they must pass into another stage. Their development, Kinnell suggests, may not be as visible or physical as the tadpole's; it occurs, finally, when they understand that one can rejoice over having to die, or losing loves, because "everything changes." And the change Kinnell says humans make is like that of the tadpole: "we go from life / into life, // and enter ourselves / quaking."

Kinnell's use of "I" is intended as the voice of "anyone, just a person." The fact that his "I" is not a specific person—himself, say—distinguishes it from the confessional mode. Further, like Berryman's "I" and Whitman's, it acts as a "third person" in the sense that it could be "anyone," and it therefore is more largely representative than it would be if confined to one personal point of view. That

Kinnell intends his "I" to act as a representational voice aligns his practice closely with Berryman's. Yet where Berryman often denied that his personal self (the John Berryman with a social security number, who brushes his teeth) was the persona he created for the poems, Kinnell acknowledges portraying autobiographical experiences in his verse, but using those experiences to suggest that what is one man's history is common to all. He remarked to William Heyen and Gregory Fitz Gerald:

> Often a poem at least starts out being about oneself, about one's experiences, a fragment of autobiography. But then, if it's really a poem, it goes deeper than personality. It takes on that strange voice, intensely personal yet common to everyone, in which all rituals are spoken. A poem expresses one's most private feelings; and these turn out to be the feelings of everyone else as well. The separate egos vanish. The poem becomes simply the voice of a creature on earth speaking. (6)

"Lost Loves," then, is just such a poem, one in which Kinnell begins with a seemingly personal moment—an autobiographical fragment, perhaps—of musing over his private loves: favorite poems, people, and places he has been. But the poem's universality of theme makes the one personal feeling "common to everyone." When the speaker of that poem says "I can rejoice that everything changes," the "I" is speaking for everyone, and therefore the phrase that follows, "that we go from life into life, and enter ourselves," is inclusive of everyone, hence the "we" and "ourselves." The "separate egos" of the personal "I" and of "them," in reference to all others but the personal self, have—as Kinnell suggests—vanished in this poem.

Kinnell clarified, to Dodd and Plumly, his use of the "I" as meaning "anyone, just a person," or, to use Berryman's reference, as meaning another, "third," person:

> I haven't consciously invented a protagonist or mask. Yet the act of writing a poem that one hopes will speak for others as well as oneself tends to create something like a persona. So Whitman becomes "a kosmos, one of the roughs." And even Wordsworth, in *The Prelude*, who tries to write accurate autobiography, becomes a kind of exemplary case. (50–1)

With this in mind, let us now return to the other poems in *Body Rags* that concentrate on the "I" as a voice speaking "for others as well as oneself," and in which animals become fused with this "I."

In "Night in the Forest," the first person speaker ponders his and his companion's natural origins. In the first stanza, which follows, the speaker compares his sleeping companion to a larva in a cocoon:

> A woman
> sleeps next to me on the earth. A strand
> of hair flows
> from her cocoon sleeping bag, touching
> the ground hesitantly, as if thinking
> to take root.

The cocoon, a silky, protective covering spun by larvae during one stage of their development, is the metaphorical agent for the sleeping bag. The woman's strand of hair "touching / the ground hesitantly, as if thinking / to take root" is the same gesture a larva takes when deciding upon the best place to attach itself in order to begin spinning its cocoon. The forest, being close to nature, seems to allow the speaker to make this comparison, but he ends the poem with one more unlikely:

> I can hear
> a mountain brook
> and somewhere blood winding
> down its ancient labyrinths.

The parallel of the brook and blood "winding / down its ancient labyrinths" calls forth that the speaker feels somehow more aware of his primordial beginning at this moment in the forest as if this night has metaphorically transformed him and the woman back to more natural states of existence. Again, as in "Lost Loves," characteristics of animals (here, insects or worms) are attributed to the human woman. And, if the "I" of this poem "speaks for others," this closing stanza implies that each of us shares a common heritage that has been recalled by a lone person spending a night in the forest.

In each of the last two poems of *Body Rags*, "The Porcupine" and "The Bear," Kinnell makes a direct association between the first person speaker and the poem's title animal. In reference to that collection, Kinnell told Heyen: "...there are many animals in my poems. I've wanted to see in themselves and also to see their closeness to us" (5). In both poems, the speaker is drawn close to the animal by witnessing its death, and in doing so the speaker assumes the animal's experience of dying. The speaker, then, becomes the animal, as Kinnell remarked to Dodd and Plumly:

For me those animals had no specific symbolic correspondence. I thought of them as animals. Of course I wasn't making zoological portraits. "The Porcupine" tries to establish explicit connections between us and porcupines. In both "The Porcupine" and "The Bear" the one speaking actually becomes the animal. Whenever we identify with some thing or some animal, it at once begins to represent us or some aspect of us, and so is on its way to becoming a symbol, even if exactly what it represents can't be specified. (56)

Not only does the speaker become the animal in each poem, but in doing so becomes representative of man's primitive origin, by which we know Kinnell to mean some existence that is pre-human—a bear-like existence in Fergus's case.

Let us turn to the poems themselves in order to make these general assertions more clear. In the second section of "The Porcupine," the speaker outlines the ways in which humans are like porcupines:

> In character
> he resembles us in seven ways:
> he puts his mark on outhouses,
> he alchemizes by moonlight…
> he uses his tail for climbing,
> he chuckles softly to himself when scared,
> he's overcrowded if there's more than one of him per five acres,
> his eyes have their own inner redness.

This is one of the few instances of the book where Kinnell neither personifies the animal nor, in an inverted personification, attributes animal traits to man. There is much comedy in these lines in which the speaker simply states what he has perceived to be seven characteristics of the porcupine that resemble man's. Although some may apply to selected humans (feeling overcrowded if more than one per five acres, for example), it must be remembered that Kinnell believes that, in a poem, "one's most private feelings turn out to be the feelings of everyone else as well," that the seemingly personal is common to everyone. The implication here, as it was in *The Book of Nightmares*, "Lost Loves," and "Night in the Forest," is that humans are not much different from animals. The speaker therefore "connects" humans to animals in an attempt to show "their closeness to us."

In the poem's next section, the speaker describes those things that the porcupine "adores":

> Adorer of ax
> handles aflow with grain, of arms
> of Morris chairs, of hand

crafted objects
steeped in the juice of fingertips,
of surfaces wetted down
with fist grease and elbow oil,
of clothespins that have
grabbed our body-rags by underarm and crotch...

The porcupine adores wood forms crafted by man, preferring these artificial shapes to wood in natural forms. Anything that man has made, it seems, the porcupine adores because he enjoys the taste of man's smell, "the juice of fingertips," the "fist grease and elbow oil," and the smell of "underarm and crotch" that seep into clothespins. The speaker is amazed that the porcupine finds the natural beauty of the forest unappealing, boring even, and that instead he is "astonished" by man's "hand crafted objects":

Unimpressed—bored—
by the whirl of the stars, by *these*
he's astonished, ultra-
Rilkean angel!

for whom the true
portion of the sweetness of earth
is one of those bottom-heavy, glittering, saccadic
bits
of salt water that splash down
the haunted ravines of a human face.

Kinnell explicated this passage for us in response to an interview question of Margaret Edwards:

I was thinking—as I seem to do often—of the Ninth Elegy, where Rilke tells how the angels are attracted by ordinary, earthly things. The porcupine eats anything with salt in it—generally things we've handled a lot, that the salt of our sweat has soaked into. So, like Rilke's angels, the porcupine loves axe handles, doors, chair arms, and so on. A porcupine once ate the insulation off all the wires in my pickup truck, for the road salt. But it's mostly wooden things they like. Once they actually ate their way through the cellar door of this house. If they had climbed the stairs into the house itself, they would have reduced the place to rubble, since it is splashed—floor, walls, and ceiling—with my sweat. As it happened they didn't get in, because they ate down the cellar stairs on the way up. Farmers regard them as pests, and kill them on sight.
(111–12)

The section following, then, begins a narrative of a porcupine's death from having been shot three times by a farmer. The speaker watches the porcupine fall from the tree where he was "dozing" when the farmer shot him on sight: "On / the way down it tore open its belly / on a broken / branch, hooked its gut, / and went on falling." That night, after witnessing this shooting and the subsequent bloody death of the porcupine (upon landing on the ground after its fall, the porcupine "sprang to its feet, and / paying out gut heaved / and spartled through a hundred feet of goldenrod / before / the abrupt emptiness"), the speaker remembers a passage from the Avesta, ancient scriptures of Persia:

> The Avesta
> puts porcupine killers
> into hell for nine generations, sentencing them
> to gnaw out
> each other's hearts for the
> salts of desire.

The punishment for killing a porcupine—if the reason is because its desire for human salt is bothersome—is that of being given that very desire. These porcupine killers will crave "each other's heart / for the salts." These lines, and the succeeding stanza, suggest two of Kinnell's consistent themes: that humans are closely related to animals; in hell, they act like porcupines—they are punished by having to act in the same way they punished the porcupines for behaving—and, second, that an act of one human is attributable to all, that one person's experience—even though it may be an individual act—is common to everyone, just as the "I" is a representative voice.

In the lines that follow, the speaker has trouble getting to sleep because of the guilt he assumes for the farmer's killing of the porcupine, and when he does, his nightmarish dreams turn him into a porcupine:

> I roll
> this way and that in the great bed, under
> the quilt
> that mimics this country of broken farms and woods,
> the fatty sheath of the man
> melting off,
> the self-stabbing coil
> of bristles reversing, blossoming outward—
> a red-eyed, hard-toothed, arrow-stuck urchin
> tossing up mattress feathers,

pricking the
woman beside me until she cries.

Although a metamorphosis has occurred, complete with the speaker having acquired quills which prick the woman beside him, some of his "character traits" remain unchanged—such as being "red-eyed" and "hard-toothed"—because they are common to both humans and porcupines, as indicated in an earlier stanza in the poem. Also his "pricking" the woman is a sexual suggestion, something the speaker can do either as a porcupine or a human. And the speaker-turned-porcupine now has an overwhelming desire to eat that which tastes of human salt so tears apart the bed, "tossing up mattress feathers" in his hungry assault on it.

The following stanza presents the speaker in a curious state of existence; that is, as he describes some of his life's experiences, those of his human life and those of his life as a porcupine become inseparable. How he has lived as a human also comprises his history as a porcupine:

In my time I have
crouched, quills erected,
Saint
Sebastian of the
scared heart, and been
beat dead with a locust club
on the bare snout.
And fallen from high places
I have fled, have
jogged
over fields of goldenrod,
terrified, seeking home,
and among flowers
I have come to myself empty, the rope
strung out behind me
in the fall sun
suddenly glorified with all my blood.

His being beaten "with a locust club / on the bare snout" and having "jogged / over fields of goldenrod," for example, parallel the experience the porcupine underwent when shot and killed by the farmer. But they also represent, metaphorically, those things in life the speaker faced as a human; also, the speaker, who in his human form witnessed the dying of the porcupine, relives that experience in the form of a porcupine (albeit one that can speak). What he saw as a human, he now, as a porcupine, has experienced. The speaker's conception of his selfhood, then, has embraced that of the porcupine whom he saw killed. Therefore, the speaker does not merely transform into a porcupine—as Gregor Samsa transformed into a gigantic insect in Kafka's story—he rather "joins" with one in particular, the one he saw die that day, making their separate lives one life, one history—as long as the speaker continues this dream. The speaker goes beyond becoming an animal to "connect" with it, actually, as Kinnell suggested. And this union has allowed the human speaker to expand his self-awareness, his notion of selfhood, so that the civilized human can perchance regain his trust in "life's natural rhythms," learn to overcome the nightmare of dying—something that adult humans fear but nevertheless bring freely to troublesome porcupines.

The speaker-porcupine in the final stanza, having learned what it is to die as the porcupine did, expresses the vision and feelings of the porcupine, how the natural world appears to him upon his death. The speaker, or poet, can end the poem with this final vision from the porcupine's perspective because he has entered fully the scope of the porcupine's existence and thus his own:

> And tonight I think I prowl broken
> skulled or vacant as a
> sucked egg in the wintry meadow, softly chuckling, blank
> template of myself, dragging
> a starved belly through the lichflowered acres,
> where
> burdock looses the arks of its seed
> and thistle holds up its lost blooms
> and rosebushes in the wind scrape their dead limbs
> for the forced-fire
> of roses.

The speaker-porcupine is "softly chuckling" as he advances towards death; it is not to be feared. In these dying moments, there is an illumination, an increase in the intensity of life, a concentration on the regenerative energies of nature, so much so that even the "dead limbs" of the rosebushes are seen in the eyes of the dying speaker-porcupine as "the forced-fire of roses," not as something dead and permanently lost. The human, because he has connected with the porcupine in this strange way, has learned what Kinnell said about "I Heard a Fly Buzz," that in "the dying moment, everything the poet knew on earth is transfigured..., which brings the strange brightening, this last moment of increased life."

The range of the persona mode of voice has been extended by Kinnell to include the "extra-human," not just the nonhuman animal. The speaker-turned-porcupine is, if viewed in light of Kinnell's theories as previously outlined, now more of a complete human being, one having reached back and connected with his primordial notion of self. And in the next poem, "The Bear," these themes are again explored using the persona mode of voice in much the same way.

"The Bear" is a narrative poem, structured in seven parts and, like "The Porcupine," the human speaker through his dream transforms into an animal; unlike "The Porcupine," however, the speaker is directly responsible for killing the bear. The "I" of the poem then is both the universal voice, the Whitmanesque representative "person, anyone," whom Kinnell hopes "dissolves" like the "I" of "Song of Myself" in a moment of self-transcendence, and the voice, moving even further beyond this transcendence, of the animal, the bear. The voice of this poem is of the persona mode in that the animal is the mask for the "I" and the "I" is a mask for all humans because it is, like the Whitman voice of "I was the man, I suffered, I was there" where he "dissolves into the air and into the ground" and finally to "disappear into someone else" (Kinnell's analysis), the voice of the one, individual experience which evokes feelings common to everyone. Let us turn to the poem to see how the voice functions in this way.

The first section opens the narrative with the speaker coming upon "some fault in the old snow" that the bear has used for hibernation during the winter. The speaker "glimpses bits of steam" and recognizes those vapors as the smell of bear:

> In late winter
> I sometimes glimpse bits of steam
> coming up from
> some fault in the old snow
> and bend close and see it is lung-colored
> and put down my nose
> and know
> the chilly, enduring odor of bear.

The speaker has done this before; he "sometimes" comes across a hibernating bear while outdoors "in late winter," which implies that soon the bear will awaken. The steam rising from the fault is the sleeping bear's exhalation of breath, which is to the speaker an "enduring odor." It endures in the mind of the speaker as well as being a lingering scent. The bear is nearly awake, yet still asleep, which will be associated with the "nonexistent" state of pre-birth later in the poem. Consequently, the bear's odor is something the speaker "knows," both because he has smelled it before and because it holds a special recognition for him, a "chilly" glimpse, perhaps, into his pre-birth existence. This becomes more evident much later in the poem, however.

In the next section, the dramatic action of the poem begins. Knowing that the bear will soon rise and search for food, the speaker plans his hunt:

> I take a wolf's rib and whittle
> it sharp at both ends
> and coil it up
> and freeze it in blubber and place it out
> on the fairway of the bears.

The speaker is engaged in a primitive form of bear hunting—one still practiced by certain Eskimos in this country. In the ensuing stanzas, the speaker describes his tracking of the bear, beginning when the wolf's rib wrapped in blubber "has vanished"—that is, when the bear has eaten it:

> And when it has vanished
> I move out on the bear tracks,
> roaming in circles
> until I come to the first, tentative, dark
> splash on the earth.

The hunter finds the bear's trail, which is marked for him by the bear's spitting up of blood caused by the sharpened wolf's rib he has swallowed, and follows him:

> And I set out
> running, following the splashes
> of blood wandering over the world.
> At the cut, gashed resting places
> I stop and rest,
> at the crawl-marks
> where he lay out on his belly
> to overpass some stretch of bauchy ice
> I lie out
> dragging myself forward with bear-knives in my fists.

In tracking the bear, the speaker mimics the behavior of the animal: He rests when the bear does, crawls where the bear crawls. In the next section, the reason for the hunter's diligence is made apparent:

> On the third day I begin to starve,
> at nightfall I bend down as I knew I would
> at a turd sopped in blood,

> and hesitate, and pick it up,
> and thrust it in my mouth, and gnash it down,
> and rise
> and go on running.

The hunter tracks the bear because he is starving; he is motivated by his instinct of survival which generates his impulse to eat the bear's blood-sopped turd, in which the wolf's rib is concealed, to sustain him until he can get something more. This is in contrast with the farmer's gratuitous killing of a porcupine dozing in a tree.

The bear finally dies in the poem's next section just as the hunter catches up with him:

> On the seventh day,
> living by now on bear blood alone,
> I can see his upturned carcass far out ahead,
>   a scraggled,
> steamy hulk,
> the heavy fur riffling in the wind.
>
> I come up to him
> and stare at the narrow-spaced, petty eyes,
> the dismayed
> face laid back on the shoulder, the nostrils
> flared, catching
> perhaps the first taint of me as he
> died.

The bear's "catching the taint" of the one responsible for his death parallels the speaker's smelling the bear's odor at the beginning of the poem which originated the hunt. In that the speaker refers to his own scent as "taint," he betrays his guilt over having killed the bear, in a particularly deceptive way, in order to survive. Because the bear was hungry, he ate the wolf's rib thinking it was blubber only; and the bear having done so in turn enables the speaker to allay his own hunger, which he does as described in the following stanza:

> I hack
> a ravine in his thigh, and eat and drink,
> and tear him down his whole length
> and open him and climb in
> and close him up after me, against the wind,
> and sleep.

Having been starving for days, the speaker madly gorges himself on the bear blood and flesh, and he wildly mutilates the remaining carcass to use it as protection from the cold. Here, wrapped inside the dead bear (and having eaten the wolf's rib earlier) the speaker begins his dream in which he becomes the bear he has just killed:

> And dream
> of lumbering flatfooted
> over the tundra,
> stabbed twice from within,
> splattering a trail behind me,
> splattering it out no matter which way I lurch,
> no matter which parabola of bear-transcendence,
> which dance of solitude I attempt,
> which gravity-clutched leap,
> which trudge, which groan.

The speaker, presently experiencing in his dream the same pain he brought to the bear, notes that even if he were to transcend himself, he would still remain "stabbed twice from within," still splatter a trail behind him. That is, even though the bear (the original animal, not the speaker-turned-bear) may have succeeded in his "bear-transcendence" and become the speaker, say, or any human, he would still feel the pain the way the speaker does now. The bear cannot escape the destruction of the wolf's rib already inside him, and the human cannot escape the burden he must carry for having killed the bear.

The dream continues to its end in the next section:

> Until one day I totter and fall—
> fall on this
> stomach that has tried so hard to keep up,
> to digest the blood as it leaked in,
> to break up
> and digest the bone itself: and now the breeze
> blows over me, blows off
> the hideous belches of ill-digested bear blood
> and rotted stomach
> and the ordinary, wretched odor of bear,
>
> blows across
> my sore, lolled tongue a song

or screech, until I think I must rise up
and dance. And I lie still.

The breeze brings his own smell, "the ordinary, wretched odor," back to him and
it "blows across" his tongue, acting as an agent for a song—or a poem. He believes
this to be his own scent because, still dreaming, he of course is a bear. But actually,
it belongs to the real bear—who is not dead, but still in hibernation in the fault of
the old snow—and it brings the speaker out of his reverie which, as it turns out in
the next stanza, he has been experiencing all along. He has not hunted and killed
the bear; the hunt and the speaker's subsequent dream were in fact an imaginative
flight. He has not left the site of the bear in hibernation which he came upon in
the first stanza. The "odor of bear" brought about a "song" in that it led to a reverie which became the making of a poem. The speaker "awakens," then, to both
the dream within his daydream and from the daydream itself:

> I awaken I think. Marshlights
> reappear, geese
> come trailing again up the flyway.
> In her ravine under old snow the dam-bear
> lies, licking
> lumps of smeared fur
> and drizzly eyes into shapes
> with her tongue. And one
> hairy-soled trudge stuck out before me,
> the next groaned out,
> the next,
> the next,
> the rest of my days I spend
> wandering: wondering
> what, anyway,
> was that sticky infusion, that rank flavor of blood, that
>   poetry, by which I lived?

This last image of the dam-bear cleaning her cubs after birth, "licking / lumps of
smeared fur / and drizzly eyes into shapes"—a manifestation of the generative energies of nature—leaves the speaker questioning why he envisioned killing this
bear while actually in the presence of her delivering her young. So he spends the
rest of his days "wondering" about this apparent contradiction which comprised
the poem's dramatic situation. The "sticky infusion, that rank flavor of blood" refers to the connection the speaker made with the bear both while hunting it—eating its blood to keep from starving, crawling as the bear did, etc.—and when

"becoming" the animal in his dream, making it his persona. In both instances, the speaker has bonded with the bear's life, pain, vision of the world. For Kinnell, the essence of a poem is "the wasted breath," that which dies. In becoming a dying bear in his dream, the speaker increases the intensity of his life; he experiences an illumination of the moment, culminating in the cubs' birth. And their birth begins—as it begins all humans' and animals'—their first stage of dying (another parallel in the poem's careful symmetry).

The speaker has broadened his notion of selfhood through the persona mode of voice. "The Bear," appearing last in *Body Rags*, which immediately preceded *The Book of Nightmares*, can be viewed as the prelude of the Fergus section of that latter collection. The bear from which Fergus separates, when he gains his pre-birth consciousness, symbolizes humans' primitive origin, the final existence before consciousness and before birth. In "The Bear," the speaker connects—"infuses"—with this notion of his origin by assuming the persona of the animal, and he therefore learns something about—enough to keep him questioning for the rest of his days—his own "nonexistence," the time of his pre-birth. In this, Kinnell's purpose for the poem is much that of Robert Bly's intention for archetype recognition (although Bly achieved his in the confessional mode of voice, as we will see in the last chapter).

Kinnell intends the speaker of "The Bear" to voice concerns we all share—in a similar sense to Berryman's intention for Henry as the spokesperson of his age—and to experience that for which we have a common feeling. Any "autobiographical fragment," as with Berryman/Henry, or any idiosyncratic notion of self and origin, as with Kinnell/animal personas, may begin as the personal, but if the poem is successful in "touching others' feelings" as Kinnell thought his "I" poems must do, it extends outward to become perhaps even a universal expression. By using the persona mode of voice, Kinnell has propelled the personal vision to move beyond the human into the animal realm, and thus has enlarged the world of the individual "I," regardless whether or not it is a Whitmanesque, representative voice.

SOME POETS WHO USE mainly another "voice" or mode, like Lowell and Strand, also find reason to use the persona mode at times. Lowell was given the nickname "Caligula" while he was at St. Mark's and it stayed with him—at least as the shortened "Cal"—all his life. In his poem "Caligula," from *For the Union Dead*, he used what he termed his "namesake" as his persona:

> My namesake, Little Boots, Caligula,
> you disappoint me. Tell me what I saw
> to make me like you when we met at school?
> I took your name—poor odd-ball, poor spoiled fool,
> my prince, young innocent and bowdlerized!

The poem's voice, which begins in this passage as confessional, merges into its subject and transforms into the voice of the persona: "I took your name—poor odd-ball, poor spoiled fool...." Both the Caligula whom Lowell discovered in his bowdlerized texts and the young Lowell at St. Mark's can fit the description of "poor odd-ball, poor spoiled fool," and it is just such a description of Caligula that allows Lowell to identify himself with the ancient Roman. Once this merging of the two has been established in the poem, Lowell can employ Caligula for his mask as a means of self-exploration without being confessional. For example, when he depicts Caligula's sufferings, he also expresses his own:

> What can be salvaged from your life? A pain
> that gently darkens over heart and brain,
> a fairy's touch, a cobweb's weight of pain,
> now makes me tremble at your right to live.
> I live your last night. Sleepless fugitive...

Consequently, the subject of Lowell's poem, Caligula, becomes the persona through which Lowell can comment on himself.

His poem "The Nihilist as Hero," from *History* (1973), presents a similar use of the persona mode:

> Life by definition breeds on change,
> each season we scrap new cars and wars and women.
> But sometimes when I am ill or delicate,
> the pinched flame of my match turns unchanging green,
> a cornstalk in green tails and seeded tassel....
> A nihilist wants to live in the world as is,
> and yet gaze the everlasting hills to rubble.

The nihilist is the subject of the poem; that he is a "hero" means that he is also the poem's protagonist. The speaker identifies with the subject of the poem: "A nihilist wants to live in the world as is, / and yet gaze the everlasting hills to rubble," which is precisely what the speaker wants when he says: "Life by definition breeds on change... / But sometimes when I am ill or delicate, / the pinched flame of my match turns unchanging green." As in "Caligula," the speaker uses the poem's subject as a persona; and it is this persona, this nihilist, which illuminates for us the

speaker's vision of the world. The nihilist and the poem's speaker are "heroes" because they both want to witness change which "breeds life": The speaker says "we
scrap new cars and wars and women"—the "we" of course includes the nihilist—
and the nihilist wishes to "gaze the everlasting hills to rubble." The nihilist, therefore, can be viewed as a persona for the speaker since his remarks and those of the
speaker are essentially identical.

More like Kinnell than Lowell, Mark Strand uses an animal persona in his
poem "Eating Poetry," from *Reasons for Moving*, but unlike Kinnell, Strand uses it
more surrealistically and to convey a sense of the absurd:

> Ink runs from the corners of my mouth.
> There is no happiness like mine.
> I have been eating poetry.
>
> The librarian does not believe what she sees....
>
> The poems are gone.
> The light is dim.
> The dogs are on the basement stairs and coming up....
>
> She does not understand.
> When I get on my knees and lick her hand,
> She screams.
>
> I am a new man.
> I snarl at her and bark.
> I romp with joy in the bookish dark.

The narrator-dog, as the poem's voice, assumes the human characteristic of
speech, yet does not read poetry. In that his senses are skewed in comparison with
the human librarian's, his pleasure derives from eating, not reading, poetry. The
voice of "Eating Poetry" sounds human and appears to be so, but then transforms
("I get on my knees and lick her hand"), acts more like a dog, and finally tri-
umphs over the horrified librarian. In Strand's poetic world—of which we shall
see more in the next chapter—the surreal is significant; it is a world in which a
dog's perception often can be more true than a human's. To survive in such a
world portrayed in poetry as a kind of "theatre of the absurd," a world in which
dogs are "coming up" to control the library, one must adopt the appropriate persona.

Four

∾

The Self-Effacing Mode

THE PREVIOUS TWO CHAPTERS have shown the different modes a poet can use to project himself or herself in verse in order to achieve an expression of self that otherwise would not be possible apart from these modes. That is, when using the confessional voice, a poet is free to explore his or her personal life and history, knowing, however, that private revelations of autobiography will be shared publicly with the reading audience. The persona mode presents an alternative. The poet who uses this voice chooses to sheathe himself or herself—emotions, experiences—by allowing a narrator (who often will have a name other than the poet's own: Mauberley, Henry, Robinson) to speak for him or her so that the poet's private self-reflections need not be tempered to the anticipated response of an audience.

The self-effacing mode of voice offers yet another option for the poet engaged in self-examination: It attempts to be impersonal while speaking of personal concerns. Whereas poets of the confessional and persona modes propel themselves into their poems, the poet of the self-effacing mode selects a voice and technique intended to absent himself or herself from the poem.

Mark Strand, who will serve as the exemplary poet of the self-effacing mode, has directed much of his poetry to themes of personal absence and nullity. To correspond to these themes, he has tried to efface himself from his poetic voice. Of course, no poet can actually "efface"—obliterate—himself or herself from the poem. Any poem is a direct manifestation of the poet's presence, or, as Richard Hugo, in his essay "Statements of Faith," once said in commenting on an idea of Williams: "...writing [is] a slow, accumulative way of accepting one's life as valid.... When you write you are momentarily telling the world and yourself that neither of you need any reason to be but the one you had all along" (72). Yet the poet working in the self-effacing mode can appear to be exploring matters of the self with an objectivity that neither the confessional nor persona voice can accomplish. Because the self-effacing poet regards himself distinct from the personal self he portrays in the poem, he might be said to write of biographical, rather than autobiographical matters, which is perhaps as close to self-effacement as a poet can get. Strand uses this mode of voice to explore his relationship to contemporary life and to understand his identity, his self-concept, in a world that he sees—having long become familiar with the post-nuclear *angst* which made the world one of terror to Kees—in surreal, but not horrific terms. In a world that is surreal, or absurd, it is Strand's notion, one must remove oneself far from it in order to discover one's role in relation to the world.

Whereas Strand begins his search for this discovery outside his personal experience in the world, Charles Simic arrives at the self-effacing voice in an opposite manner. Simic begins with his personal experience, but because the world is seemingly surreal to him, he grows increasingly alienated from it, and eventually his personal relationship to the world becomes impersonal. Speaking of how to recreate his life experiences in his poetry, Simic told Richard Jackson:

> I find that in my own poems I tend to abandon the original cause or the visible aspects of the original cause and follow wherever the poem leads. That's why my poems often seem impersonal. It is not clear who the "I" is. It doesn't seem necessary for me to equate that "I" with myself. I follow the logic of the algebraic equation of words on the page which is unfolding, moving in some direction. (22)

The identity of Simic's "I" is not clear because it cannot be "equated" with his personal experience. Therefore, unlike the confessional voice which can be attributed to the poem's speaker (whether it is the poet or the poetic, personal self he has created for the public audience) and the persona voice which belongs to a specific poetic character (like Henry or Robinson) or narrator (the "I" as universal spokesperson), the voice of the self-effacing mode is impersonal, belonging to no one—or group—discernible. Simic does not intend his "I" as himself or anyone else because in a world which renders experiences impossible for him to record in his poetry—as the confessional and persona poets do—a personal voice would be inappropriate. Simic does not have a personal relationship to that which he experiences in the alien world of the absurd, as we shall see later in the chapter.

Having a more definite sense of the world as "real," rather than surreal, which is to say, regarding personal experience as neither something from which to retreat (as Strand does) nor to abandon (as Simic does), David Ignatow uses the self-effacing voice to expand from a complete absorption in his own person in order to extend his conception of self outward to his relation to the community. As the critic Ralph J. Mills, Jr., has written:

> Ignatow constantly explores his inner life, carrying what he finds into the light, bearing whatever pain it may cause him. But such self-examination is just one side of the coin in his poetry; the second side involves him in the lives of others, for his aim, beyond the earliest poems, is to become a poet of the city, specifically, of New York, to make himself, as he says, "the metaphor of his community." Awareness of identity and of self-integrity depend not simply upon the ability to scrutinize with honesty and care one's inward being but also on the capacity for extending the self outward into immediately surrounding existence. "My kind of writing forces me to go out among people," Ignatow remarks. "I'm not a social poet. I'm a poet of individuality and I only know my individuality by interacting with others. I can't do less than respond as I'm made to respond by environment. Yet I'm conscious, as a poet, of exactly what's happened to me." Precisely here, at the margin of daily existence, where the self encounters others or turns away to look within, the elements of his experience take the shape of a unique poetic articulation. (374)

Ignatow differs from the persona poet, whose "I" voice acts universally as representative of the modern person, in that he is able to leave his "awareness of identity and of self-integrity"—by using the self-effacing mode of voice—in order to become "the metaphor of his community" in an attempt to extend this concept of self-identity "outward into immediately surrounding existence." That he accomplishes this will be shown by an analysis (to come later) of specific poems, but let us now turn to Mark Strand's concept of selfhood and how it functions to establish his method of self-effacement in his poetry.

MARK STRAND

IN HIS SHORT COLLECTION of idiosyncratic musings in verse form, *The Sargeantville Notebook* (1973), Strand included the following curious statement:

> The ultimate self-effacement is not
> the pretense of the minimal,

but the jocular considerations of the maximal
in the manner of Wallace Stevens.

Strand admittedly has long admired Stevens's work, and read Stevens even before
beginning to write his own poetry. (He once remarked to Wayne Dodd: "I discovered I wasn't destined to be a very good painter, so I became a poet. Now it didn't
happen suddenly. I did read a lot, and I had been a reader of poetry before. In
fact, I was much more given to reading poems than I was to fiction and the book
that I read a lot, and frequently, was *The Collected Poems of Wallace Stevens*" [55].)
Perhaps Strand, in commenting on what constitutes the "ultimate self-effacement," regards Stevens as a belated Romantic poet, as does Harold Bloom, in that
the ostensibly private reflection, which is the subject of the poem, expresses emotions or ideologies that are in fact diffuse. I make this parallel by suggesting that
Strand means "the minimal" to be the private, or individual, concern so that a
pretense of such occurs when a poet argues for his own life experiences as reflective of a larger than personal theme, and that his phrase "the jocular considerations of the maximal" means the viewing of global concerns with some degree of
wit, with a touch of the absurd. A poet betrays his "pretense of the minimal" when
he tries to be an impartial observer, a chronicler of an event he has witnessed or of
a landscape he has seen; his presence in the poem—his personal "I" speaker—ne-
gates his intended impartiality, or objectivity, towards his subject. In chapter 2 we
saw this "pretense of the minimal" in Lowell's "The Mouth of the Hudson," where
the speaker regards "the single man's" and "the Negro's" concerns as his own finally.

Strand reads Stevens, however, as having successfully avoided such pretense
by constructing poems that begin about another's concerns, then move outward
to embrace universal questions: "Peter Quince at the Clavier," "Le Monocle de
Mon Oncle," and "The Paltry Nude Starts on a Spring Voyage" are a few examples
from his early work. These jocular titles lead us to poems of "maximal" subject
matter; in each, Stevens's presence is not visible. Each poem concentrates on the
individual named in its title; consequently, Stevens's discussion of universal matters is filtered through his representation of these paltry and jocular characters.
Yet these poems of Stevens employ a particular individual—Peter Quince, the
"Oncle," the Nude—(and none acting as a persona) in order to achieve his measure of self-effacement. In this sense, these figures are like *dramatis personae*. Yet
Strand's objective is to achieve the same extent of impartiality, and impersonality,
while using an "I" speaker that is neither a persona (that is, a representative "I"
speaking in behalf of all) nor one that is entirely confessional.

Another phrase from *The Sargeantville Notebook* explains how such an "I" can function in personal poetry: "The poet could not speak of himself, / but only of the gradations leading toward him and away." If the poet explores that which leads toward him and away from him, he will come to a better understanding of himself. Strand has written further about this in "A Statement about Writing":

> Ideally, it would be best to just write, to suppress the critical side of my nature and indulge the expressive. Perhaps. But I tend to think of the expressive part of me as rather tedious—never curious or responsive, but blind and self-serving. And because it has no power, let alone appetite, for self-scrutiny, it fits the reductive, dominating needs of the critical side of me. The more I think about this, the more I think that not writing is the best way to write.
>
> Whether I admit it or not, I write to participate in the delusion of my own immortality which is born every minute. And yet, I write to resist myself. I find resistence irresistible. (317)

His use of the phrase "which is born" is ambiguous; it could likely mean that his delusion of immortality is that "which is born every minute," or, perhaps, that his immortality is born every minute that he writes.

Whichever is intended, his stated goal is to "resist" himself. Because his expressive part is blind to everything except that which is self-serving, his critical side is necessary for self-scrutiny, self-definition (which, according to Strand's notion, is reductive), and it is this side that "dominates." The need for self-scrutiny, for self-definition, is separate from the self-serving impulses. It is this critical side that helps Strand control the tone of his poems which in turn contributes to the seeming absence of self, or rather, the impersonal voice, of the "I" speaker. Strand, in concentrating on self-scrutiny (the critical side of his nature), can resist himself; that is, he can resist the more personal, intimate tone which is expressive and self-serving. For this reason, that he writes to resist himself, Strand, as we shall see later in the chapter, mocks the extremely personal indulgences of poets like Adrienne Rich or Anne Sexton, to name but two. Although self-definition is reductive, and therefore mostly contrary to self-scrutiny—in that one should, presumptively, expand one's self-awareness through such scrutiny, not limit oneself to a single, finite, definition—it cannot be avoided since it is a "dominating need" of Strand's critical nature.

Consequently, he does attempt self-definition in his work, yet it is neither finite nor reductive. Strand's speaker defines himself by all that he is not. Consider this early poem, "Keeping Things Whole" from *Reasons for Moving* (1968)— this poem (with the title "A Reason for Moving") was included originally in his

first book, *Sleeping with One Eye Open* (1964), a limited edition—in which the "I"
speaker defines himself by his absence:

> In a field
> I am the absence
> of field....
>
> Wherever I am
> I am what is missing....
>
> We all have reasons
> for moving.
> I move
> to keep things whole.

Strand's sparse use of words, regular syntax, and simple prose sentences (six comprise the poem) are appropriate aesthetic choices; each helps to reflect the
speaker's feeling of absence. The poem's content is the speaker's self-scrutiny
which leads to his self-definition: "I am what is missing." The speaker character-
izes himself by a description of absence; he defines himself in terms of that which
is not present: "In a field / I am the absence / of field." Yet the poem enumerates
particulars of the physical world: a field, the air. And although the speaker is part
of physical reality, he considers himself a void. When standing in a field, he has no
relationship to it other than using it to illustrate what he is not. The speaker is obviously alienated from the physical world; he represents a nothingness, someone
unable to mark his presence: "the air moves in / to fill the spaces / where my
body's been." Of this self-definition, Harold Bloom has written: "Beneath the
grace, this is desperate enough to be outrageous. This 'I' might wish he were
asleep elsewhere as well as here, and so be no man rather than two. His absence
seems a void that his presence could not fill, or a wound that his presence could
not heal" (135).

In Strand's *The Monument* (1978), prose represented as the work of an
anonymous author who addresses his future translator, giving him instructions
how the work should be best represented in order to ensure the author's immortality, a particular passage (#9) explains further the concept of nothingness. It begins with an epigraph taken from Wallace Stevens's "The Man with the Blue
Guitar":

> *...Nothing must stand*
>
> *Between you and the shapes you take*

When the crust of shape has been destroyed.

You as you are? You are yourself.

It has been necessary to submit to vacancy in order to begin again, to clear ground, to make space. I can allow nothing to be received. Therein lies my triumph *and* my mediocrity. Nothing is the destiny of everyone, it is our commonness made dumb. I am passing it on. The monument is a void, artless and everlasting. What I was I am no longer. I speak for nothing, the nothing that I am, the nothing that is this work. And you shall perpetuate me not in the name of what I was, but in the name of what I am.

Since this passage suggests the absence of the author ("what I was I am no longer" and "the nothing that I am"), that which the author "passes on" in leaving behind his work—his monument—is a "void, artless and everlasting." His work is artless because it is prose—uncomplicated, simple sentence patterns—and everlasting because the translator places it in the world's literary canon. Strand said in an interview with Frank Graziano that *The Monument* represents a notion of "the desire for immortality":

That sounds rather grand...and making fun of it at the same time. I mean there are moments in one's life when one would like a guarantee that he will be read after he's dead. I thought this would be a clever way of doing it; writing a text for the translator who might...not be interested in the rest of one's work, or maybe just interested in the rest of one's work and telling him don't be, just do this.... [S]o I started writing *The Monument* and it became less and less about the translator of a particular text, and more about the translation of a self, and the text as self, the self as book. (37)

The words in themselves may not require linguistic translation, but as representative of the author—his immortal self—they do require a translation (in much the spiritual use of the term) into the future, towards immortality. Strand, speaking from the point of view of *The Monument's* "author," continued, in that interview: "[I]t's more than the things I've written, it's more than the text, it's my self that has to be continued. It's my self that has to be created again; the illusion has to be that I am doing it again, so that the translator in *The Monument* is my self, takes on an identity. It's not really being read in the future; that's what initiated *The Monument*. I mean I don't really care one way or the other, in truth" (37-8). What the author wishes to have translated, finally, is nothing: "I speak for nothing, the nothing that I am, the nothing that is this work. And you [he tells his translator] shall perpetuate me not in the name of what I was, but in the name of what I am"—nothing, whose work is a void. This is one way Strand is "making fun" of his fictional author's desire for immortality.

In a later passage (#22) in *The Monument*, the author more openly discusses the self's absence (and closely following this passage, the author insists on referring to himself only in the third person, thereby becoming in fact "absent" from his own text):

> This poor document does not have to do with a self, it dwells on the absence of a self. I—and this pronoun will have to do—have not permitted anything worthwhile to be part of this communication that strains even to exist in a language other than the one in which it was written. So much is excluded that it could not be a document of self-centeredness. If it is a mirror to anything, it is to the gap between the nothing that was and the nothing that will be. It is a thread of longing that binds past and future. Again, it is everything that history is not.

The speaker attains self-effacement in that he removes himself from the restrictions of the present ("What I was I am no longer") and attempts to become that which is expected in the future: "the nothing that will be." In Stevens's terms, "you are yourself" when you have reached the "shape" after "the crust of shape has been destroyed." That is, one understands a knowledge of self when the binding forces, which define oneself presently, are removed and a new shape for the future is created with anything left.

This is the speaker's purpose in "Giving Myself Up" from *Darker* (1970), in which the chantlike phrasing is incantatory and serves to simulate what might be an Eastern religious meditation of self-negation:

> I give up my eyes which are glass eggs.
> I give up my tongue.
> I give up my mouth which is the constant dream of my tongue.
> I give up my throat which is the sleeve of my voice....
> I give up my clothes which are walls that blow in the wind
> and I give up the ghost that lives in them.
> I give up. I give up.
> And you will have none of it because already I am beginning again
>   without anything.

This poem comprises a rather complete list and is indicative of many characteristics common to Strand's work of self-scrutiny we have discussed so far. It is "artless" because it is lengthy and repetitive (both tire our patience); the intentional craft—that is, his choice of simple prose statements—contributes to this. Richard

Howard's remarks about Strand's "Elegy for My Father," from *The Story of Our Lives* (1973), may help to explain the use of prose in "Giving Myself Up":

> Strand divides to conquer, divides the self to conquer the self.... [F]or the price of experience, experience which Blake has told us cannot be bought for a song, is negation. Which is why Strand writes his lament not in verse but in the very dialect of negation, in prose, the one linguistic medium out to eliminate itself, to use itself up in the irrecoverable rhythms of speech rather than in the angelic (or ecstatic) measures of repetition and return." (599)

But Strand's aesthetic in "Giving Myself Up," on closer examination, is one of luscious phrases, increasingly so as the speaker gives up more of himself, so that the very act of self-negation becomes celebratory of his existence. In this poem—as with many of Strand's—the clear images and language can lull the reader away from its more complex intentions. Thematically, then, the poem indicates the speaker's self-divesture, but its craft can be suggestive of the contrary.

Still, the speaker of "Giving Myself Up" sounds like a programmed machine, or someone in a trance, devoid of emotional anguish or excitement, and with an unchanging, stoic personality. Although an "I" is indeed giving himself up in the poem, it is an impersonal one, betraying a subdued wit just once by a quip of sarcasm in the final line. That the speaker begins "again without anything" is his declaring a state of nothingness (which parallels similar declarations: "the nothing that I am," and "the nothing that will be" from *The Monument*).

Finally, like the speaker of "Keeping Things Whole," the speaker of "Giving Myself Up" is apparently alienated from the physical world because there is no mention of it except in relation to various parts of his body. In giving himself up, the speaker only considers physical reality in terms of his body; he only knows the world in this way. When he gives up his smell, he leaves behind "a stone traveling through rain"; giving up his clothes means relinquishing "walls that blow in the wind," and his lungs are "trees that have never seen the moon." It is a solipsistic perception of the physical world; his place in it is determined by his presence or absence. When Graziano asked Strand about solipsism in his work, he replied: "I think a lot of contemporary poetry is solipsistic in that reality is a subjective determination and that we write about our vision of the world as if it were the world" (32). So Strand's definition is close to the metaphysical theory of solipsism which is, succinctly stated, that all real entities (that which we see) are only modifications of the self, states of our mind. This seems reasonably applicable to the speaker of "Giving Myself Up," who may have, in actuality, given up nothing more than his way of viewing himself in relation to physical reality. He therefore is ready to begin "again without anything," which is to say from a fresh perspective, a new state of mind.

That Strand manifests his critical side, his nature for self-scrutiny—particularly his penchant for "resisting" himself through his themes of nullity and absence and by means of his aesthetics which include an impersonal speaker, one who is stoic and solipsistic—has led Linda Gregerson, in writing of "Giving Myself Up," to remark:

> When Mark Strand reinvented the poem, he began by leaving out the world. The self he invented to star in the poems went on with the work of divestment: it jettisoned place, it jettisoned fellows, it jettisoned all distinguishing physical marks, save beauty alone. It was never impeded by personality. Nor was this radical renunciation to be confused with modesty, or asceticism. The self had designs on a readership, and a consummate gift for the musical phrase. (90)

Except for the suggestion that Strand's musical phrasing (that is, his chanting) is a "consummate gift," I would think this assessment fairly describes Strand's intentions, primarily in *Darker*.

Another poem similar in meaning to "Giving Myself Up" is "The Remains," from the first section of *Darker* (which section is also titled "Giving Myself Up"). In this poem, the speaker empties himself of his life, or continues his "work of divestment":

> I empty myself of the names of others. I empty my pockets.
> I empty my shoes and leave them beside the road....
>
> Time tells me what I am. I change and I am the same.
> I empty myself of my life and my life remains.

This is perhaps closer in content and tone to Stevens's lines from "The Man with the Blue Guitar," used to introduce *The Monument* passage concerning the speaker's change to nothingness, which lines were: "When the crust of shape has been destroyed. / You as you are? You are yourself." In "The Remains," the speaker pronounces: "I change and I am the same." Like Lowell in "Memories of West Street and Lepke," Strand's speaker traces his "seedtime" attempting to determine, as he states, "what I am." The tone of this poem, however, strikingly contrasts with that of the confessional mode of voice. Whereas Lowell's is immediately personal (as documented by the autobiographical content of the poem and by the urgency of the voice, the sense of personal drama evoked by the tone of the first person speaker), Strand's tone is controlled to the extent of making the speaker—

again—stoic, and his words flat, neither urgent nor passionate. His rhetorical questions (which he proceeds subsequently to answer) and his self-revelations as simple pronouncements of fact make Strand's tone here, like that of "Giving Myself Up," one reflective of the impersonality of the speaker. One level of absence has been reached in these poems, then, in that the personal has been removed from the "I." Strand has invented a self "to star" in these poems of self-divestiture. The self invented by Lowell—or any poet of the confessional or persona modes— is one for public representation, to use Trilling's argument, but it remains a personal self that is closely connected to the poet.

Strand's poetic self, and the voice of that self, achieve for him the peculiar tone of the poems of *Reasons for Moving* and *Darker*, a tone so different from that of the speakers of the confessional or persona modes that it is at once bolting and impressive to most readers. Bloom has written:

> The irreality of Borges, though still near, is receding in *Darker*, as Strand opens himself more to his own vision. These poems instantly touch a universal anguish as no "confessional" poems can, for Strand has the fortune of writing naturally and almost simply (though this must be supreme artifice) out of the involuntary near solipsism that always marks a central poetic imagination in America. An uncanny master of tone, Strand cannot pause for mere wit or argument but generally moves directly to phantasmagoria, a mode so magically disciplined in him as to make redundant for us almost all current questers after the "deep image."

Others have commented on Strand's "uncanny mastery of tone": Linda Gregerson writes, "Strand undoubtedly studied something of tone from Donald Justice, whose perfect elegance is always perfectly double. Justice has polished a surface in order to aggravate the discrepancies between manner and tone, has cultivated, in other words, the inherent ambiguity of perfect manners" (92). Peter Stitt, in his essay "Stages of Reality," feels that the poems from *Sleeping with One Eye Open* "introduce us, inevitably, to the characteristic speaking voice of nearly all early Strand poems—the consciousness through which everything seen, thought, felt, is filtered. Undoubtedly, this character is very nearly identical to Mark Strand himself, and yet to equate him with Strand would be to deny the role the imagination plays in these, as indeed in all poems, however directly 'confessional' they may appear to the naive reader" (201-2). Of that first collection, Richard Howard, in *Alone With America*, writes: "By writing an existing language as if it were his own invention, by confiding his endurance of dissolution to traditional discourse, Strand achieves...the spooky sense that he is being written by someone else, by some*thing* else, an energy his own only in that it moves *through* him, for it does not proceed from him.... [These poems] register a collapse, a defeat, a disintegration of the identity they are concerned to disclose, they do so with the tenantless decorum of alienation, of *otherness*..." (591-2). And Stanley Plumly, in his review of *Darker*, observed, "If there is a poetry of the absurd, Strand is its present master.... [I]t is the artifice, the revelatory means of Strand's special madness, that defines his intention and achievement. 'The Sleep,' for example, reminds us of nothing really new.... What is profound, of course, is the execution of the perception, especially Strand's marvelous ability with timing and tone" (79).

Strand, too, is conscious of his voice—which ultimately determines tone—and felt that in *Darker* he had achieved some "mastery" of it. When Plumly, in an interview, commented: "I have a greater sense of speaking voice, say, direct to Mark Strand in *Darker*," Strand replied: "I agree.... There are other voices in *Reasons for Moving*. There are other voices in *Darker*, too, but I think that I don't rely on them; I think I use them with—I don't want to say greater control—but I use them because I've chosen to" (61), which is to say in essence that in *Darker* Strand believes he achieved a control of voice. In choosing a voice, or speaker, for each poem, he has eliminated the possibility that his subject matter dictate to him which voice to use. (Some subjects—such as Lowell's from the *Life Studies* poems we have discussed—demand a particular, confessional voice appropriate to the poem's content.) Strand's *Darker* poems, however, begin with an impersonal self as its voice, regardless of the individual poem's subject. The voice is "direct to Mark Strand" because it reflects his personal inquiry of the self. His "uncanny mastery of tone" is a result of his poems' subjects: impersonality, self-negation, and absence. But if he is hesitant to "say greater control," he is willing to label his voice as "restrained." In attempting to determine the influence other poets have had on his work, Strand told Richard Vine and Robert von Hallberg: "...it has to do with a certain *tone*, a tone I associate with George Herbert: a kind of restrained, but not withheld, conversational tone, not inelegant, not elegant, and very hard to maintain" (130).

Strand's tone, then, is determined by the self he defines in his poems—the impersonal, the self of absence—who is also the poem's speaker. His craft, specifically his use of the impersonal "I," and his subject, the quest for self-definition and thus fulfillment, function in tandem to effect the "restrained, but not withheld" tone. A detailed examination of this unique tone will better define the self-effacing "I."

In Strand's early poetry, the speaker's purpose is to discover his place in the contemporary world and his relationship to it. Having found neither (as has been shown in such poems as "Keeping Things Whole" and "Giving Myself Up"), he alters himself—rather than the world—and strives for his other self, a void of a self, one of nothingness, for, as Octavio Paz has written of Strand's *Selected Poems* (1980): "To be alive is to be absent from oneself—or, an extreme and desperate means of being present to oneself. The poetry of Mark Strand explores the *terra infirma* of our lives. Fascinated by emptiness, it is not strange that he should conceive the poem as a description of absence; but at the same time his vision continually stumbles against the blunt, obtuse reality of things and beings irrevocably trapped in brute existence." That one self, the one present in the physical world, who is paranoid and alienated, can transform into another self, the "other," absent from any relationship to the world, was suggested by "The Remains," or his poem "The Guardian" which concludes: "Guardian of my death, // preserve my absence. I am alive."

Since tone is determined by the speaker (as I. A. Richards instructed us, it is the attitude the speaker adopts towards the poem's subject) and because the speaker in these early Strand poems defines himself in terms of absence, an impersonal "I"—which is to say the self-effacing voice—results. However, in Strand's poems, subject matter is not the sole determination of the voice's tone; the speaker's wit and sense of the absurd also contribute. In analyzing this tone, let us first consider the speaker's sense of alienation further, then the ensuing pursuit of his "other" or double self—a pursuit resulting from the speaker's alienation—and finally his notion of the absurd. Each operates towards formulating Strand's voice of self-effacement.

That Strand's "I" finds the world alien, and himself so afraid he is unable to cope with it, was evident in the poem "Sleeping with One Eye Open" in which the "I" expresses his abject paranoia, as this selection shows:

> It's my night to be rattled,
> Saddled
> With spooks....
>   Oh I feel dead,
> Folded
> Away in my blankets for good, and
> Forgotten.
> My room is clammy and cold,
> Moonhandled
> And weird. The shivers
> Wash over
> Me, shaking my bones, my loose ends

> Loosen,
> And I lie sleeping with one eye open,
> Hoping
> That nothing, nothing will happen.

Although the speaker's phobias keep him awake, he remains composed enough to tell us of them by way of rather clever, end-rhymed couplets (including slant rhymes and off rhymes), the last three lines comprising a closure rhyming "open," "hoping" and "happen"—hardly the phrasing of an acutely paranoid insomniac. Strand's playful sense of the absurd—evident here by his attributing ingenious speech patterns to his speaker whose "bones are shaking"—informs this otherwise disturbing monologue of a frightened man.

The same fears are expressed more solemnly in "When the Vacation Is Over for Good" which concludes with the speaker wondering "just what it was / That went so completely wrong, or why it is / We are dying," and in "Violent Storm" (both from *Sleeping with One Eye Open*) in which the speaker proclaims of the "long night sweeping over these trees" that:

> for us, the wide-awake, who tend
> To believe the worst is always waiting
> Around the next corner or hiding in the dry,
> Unsteady branch of a sick tree, debating
> Whether or not to fell the passerby,
> It has a sinister air.

Earlier in the poem, the speaker alludes to the "us" as "nervous or morbid," and their unquieting considerations are held in contrast to "Those who have chosen to pass the night / Entertaining friends / And intimate ideas in the bright, / Commodious rooms of dreams." These people are oblivious to the sinister air, apparently; they:

> Will not feel the slightest tremor
> Or be wakened by what seems
> Only a quirk in the dry run
> Of conventional weather. For them,
> The long night sweeping over these trees
> And houses will have been no more than one
> In a series whose end
> Only the nervous or morbid consider.

In this direful world, the speaker tries to define himself in relation to his place in it. Ultimately finding that he is alienated from any physical part of the world—in a field, he is nothing but the absence of field—the speaker chooses what he believes to be the last recourse: to absent himself from the world, but to do so without actually dying. Consider "The Guardian," a short poem from *Darker*, the last lines of which we have already seen:

> The sun setting. The lawns on fire.
> The lost day, the lost light.
> Why do I love what fades?
>
> You who left, who were leaving,
> what dark rooms do you inhabit?
> Guardian of my death,
>
> preserve my absence. I am alive.

Only in absence, freed of his former, confining, fear of night, does the speaker feel alive. He now loves the "lost light"; he now chooses to inhabit dark rooms in an effort to preserve his absence from the reality of the physical world. There is a spiritual sense, too, to the reference of the mysterious "dark rooms"; it is in them that the speaker believes he can retain life. The problem, therefore, is one of transcendence. The killing of oneself, or physical death resulting from any cause, would preclude discovering the life one finds in absence, in the dark rooms of nothingness.

In "The Remains," a poem of self-divestiture as we have seen, the speaker encounters this problem, finds no solution, and finally realizes: "I change and I am the same. / I empty myself of my life and my life remains." Bloom, in his essay "Dark and Radiant Peripheries," has written of this poem that what "remains" is:

> everything about the self that ought to have only posthumous existence, when the poet will survive only in the regard of other selves. But this dread (which is one with the reality of him) is that already he survives only insofar as he has become an otherness capable of extending such regard.... "The Remains" is a poem written by Strand's *alastor* or Spirit of Solitude, his true voice of feeling. Its despairing wish—to be delivered from the self's prison without abandoning a self that can be embraced only when it in prison lies—is repeated throughout *Darker* in many superb modulations....
>
> The mode is phantasmagoria, of which the American master will always be Whitman.... Closer to Strand...is the Stevens who charted the "mythology of self, / Blotched out beyond unblotching." Strand's peculiar courage is to take up the quirky quest when "amours shrink / Into the compass and

curriculum / Of introspective exiles, lecturing," concerning which Stevens warned: "It is a theme for Hyacinth alone." Throughout *Darker*, Strand's risk is enormous. He spares us the opaque vulgarity of "confessional" verse by daring to expose how immediate in him a more universal anguish rages.... (138-9)

What Bloom calls "the opaque vulgarity of 'confessional' verse," Strand feels is "the pretense of the minimal," as suggested earlier. Instead, Strand's speaker becomes an "otherness"—which is his final achieving of absence—only after some struggle with his double, in various guises, or this other self, who seeks entrance to (what he calls in "The Guardian") the "dark rooms" which will ensure his absence and thus his life. So afraid of the emergence of this "other" that, at one point, the speaker of "The Tunnel" (from *Sleeping with One Eye Open*) threatens suicide to scare it away:

> A man has been standing
> in front of my house
> for days. I peek at him
> from the living room
> window and at night,
> unable to sleep...
>
> I weep like a schoolgirl
> and make obscene gestures
> through the window. I
> write large suicide notes
> and place them so he
> can read them easily....
>
> I feel I'm being watched
> and sometimes I hear
> a man's voice,
> but nothing is done
> and I have been waiting for days.

Again the speaker is frightened, unable to sleep, yet again he retains his wit. He "weeps like a schoolgirl" hoping to discourage his pursuer, and the public display of his "large suicide notes" is a jest aimed towards the "tragic generation" of poets, those whom Berryman elegized in *The Dream Songs*, and whose verse Bloom criticized as "opaque vulgarity." Strand, I would think, inclines to agree with Bloom, as evident by his contrasting style of voice and by these remarks to Plumly: "...one of the horrifying things about many poets is that they lost, somewhere

along the line, in the fervor of the inner debate, the idea of poetry.... They become, in fact, 'chroniclers' or 'notators.' They write notebooks or leaflets or what
have you" (59). The intent, certainly, of "The Tunnel" is not to chronicle a personal experience, but to explore the terror—here presented in a mildly surreal circumstance—of confronting one's otherness, which nevertheless must be faced
eventually if (to use Bloom's phrase) one is to be "delivered from the self's prison
without abandoning a self that can be embraced only when it in prison lies,"
which is to echo Strand's line from "The Guardian": "preserve my absence. I am
alive."

    Strand's speaker, then, faces the challenge of transcendence, of absenting
himself while still physically alive—what Bloom in referring to "The Remains"
called becoming "everything about the self that ought to have only posthumous
existence." This transcendence is close to being the "ultimate self-effacement" for
one escapes from oneself in order to fill the void of not knowing oneself, and thus
not knowing—and, consequently, fearing—one's relationship to the physical
world, as Paz wrote: "To be alive is to be absent from oneself—or, an extreme and
desperate means of being present to oneself." The world must be illuminated,
made less threatening, before the speaker can complete the process of becoming
"alive." For Strand, who inverts the notion of one's presence (as one's absence),
that which is dark is most illuminating. *Darker*, finally, traces the process of the
speaker's transcendence to the other—a process that includes his abandoning fear
and gaining confidence—and in doing so, he reaches an understanding of self-
definition. "Mark Strand's vision of [the world] is something like a photographic
negative," writes James Crenner. That darkness is inviting to the speaker is shown
in the seventh of "Seven Poems," which also serves as *Darker's* epigraph:

> I have a key
> so I open the door and walk in.
> It is dark and I walk in.
> It is darker and I walk in.

Crenner has written of *Darker*: "It is as though your daily life has been translated
into a haunted house, where the daylight is so bright you can barely make anything out, all bleached to a sameness; then the thunder rumbles and suddenly
there is a bolt of darkness in which, for an instant, the heavy furniture and the
corpse and the monster stand out clearly. The darker the clearer" (85). The analogy of the haunted house is a becoming one, for it suggests the witty and sometimes absurdly surreal vision of the speaker in many of these poems.

The process of becoming an "otherness" is that of disappearing into darkness, for in darkness lies life:

> The present is always dark.
> Its maps are black,
> rising from nothing,
> describing...
>
> the black, temperate
> necessity of its completion.
> As they rise into being
> they are like breath.
>
>   (from "Black Maps")

Or, the act of diminishing is one of becoming:

> Out of breath
> I will not rise again.
>
> I grow into my death.
> My life is small
> and getting smaller. The world is green.
> Nothing is all.
>   (from "My Life")
>
> Flowers bloom.
> Flowers die.
> More is less.
> I long for more.
>   (from "The One Song")

The double self, the other, is addressed in "My Life By Somebody Else." The speaker, having tried various ways to lure the other out in the open, grows increasingly frustrated; the poem's concluding stanzas follow:

> The days drag on. The exhausted light falls like a bandage
> over my eyes. Is it because I am ugly? Was anyone
> ever so sad? It is pointless to slash my wrists. My hands
> would fall off. And then what hope would I have?
>
> Why do you never come? Must I have you by being
> somebody else? Must I write *My Life* by somebody else?
> *My Death* by somebody else? Are you listening?
> Somebody else has arrived. Somebody else is writing.

The two poems previous to "My Life By Somebody Else" in *Darker* are in fact "My Life" and "My Death"; all three are part of that book's final section which is also titled "My Life By Somebody Else," as if Strand is implying that his speaker, having discovered the means of transcendence earlier in the book (that is, by seeking darkness, by diminishing), has now become "somebody else," the otherness he sought. Here Strand has achieved self-effacement on at least three levels: Mark Strand is not projecting himself in this grouping of poems (collectively as "My Life By Somebody Else"), as the confessional or persona poet does. If we can continue to assume that Strand's work has been towards self-divestiture, then the life referred to in these poems is strictly invention, and Strand frequently injects moments that are not quite believable, or which are surreal or absurd, to emphasize the difference between the life presented in the poem by the speaker and the poet's actual (public) life. Further, the speaker of the poems is suggesting that that life is not really his either, but that it is controlled—it is being authored—by somebody else. And still another level of self-effacement is reached when, within the individual poem "My Life By Somebody Else," a separate presence takes over that which the speaker has been writing. If it is necessary, as the speaker wonders, for "My Life" and "My Death" to have been written by somebody else before the otherness can appear, then that otherness, by appearing at the end of "My Life By Somebody Else," has taken control of not just that one poem, but the entire grouping.

Both Strand and his speaker have been effaced from these poems. Crenner gives his perspective of the speaker's confrontation with his otherness as he writes of "My Life By Somebody Else," in which Strand, Crenner argues, has "dramatized, with characteristic mastery of tone ('You must have hated me for that'... 'Was anyone / ever so sad?') the self/self dichotomy," and continues that:

> One is reminded of Borges' "Borges and I," in which the narrating "I" speaks of the Borges to whom everything real happens and in whom the "I"—rather than in itself—has its being. The "I" concludes the piece with, "I do not know which of us has written this page." But Strand here goes even Borges one better, beginning with two selves and ending with three (or maybe one)! The process of recording the cat-and-mouse game between the I and the missing self leads to the arrival of a third party, a "someone else" who by the end of the poem is writing the poem. We might recognize this "someone else" as the only possible union of the other two, a union which takes place only in the act ("writing") of the poem. This is poetry as revelation. (88-9)

Strand wants us to think of Borges. In his previous collection, *Reasons for Moving*, Strand takes as his epigraph Borges's phrase: "[W]hile we sleep here, we are awake elsewhere and that in this way every man is two men." There are several poems following that concern Strand's notion of a double self—one is "The Tunnel" (originally appearing in *Sleeping with One Eye Open*) which we have already seen. Others are "The Whole Story" (also first included in *Sleeping with One Eye Open*) and "The Man in the Mirror"; none, however, is a "dramatization" in the manner of "My Life By Somebody Else." Instead, each considers the notion of otherness accompanied by Strand's sense of amusement.

Strand, when giving a public reading of "The Whole Story," will often tell of the poem's genesis, that as a young poet he showed his work to a much older (and famous) poet who told Strand not to repeat himself in his poems; that advice forms the poem's epigraph: "I'd rather you didn't feel it necessary to tell him, 'That's a fire. And what's more, we can't do anything about it, because we're on this train, see?'" A selection from the poem follows:

> How it should happen this way
> I am not sure, but you
> Are sitting next to me,
> Minding your own business
> When all of a sudden I see
> A fire out the window.
>
> I nudge you and say,
> "That's a fire. And what's more,
> We can't do anything about it,
> Because we're on this train, see?"
> You give me an odd look
> As though I had said too much.
>
> But for all you know I may
> Have a passion for fires,
> And travel by train to keep
> From having to put them out.
> It may be that trains
> Can kindle a love of fire.

The poem does not exist solely for its humor although some is rather revealing of human behavior. The speaker, for example, repeats verbatim, in the context of the poem, the dialogue already quoted in the epigraph. That is, the speaker cannot cease repeating himself even in a poem that attempts to justify such refrains, claiming that they are useful in recovering "the whole story." But the large theme operative here concerns the dialogue the speaker has with himself—with his other self, specifically, as the last lines of the poem indicate. He has been talking to his reflection he sees in the window. In his oral introduction to this poem, Strand tries to make us believe the dialogue is between the speaker and the older poet who, thinking the speaker has said "too much," gives him an "odd look." Yet the speaker is attempting to understand his immediate situation of helplessness, and so considers all the possibilities in order to justify his not being able to "do anything about it, because we're on this train." The "we" therefore would be the rational self and the emotional, or impulsive, self.

Further, the poem is in part a response to the older poet, informing him not to assume that repetition is unintentional and valueless. The speaker comes to some tentative understanding—if that understanding is only an awareness of the endless possibilities of the situation—by conducting this dialogue, complete with the repetitive thoughts and words to which any of us is prone, particularly when thinking to ourselves.

The personal "I" has been effaced by confusing its identity; it has two selves in this poem (maybe several more in a poem like "My Life By Somebody Else"). The controlled tone—without lineation, the prose is even, unemotional, matter of fact, as these lines near the end of the poem show : "And then again / I might be wrong. Maybe / You are the one / Who loves a good fire. Who knows?"—and the speaker's sense of the absurd ("I may have lied about the fire"), that the entire poem has been a hoax, also contribute to the self-effacement of the voice. What Strand would have us believe initially is that a poem of personal experience becomes yet another type of self-divestiture poem.

"The Man in the Mirror" presents another "self/self" confrontation. This long (five pages) poem—the final one in *Reasons for Moving*—is seemingly a "dialogue" between the selves, but since we never hear directly from the other self, the man actually "in the mirror," it is more a slow, quiet monologue of the "I" addressing his reflection as "you." Still, the speaker's reflection alone is insufficient for a self-confrontation because earlier in the poem, the speaker says "the mirror was nothing without you," then adds later:

> I remember how we used to stand
> wishing the glass
> would dissolve between us,
> and how we watched our words

cloud that bland,
innocent surface,
and when our faces blurred
how scared we were....

You never spoke
or tried to come up close.
Why did I want so badly
to get through to you?...

It will always be this way.
I stand here scared
that you will disappear,
scared that you will stay.

The speaker here is not "scared" in the same way as the paranoiac in *Sleeping with One Eye Open*, but is afraid of losing contact with his otherness and of that which the otherness has to reveal about the speaker's self-identity. In "The Tunnel," the speaker urges the other self to leave; here the speaker is weary of the ensuing consequences if the other does so. The speaker has matured; his tone, not comically absurd, but serious (and without the emotional urgency of the confessional voice), is indicative of the surreal content: "we watched our words / cloud that bland, / innocent surface" of the mirror, rather than the speaker's physical breath, which in turn causes the reflection to blur.

Strand's aesthetic, his technique of craft, is enmeshed with his themes of self-discovery. To be is to be nothing—which, of course, echoes Stevens's final line from "The Snow Man": the listener, "nothing himself," stands watching the "Nothing that is not there and the nothing that is." The self-effacing mode of voice serves to define Strand's speaker's growth from alienation to achieving absence from the physical world without physically dying, and it mirrors each poem's content. As the speaker becomes less afraid of his otherness, his tone becomes less comic. The speaker's reaction to his estranged world was that of humor, but as he began to better understand his relationship to it, the world seemed less strange, and his place in it more definite ("In a field / I am the absence / of field."), no longer befitting a humorous response.

Strand told Richard Jackson that "the act of writing is itself a metaphor for the way we relate to the hidden resources of our lives. A truly exciting poem has something evasive or mysterious at the core, and it succeeds in suggesting to us that the core is essential to our being. But that core's absence reminds us of how precariously we exist in the universe that evades us, that is always beyond us" (13–14). The

speaker of "The Man in the Mirror" ends his monologue by articulating this pre-
cariousness. That Strand's craft informs his poems' subject matter is stated best
by Strand himself when writing of Donald Justice's work for *Contemporary Poets:*

> From the very beginning Justice has fashioned his poems, honed them down,
> freed them of rhetorical excess and the weight, however gracefully sustained,
> of an elaborate diction. His self-indulgence, then, has been with the possibili-
> ties of the plain statement. His refusal to adopt any other mode but that
> which his subject demands—minimal, narcissist, negating—has nourished
> him....
>
> If absence and loss are inescapable conditions of life, the poem for Jus-
> tice is an act of recovery. It synthesizes, for all its meagreness, what is with
> what is no longer; it conjures up a life that persists by denial, gathering
> strength from its hopelessness, and exists, finally and positively, as an emblem
> of survival. (818)

Strand well could be assessing his own work here; he said to Plumly of Justice:
"I've learned a lot from him. And I think he's learned some things from me, too.
We share some of the same subject matter and give each other poems—that is,
ideas for poems" (66-7). It is true of Strand's technique, too, that he refuses "to
adopt any other mode but that which his subject demands—minimal, narcissist,
negating," and the mode to convey such subjects is the self-effacing voice, which
Strand achieves, as we have seen demonstrated by his poems so far discussed, by
his themes of self-definition and his tone. The self-effacing "I" is a matter of technique, but it is a technique available only for use in certain poems whose content
allows for it. In "Keeping Things Whole," the "I" is self-effacing because the
speaker's definition of himself—the subject of that poem—is one of effacement,
or absence from his presence in the physical world. In "My Life By Somebody
Else," the "I" is self-effacing because the poem's subject suggests a confusion of
personal identity, an indefiniteness of the speaker-composer of the poem. And in
"The Whole Story," the comic tone becomes the subject; the ultimate joke of the
poem is the speaker's disavowal of the subject of the fire—that is, his effacement
from the poem's original subject.

Strand achieves the truly "ultimate" self-effacement in some of his translations, however. In something of the reverse of the intention of the speaker of *The
Monument,* who desires immortality by being spiritually "translated" through his
work which survives him, Strand at times leaves behind the author whose poem
Strand literally translates. Consider "The Dirty Hand" from *Reasons for Moving.*
Following the poem's title, in parentheses, is the inscription "after Carlos Drummond de Andrade," yet we can assume it is Strand's own composition because he

does not indicate otherwise. The poem is, however, neither a response to Drummond, an engagement of poetic dialogue with him, nor an adaptation in, say, the manner of Lowell's *Imitations* (1961) as might be thought considering the inscription. In 1976, Strand published the following translation of "The Dirty Hand" in *Another Republic*, in which he presented the poem as a translation of Drummond's. Strand's is very closely a literal rendering; I have compared it to John Nist's literal translation of it found in Nist's *In the Middle of the Road* (1965). Here is a selection of Strand's translation from *Another Republic*:

> My hand is dirty.
> I must cut it off....
>
> I used to keep it
> out of sight,
> in my pants' pocket.
> No one suspected a thing.
> People came up to me,
> wanting to shake hands.
> I would refuse
> and the hidden hand
> would leave its imprint
> on my thigh.
> And I saw
> it was the same
> if I used it or not.
> Disgust was the same....
>
> It is impossible
> to live with this
> gross hand that lies
> on the table.
> Quick! Cut it off!
> Chop it to pieces
> and throw it
> into the ocean.
> With time, with hope
> and its intricate workings
> another hand will come,
> pure, transparent as glass,
> and fasten itself to my arm.

The following is the text of what Strand implies is his own poem, "The Dirty Hand" ("after Drummond"), published eight years prior to the appearance of his translation we have just seen:

> My hand is dirty.
> I must cut it off....
>
> I used to keep it
> out of sight,
> in my pants pocket.
> No one suspected a thing.
> People came up to me,
> wanting to shake hands.
> I would refuse
> and the hidden hand,
> like a dark slug,
> would leave its imprint
> on my thigh.
> And then I realized
> it was the same
> if I used it or not.
> Disgust was the same....
>
> It is impossible
> to live with this
> gross hand that lies
> on the table.
> Quick! Cut it off!
> Chop it to pieces
> and throw it
> into the ocean.
> With time, with hope
> and its intricate workings
> another hand will come,
> pure, transparent as glass,
> and fasten itself to my arm.

Strand makes his claim of authorship based on four changes in Drummond's text: In line three of the second stanza, "Strand's" poem reads "in my pants pocket," his translation of Drummond is "in my pants' pocket" (the poems were published by different presses; I am discounting the allowance for "house style"); in line nine of the same stanza, Strand includes "like a dark slug," which was omitted from his translation; in line twelve, also of that stanza, Strand writes "And then I realized" instead of the "And I saw" of his translation; and the last change, in the penultimate line of stanza three, reading "lethargic and crablike" in Strand's "The Dirty Hand," was omitted from his translation.

If these differences are slight, they are enough to alter (however slightly) the tone and emphasis of the poem. The voice of Strand's translation of Drummond betrays a Christian sensibility. That is, Drummond clearly means to suggest, in part, "if thy hand offend thee, cut it off" from the Gospel of St. Mark, 9:43. Strand's poem is different—that is, taken from, or "following" Drummond—because Strand now emphasizes, by adding two more lines of description to the hand (making it more definitely metonymic), the slothfulness of the human condition, and, by implication, the desire for something supernatural to replace it.

But this is mere justification. Strand has implied that his early version of "The Dirty Hand" is his own poem, not Drummond's. (And such a claim is almost believable given that Strand's flat style—the result of his careful and complete tonal control—makes all his early poems read as though they were themselves translations.) Nothing could be more self-effacing than to remove oneself nearly entirely from the poem—from conceiving it, from actually writing it. Strand uses Drummond to author Strand's poem: the ultimate, and most absurd, act of self-effacement.

Strand freely admits to "basing" some of his poems on his reading of others' work. "Reading," he said to Graziano, "is as much a part of experience as walking down the street or talking to people or anything. It's part of life.... [S]ometimes I don't know whether I read something or experienced it" (39–40). Strand's "jocular consideration" is to subvert the essence of the confessional and persona poets who rely so greatly on personal experience. Strand's personal experience of reading others' work—and taking their ideas, that is, their experiences—becomes the subject of his work. He continued in the same interview:

> ...the first of the "Night Pieces" [from *The Late Hour* (1978) is] a version of a paragraph toward the end of *Bleak House*. Of course I changed it a lot; turned London and the Thames into New York and the Hudson and I changed a lot of details to make it more contemporary, and I added things of my own. (35)

Perhaps, then, Strand's acknowledgment—"after Dickens" follows the poem's title—is enough to suggest the affinity to the paragraph in *Bleak House*; its having been altered significantly makes it a genuine Strand poem. But consider our next example, something of "a third 'Night Piece,'" Strand says, "that was based on a reading of Leopardi." That poem, first published in *Antaeus* (Spring 1978) under the title "Poem after Leopardi," but appearing as just "Leopardi" in his *Selected Poems*—leaving the reader without much of a clue to the meaning of the one word title—follows in excerpted form:

> The night is warm and clear and without wind.
> The stone-white moon waits above the rooftops
> and above the nearby river. Every street is still
> and the corner lights shine down only upon the hunched shapes of
>   cars.
> You are asleep. And sleep gathers in your room
> and nothing at this moment bothers you.
> Jules, an old wound has opened and I feel the pain of it again.
> You are asleep and I have gone outside to pay my late respects
> to the sky that seems so gentle
> and to the world that is not and says to me:
> "I do not give you any hope. Not even hope."
> Down the street I hear the voice of a drunk
> singing an unrecognizable song
> and I hear a car a few blocks off....
> Once when I was a boy, and the birthday I had waited for
> was over, I lay upon my bed, awake and miserable, and very late
> that night the sound of someone's voice singing down a sidestreet,
> wounded me, as this does now.

Here is my literal (as closely possible) translation of Leopardi's "La Sera Del Di' Di Festa"; I have chosen to translate a bit more than just the lines Strand retains for his "Leopardi," omitting but a few lines from Leopardi's Italian text:

> The night is sweet and clear and without wind,
> And the moon poses quietly over the roofs
> And in the middle of the gardens, and reveals
> In the distance the serenity of every mountain. Oh, my woman,
> Now every path is silent, and from the balconies
> Only a rare night lamp is shining.
> You are asleep, crouched in easy sleep
> In your quiet rooms, and no care eats at you,
> And, of course, you have no thoughts of how you have
> Opened the wound in the middle of my chest.
> You are asleep: I look towards the sky, which seems benign,
> And I salute it, and salute nature which wounded me once.
> "Hope?" nature said to me. "Hope I deny you...
> Only tears will shine in your eyes."

This day was a holiday: but all its fun
You have ended with sleep, remembering perhaps
In your dreams how many took to you today,
How many you took to: it is not my name
That comes to your mind. So here I ask
What life can I look for...
Where today are our famous ancestors crying,
And the great power and armies and roar of Rome
That covered land and sea?
All is peace and silence; the world rests,
Our passions have subsided.
When I was very young, the holiday
For which I anxiously awaited came and went,
Leaving me in pain, awake, pressing my pillow;
And in the late night, a song that rose from the streets,
Dying little by little into the distance,
Pained my heart, as now.

Strand eliminates some of Leopardi's verbiage (accouterments of the early nine-teenth century), changes some of the diction to make the poem's sound and set-ting more contemporary, and ensures that the poem evokes an American, rather than Italian, evening after a holiday. Still, the situation here in "Leopardi" is re-markably that of Strand's-Drummond's "The Dirty Hand"; there is but slight dif-ference in content, and none in meaning, between Leopardi's piece and what Strand calls his own poem, one "based on a reading of Leopardi"—a very close reading, obviously. Strand's inclusion of this poem in his "New Poems" section of *Selected Poems* simply as "Leopardi," giving no clear acknowledgment to the poet whose work it is, can be justified if considering that Strand added his personal mark to the poem by addressing "Jules," his wife. (Leopardi wrote, "Oh, my woman.") Yet this makes Leopardi's "La Sera Del Di' Di Festa" appear to be Strand's, in the confessional mode of voice—particularly since it is placed in his *Selected Poems* following a grouping of his confessional poems about his child-hood in Nova Scotia—when, in fact, it is Strand at his self-effacing best.

In another instance, Strand more subtly seduces us into believing that his poem "For Jessica, My Daughter" from *The Late Hour* is confessional—he does have a daughter named Jessica (and his *Selected Poems* is dedicated to her and to Jules)—until we realize that the poem's opening in a wind storm and its theme of a father's contemplating his daughter's future are too similar to Yeats's "A Prayer for my Daughter," although the actual phrasing and specific lines of the two poems are dissimilar.

Nothing could be more jocular than to claim authorship of poems one has translated; indeed, the true author has been lost in the translation—as Drummond and Leopardi were, having been supplanted by the Strand who is actually effaced from these same poems. He could well title these: "My Poems By Somebody Else."

For Strand, such a claim of authorship is a final display of the absurd, of phantasmagoria, which helped inform the controlled tone, a tone necessary in establishing the voice of an impersonal "I," one defined by the degree to which he can achieve absence—from himself, from the physical world. The resulting self-effacing voice aids Strand in his personal inquiry into the constitution, the definition, of an individual in a contemporary world to which he feels no relationship or role other than that of filling a void. Such an inquiry—and tentative answers—could not have been effected without his use of the self-effacing voice, for, as we have seen, this voice cannot be distinguished from the self portrayed—and defined—in these poems, whoever it is Strand would have us believe is their author.

CHARLES SIMIC

CHARLES SIMIC'S WORK, FORTUNATELY, does not lend itself to the circulatory—and oftentimes confusing—exegeses that Strand's poems require. But the two poets do show common characteristics in their work, most notably the exploration of absence and the inquiry into the many, and varying, aspects of the self (besides, of course, their use of the self-effacing voice). In their jointly authored introduction to *Another Republic* (1976), an anthology of translations by "17 European & South American Writers" that Strand and Simic edited, they wrote of a theory, on which they collaborated, separating the poets represented in that collection into two distinctive categories: the mythological and the historical. They posited the following:

> The origins of the mythological vision can be seen in surrealism, which, by concerning itself with the unconscious, found a method for uncovering and using archetypal imagery. It restored to the familiar world its strangeness and gave back to the poet his role of myth maker. Thus, for the mythological poet the miraculous is close at hand, easily encountered if he pays attention, as he must, since attention is his most important faculty. For him the poem is either a phenomenological interrogation, a process by which the archetype is dismantled,... or an elaborate narrative....
>
> For the poets whose vision is dominated by historical consciousness,

> Cavafy is the great modern ancestor, since he understood perhaps better than
> any of his contemporaries that in history nothing changes except the names,
> that there are always victims, always oppressors.... Such poets bear tragic wit-
> ness to the social and political events of their time, and their work is charac-
> terized by two modes of self-expression: the lyric, which attempts to ennoble
> the suffering of those who are victimized or estranged; and the comic, which
> recognizes the absurdity of individual destinies in the presence of the great
> abstractions of history. (17-18)

If the poets whose work appears in *Another Republic* can be grouped as either representing a mythological vision or an historical consciousness, as the editors suggest, Simic's poetry represents both, oftentimes in a single poem. Consider the
following selection from "History" which opens his collection, *Austerities* (1982):

> On a gray evening
> Of a gray century,
> I ate an apple
> While no one was looking....
>
> Then I stretched my legs
> As far as they'd go,
> Said to myself
> Why not close my eyes now
>
> Before the Late
> World News and Weather.

The historical consciousness represented here is that which is documented in
Genesis, of course, and that of the personal record of the poem's speaker on a certain evening, a speaker who is a "victim" of destiny, of the history resulting from
his first Judeo-Christian parents' indiscretion. In the way this history is presented
in the poem, it is true, "nothing changes": The speaker needs to rest before watching the news. That he is about to watch the news and weather report should remind him that neither would exist had he—that is, his earlier self, the self from
which he has descended—not eaten that "small, sour apple" (while no one was
looking) "On a gray evening / Of a gray century." That he is fatigued and in need
of rest is also a consequence of eating the apple, and it emphasizes his mortality—
a further consequence. If "History" must be set against Strand's and Simic's theory, it would most nearly reflect the historical-comic classification since it is not
lyric but "recognizes the absurdity of individual destinies in the presence of the
great abstractions of history." That the speaker who said: "I stretched my legs / As

far as they'd go," back on that gray evening of that gray century (meaning, simply, that he tested God's authority), is the very speaker who says the same thing before taking a nap (meaning literally to stretch his legs) is inherently absurd. The destiny—which is mortality—of the contemporary speaker has been determined for him by one of the greatest abstractions in Judeo-Christian history—or myth. For "History" also presents a mythological vision. On one level it repeats the fall of man myth of the early Hebrew cosmogony, Genesis, and on another it uncovers for the contemporary speaker (the one about to nap before the news) an archetypal image. "History" shows that "for the mythological poet the miraculous is close at hand" in that the one voice of the poem is comprised of two separate personages, both however of a common self, one an ancestor of the other, yet joined in a single voice by the miracle of the poem.

Much of Simic's work, as "History" proves and as will be shown in greater depth by analyses of poems later in this chapter, presents both a mythological vision to uncover and use archetypal imagery in his poetry and offers an historical consciousness in so doing. Myth and history are inseparable to Simic. He studied what he called "mythic materials" in order to learn the history of myths and people of North America to better understand the mythic consciousness, or "the imagery," as he says, "that is archetypal to this continent." He began by studying "Roethke, and Roethke interested me," Simic continued in his interview with Wayne Dodd and Stanley Plumly, "especially for the material from which he created those sequences—folklore, nursery rhymes, and so forth." Then, he explains:

> ... I spent years in the New York Public Library reading folklore.... [A]nd I spent just endless hours pouring through those things, and taking out little notes.... And when I ran out of that, I started reading books on primitive religions, anthropology, God knows what. Then from that point I moved to the utopian sects, early explorers, settlers.... [This material] had to do with a theory that I started developing around that time. It seemed to me that it was necessary to locate the imagery that is archetypal to this continent, some sort of mythic consciousness that is peculiar to this place... contemporary, but in order to find the contemporary you have to go back.... Anyway, it's not so much the question of finding the native archetype, but rather the manner in which that kind of consciousness works. (208-9)

That manner is the Jungian concept of the collective unconscious, to which we will return later.

But first, an understanding of Simic's use of myth will further illustrate that his poems can be a fusion of the mythic and historic—which fusion is the basis for his self-effacing voice. Specifically, he insists that his representation of myth, in all its strangeness, be "restored to the familiar world." To accomplish this, his evocation of archetypal imagery (his mythmaking) is always connected to the real, the physical, world; therefore Simic's mythic mode unites with place, an outward manifestation of the historical world. Place, though, transcends the historic, as Simic suggested to Dodd and Plumly: "There are certain things that are absent in my poetry on purpose, things that I dislike a lot. It's a prejudice. I hardly ever give place locations, mention any names, specific contemporary references. A sort of Neanderthal atmosphere prevails, though many of the poems have their seed in specific events. The Vietnam War, for example" (216). The allusion to his creating a "Neanderthal atmosphere" is appropriate in describing this historic (place)/ mythic (time) setting for his poetry. Although he is conscious of place, which gives the poem its historical foundation, he declines mentioning it in order to add a mythic, mysterious dimension.

Simic began his investigation of archetypal imagery after reading Roethke's *The Lost Son* (1948) and *Praise to the End!* (1951), both of which contain references to folklore set aside nature—particularly the soil and flowers—and other, pastoral images as a means of ontological inquiry which included a use of archetypes. As Simic told Dodd and Plumly, before reading Roethke, "I already had an obsession and interest in minimals, and that kind of gave me the notion that I did have to begin from the beginning, find something in my own life that I understood very well and felt passionately about, something that surrounded me.... The miraculous is always here.... The pastoral elements came from.... We always had, in the family, a romantic notion of going back to the land. We thought of ourselves as peasants" (208). This "romantic notion" gives much of his poetry "a weight of European folkwisdom and mythology," about which Simic continued in the same interview: "I'm sure, because of my background, those ten years in Yugoslavia [where I was born], that something in the way I see things or select things gives it, if you will, that kind of flavor. What I draw from is not European necessarily. There is much in American folklore—the riddles, incantations, magic charms, superstitions, proverbs—which most people are not familiar with anymore" (209-10). Simic's perception of the world, from which he bases his culling of archetypal imagery ("the way I see things or select things"), is not exclusively solipsistic, as is Strand's, but empirical to the degree to which it arises out of his personal beginning in Yugoslavia. The mythic is thus joined to the historic in this sense.

One other factor, in addition to the knowledge—yet exclusion—of place and the pastoral and folklore elements, helps to make Simic's poems a combination of the mythic vision and the historic consciousness: his allegiance to the physical world. An example is the short "Poem," from his first full collection of verse, *Dismantling the Silence* (1971):

> Every morning I forget how it is.
> I watch the smoke mount
> In great strides above the city....
>
> Then, I remember my shoes...
> How bending over to tie them up
> I will look into the earth.

The speaker awakes thinking he is without restriction, free, belonging to no one; then he realizes that he is bound to the earth and that which it imposes on him. Yet the poem's simple title indicates that the subject of "Poem" may act as a metaphor of Simic's philosophy of composition. He begins each day, or each poem, thinking he has no obligation to fulfill in writing, so can follow any mythic impulse (the smoke mounting "in great strides above the city" evokes a certain mythic quality), until he remembers his commitment to the earth and the particulars of life in the physical world. Simic remarked, in commenting to Richard Jackson on his notion of an anonymous "I" in his work (which soon will be discussed):

> What I've always tried to do in these metaphysical excursions is to remember the predicament of that "I." I dislike flights of imagination that leave behind the human condition. It delights me to remember this "I" who might be trying to figure out some incredible abstract proposition about the nature of the universe, this "I" who has holes in his socks, perhaps. It is Thoreau's notion, I guess, of keeping an allegiance to the soil, to our everydayness in the same instant as we experience the transcendental. (23)

These remarks illuminate Simic's earlier phrase, that he "had an obsession and interest in minimals," a phrase he later clarified as meaning "the essentials, of forks and knives" or other inanimate objects which ensure his "allegiance to the soil, to our everydayness in the same instant as we experience the transcendental." That his poems of this type are concerned with preserving these minimals ("a kind of absolute integrity—essentials") grounds them in the history of "everydayness"; that they are used to uncover archetypal imagery makes them instruments of a mythic vision.

The poem "Stone," which is part of a grouping in *Dismantling the Silence* of poems using a particular essential of "everydayness" to illustrate an aspect of myth (consider their titles, each revealing the essential, or minimal, as the poem's subject: "Table," "The Spoon," "Fork," "Knife," "My Shoes," and so on), is one such representation of a mythic vision being disclosed to our consciousness through an act of observing the minimal:

> Go inside a stone
> That would be my way.
> Let somebody else become a dove
> Or gnash with a tiger's tooth.
> I am happy to be a stone.
>
> From the outside the stone is a riddle:
> No one knows how to answer it.
> Yet within, it must be cool and quiet...
>
> I have seen sparks fly out
> When two stones are rubbed,
> So perhaps it is not dark inside after all...
> Just enough light to make out
> The strange writings, the star-charts
> On the inner walls.

In chapter 3 Galway Kinnell, in explaining his reasons for the necessity of the persona mode of voice, said: "If you could go even deeper, you'd not be a person, you'd be an animal; and if you went deeper still, you'd be a blade of grass, eventually a stone. If a stone could speak, your poem would be its words." But Kinnell only went as far as representing the self as an animal, a bear, never a stone (even though in *The Book of Nightmares* he suggests that the stone has the spiritual significance of a saint: "*stone saint smooth stone...*"). Simic's "Stone" expresses a desire—similar to that of Kinnell—for a return to the primitive. Yet where Kinnell's intent was a change of consciousness (that is, in the way in which we could perceive of ourselves if "uncivilized" or closer to the death-sphere), Simic's is to uncover our collective unconscious, not hoping to alter us, or our perception, necessarily, but to help us define our relationship to history and myth, to understand how our lives have been partially guided, our destinies formed, by archetypal imagery. That the speaker "is happy to be a stone" declares his allegiance to the soil. And as such, the speaker considers the possibilities of that "life": sustaining strength, a source of fire, of light which leads, perhaps, to "strange writings, the star-charts / On the inner walls" of one's unconscious. Simic's sense of the primitive, then, is atavistic. The mythic vision of the speaker turned stone reveals images inherited from our most remote ancestors, images which have been forgotten by our more immediate ones.

Although the last image of the poem reflects a mythic vision of the unconscious, the "I" is still present in "Stone." (Simic said: "It delights me to remember this 'I' who might be trying to figure out some incredible abstract proposition about the nature of the universe...") The "I" retains his human, petty concerns such as what others might think of him, what their positions are, etc.—"Let somebody else become a dove / Or gnash with a tiger's tooth"; and, although the "riddle" contained inside the stone is the ultimate question in the poem—the "incredible abstract proposition"—the stone's "outside" riddle, its everydayness, is also considered: that it can absorb the full weight of a cow's stepping on it, that it survives a child's abuse. "Stone" is mythic in that its vision is obscure, abstract ("strange writings, the star-charts"), yet historic because of its speaker's literal link with the soil. "I have ideas," Simic said to Dodd and Plumly. "We live in an age unaware of its miracles, an age unable to incorporate the discoveries of science, psychology, anthropology, etc., into its common consciousness. And I would like to include these in some way. At the same time, I have a horror of abstractions—I dislike wisdom not tested through experience, anything which doesn't have its roots in the soil, so to speak" (214).

Simic binds the presentation of his mythic vision to historical consciousness—that is, the physical world—by showing "its roots in the soil" as well as his sense of place and the elements of folklore and anthropology (that we have seen) which inform his work. And a last note regarding "Stone": Its mythic dimension derives from evoking the cave writings of early man. In "History" Simic used Genesis to clarify and magnify the actions of his contemporary speaker. The poet takes from all anthropological and folk-myth sources in order to uncover archetypal imagery.

The result of a poem which combines mythic vision with historical consciousness is, as has been suggested, a speaker of the self-effacing mode, an impersonal "I." In the introduction to this chapter, Simic was quoted as saying that his poems seem impersonal because "it is not clear who the 'I' is." A poem, for Simic, or "any verbal act includes a selection, or conceptualization, a narrowing down," he said. That is, what makes the "I" personal is diminished because the poem reduces the speaker's experience in its attempt to conceptualize it. This concept is like Strand's theory that his critical nature is reductive in that it is the side best suited for self-definition. In defining the self, in exercising the critical over the expressive side, the poem's speaker becomes more impersonal. Following is Simic's justification for his theory that the poem is a "narrowing down" which consequently produces an impersonal "I" as its speaker, as he told Jackson:

Let's say someone has the experience of walking around a swamp at night, sees things he wouldn't see in another place or in the day time, perhaps feels fear, confusion. Now, he would have to be seriously deluded to believe that when he sits down to render all this that he can equal its complexity. Since what he writes doesn't equal the experience, there's this suspicion which becomes a voice, a voice that asks, "What have I experienced?" But let's say he begins to write and arrives at an acceptable equation. The problem is then with a language that is larger than his uses for it. On the one hand, it contains echoes and resonances he never suspected.... So he starts hearing two things. He hears what recreates his swamp experience, but also other things that are unexpected, that point to a different subject matter, to a different development. Here he has to make some sort of choice. I find that in my own poems I tend to abandon the original cause or the visible aspects of the original cause and follow wherever the poem leads. That's why my poems often seem impersonal. (21-2)

To begin from an experience—that is, to take from one's record of personal history—must not be allowed to dominate the poem's intention of expressing a mythic vision. The poet, if his desire is to create a myth or to uncover archetypal—or atavistic—imagery, must not impose his personal self, his history (or experience), on the mythic structure on which he intends to base his mythic vision. Simic illustrates the problem of simply "cataloging the archetypal structures" in order to "introduce mythic consciousness into poetry" with the example of a Navaho myth: "you can intellectually deduce its form," he told Jackson, "but the content, and the deeper psychological impetus for that content, would be missing. Unless you were a Navaho living when the myth was set, you could only provide a generalized content. I began to realize that these structures would be imposed from the outside.... There was something mechanical and unsatisfying in trying to fit an experience into a deliberate mythic structure" (19-20). Altering the mythic structure in order to make it "fit an experience" would be equally mechanical. The solution, therefore, is to alter the speaker's rendition of his experience (a wholly created speaker "could only provide a generalized content," consequently some measure of empiricism must be involved in suggesting that from one's experience arises a mythic vision) by abandoning "the original cause or the visible aspects of the original cause and follow[ing] wherever the poem leads," even, as it does eventually, to where the "I" becomes impersonal.

The need for the impersonality of the poem's first person speaker is the need of uncovering archetypal imagery, or of expressing the mythic vision, for ontological investigation. The "I" must become less personal even though the impetus for the mythic suggestion may be a personal experience, such as walking around a swamp at night. The poet must establish a sense of self-diminishment in the poem's speaker, or, as Richard Jackson wrote in his essay "The Presence of Absence": "Simic's mode is finally to deconstruct presence, to recede back into the growing region of emptiness…" (143). Yet this "deconstruction" is not to imply a complete removal of the presence of self in the poem, for that would make it entirely mythic, abstract, which Simic finds "empty and arbitrary." As always, this mythic intention must be balanced by an infusion of historical consciousness: From those mythic poems, Simic told Jackson, "what was missing was a test of the presence of the human being who accepts the responsibility of those visions. There is a constant dialectic in my poetry between a longing to take off on abstract flights and my concrete, physical needs. One has to consider the life of the world: the historical dimension, the horrifying history of our age. All that intrudes into poems" (23).

Simic's poem "Eraser," from *Charon's Cosmology* (1977), presents a self-diminished "I," one retaining enough presence, however, in order to test the mythic vision it voices:

> A summons because the marvelous prey is fleeing
> Something to rub out the woods
> From the blackboard sound of wind and rain
> A device to recover a state of pure expectancy…
>
> This emptiness which gets larger and larger
> As the eraser works and wears out
> As my mother shakes her apron full of little erasers
> For me to peck like little breadcrumbs

Jackson in his interview with Simic, after quoting Foucault that "language always seems to be inhabited by the other, the elsewhere, the distant; it is hollowed by absence," offered to Simic the following explication of "Eraser":

> Your own metaphors suggest such notions as silence, invisibility.… [T]he poem "Eraser" seems to talk about this—there is a "summons" motivated by the flight of a "marvelous prey." The erasing is a means to "recover a state of pure expectancy," to recover traces of what seems absent, the hollowness, the cleared place.… (22)

In "Eraser," the speaker needs to maintain a degree of presence, or consciousness, in order to evoke the clearing that is the domain of the marvelous prey. Simic responded to Jackson's remarks by defining this degree of presence—or absence—of his speaker as an "anonymity." He said:

> I've always felt that inside each of us there is profound anonymity. Sometimes
> I think that when you go deep inside, you meet everyone else on a sort of
> common ground—or you meet nobody. But whatever you meet, it is not
> yours though you enclose it. We are the container, and this nothingness is
> what we enclose. This is where Heidegger is very interesting to me. He de-
> scribes the division between the world as nothing, as what he calls the "open,"
> and any act of conceptualizing which restores the world in a particular way.
> Many of his texts are longings to experience that anonymity, the condition
> where we don't have an "I" yet. It is as if we were in a room from which, para-
> doxically, we were absent. Everything is seen from the perspective of that ab-
> sence. I suppose, in some ways, this is a mystical vision that brings to me a
> sense of the universe as an anonymous presence. (22-3)

This "anonymous" self is the unconscious, as argued by Paul Breslin, in his article "How to Read the New Contemporary Poem." Simic's self-effacing "I" is a manifestation of the absence of consciousness; this "I," from whose perspective "everything is seen," has abolished the conscious self in favor of the collective unconscious. Breslin remarks that in "reading poetry that depends so much on a revealed symbolism, rather than a symbolism created by the arrangement of the poem or the exploration of a recognizable subject...we are asked to dismiss the quotidian world and take refuge in the collective unconscious" (364), which brings us back to Simic's compelling reason for an impersonal "I" in his work: so to reveal a symbolism—that is, to uncover archetypal imagery—unknown to the conscious, the personal, self. Breslin, after citing selections from Simic's "Knife" and Bly's "Turning Inward at Last," concludes: "[T]hese poems have...a great deal to do with the collective theogonic unconscious proposed by Jung" (361). He continues that this type of poetry "represents a giving up on the outside world, a retreat from psycho-politics into a solipsistic religion of the unconscious," and that this comes "at any cost, even the abolition of social reality and the conscious self" (366).

Yet Simic's intention is to uncover archetypal imagery for the outside world, as he remarked to Dodd and Plumly: "I have an idea for a poem which...would also be ultimately accessible to everyone. I feel a certain responsibility toward other lives because it's the other lives I feel I ought to write about" (217). This differs from Bly's intended use of archetypal representation (as we will see in the next chapter) in that Bly uses his personal self—that is, the confessional "I"—to relate a mythic vision whereas Simic's speaker attempts to transcend his ego (an abolition of the conscious self, as Breslin has argued) in order to express our collective unconscious. Bly intends these images to help define his personal self; Simic intends them to be joined with our collective historic consciousness so they will complement his mythic vision.

Simic, then, needs to employ the self-effacing mode of voice to transcend the personal, conscious self of the speaker. Such a voice can better express a mythic vision which is evocative of the archetypal imagery relating to our collective unconscious. However, since Simic wants to keep this impersonal speaker "rooted in the soil," his speaker must take the form of a bifurcated self, as does Strand's. The personal self retains an historic consciousness; the other self speaks for our unconscious. Simic's "History" showed how the two can function in a poem as a remarkably unified voice. Two poems from *Charon's Cosmology* illustrate Simic's concept of the other: "The Prisoner" and "Position Without a Magnitude." In the first, the speaker lies with his lover after their picnic lunch, but senses, in this moment of intimacy, that he is a prisoner of his other self—referred to as "he"—an other always present and representative of cosmological knowledge incomprehensible to the speaker:

> He considers my hand on her breast,
> Her closed eyelids, her moist lips
> Against my forehead, and the shadows of trees
> Hovering on the ceiling.
>
> It's been so long. He has trouble
> Deciding what else is there.
> And all along the suspicion
> That we do not exist.

This other, although perhaps better understanding the nature of the universe— the leaves, the shadows of trees (the speaker only has a Romantic notion of these)—does not comprehend the love the couple shares. And the speaker has not felt the presence of this other for some time; it is suggested that the absence of this otherness can be attributed to his doubting the very existence of anything but his own "otherness." Each of us, contends Simic, has a self, which, from its "position of magnitude" like that of a star, is able to view our other self's "everydayness," our quotidian existence, from a higher perspective. This self is described in "Position Without a Magnitude," a title which suggests that in this poem, the speaker, who is in a position without magnitude, gets a glimpse of what his other self might be:

As when someone
You haven't noticed before
Gets up in an empty theater
And projects his shadow
Among the fabulous horsemen
On the screen

And you shudder
As you realize it's only you...

This other makes the speaker consider the possibility that he "doesn't have an 'I,'" as Simic was quoted earlier. "Everything is seen from the perspective of that absence"—of which the speaker thinks in "The Prisoner" possibly—"a mystical vision that brings to me a sense of the universe as an anonymous presence." Again, the vision of myth derives from an historical consciousness. The "fabulous horsemen / On the screen" is both present history (in that it is then occurring) and a Biblical allusion (chronicled ancient history). In the universe which the poem depicts, this other, "anonymous presence," is ultimately responsible for its—the poem's, the universe of the poem's—creation, as Simic suggests in "Description" (also from *Charon's Cosmology*), in which the poet (who is the poem's speaker) selects, in making his poem, only those images that derive from his "anonymous presence":

Among all the images
that come to mind,

where to begin?
Contortions, infinite shapes...

A corner where
a part of myself

keeps an appointment
with another part of myself....

This other part of himself is what finally dictates which images to select, which poems to write. Simic has already told us that his poems seem impersonal because he abandons his personal experience and follows wherever the poem leads, "the logic of the algebraic equation of words on the page which is unfolding, moving in some direction." As "Description" indicates, the poem moves toward the direction of the other, and, as Simic said: "That's why my poems often seem impersonal. It is not clear who the 'I' is. It doesn't seem necessary for me to equate that

'I' with myself," that is, with the part of himself that is personal, conscious, historical, quotidian. Simic achieves self-effacement in these poems because he moves
away from his original, personal experience towards the language of the poem.
And "language," suggests Jackson in "The Presence of Absence," "acts as a force
which alienates us from ourselves" (138). Although the self has been effaced, it remains in the poem. The other cannot control the universe of the poem entirely, as
Simic has argued in his interview with Jackson:

> I don't think the author is ever absent. The simple act of selectivity from the
> vast possibilities of language and experience introduces the author. Except
> that for me there is no *one* "I." "I" is many. "I" is an organizing principle, a
> necessary fiction, etc. Actually, I'd put more emphasis on consciousness: that
> which witnesses but has no need of a pronoun. Of course, consciousness has
> many degrees, and each degree has a world (as an ontology) appropriate to it-
> self. So, perhaps, the seeming absence of the author is the description of one
> of its manifestations, in this case an increase of consiousness at the expense of
> the subject? It's a possibility. (25-6)

There are two ways, then, in which Simic accomplishes the self-effacing mode of
voice: The first, as we have seen, is the transcendence of his ego in order to uncover mythic visions of the collective unconscious, and the second is in allowing
the language to invoke the presence of the other self, the result of a poem composed of a language, he told Jackson, that "is not mine.... [T]here is something
that precedes language.... [T]here is a state that precedes verbalization, a complexity of experience that consists of things not yet brought to consciousness, not
yet existing as language but as some sort of inner pressure" (21).

   That "something precedes language" brings Simic to the collective unconscious which is revealed through the other, that which awaits beyond the transcendence of the ego. This other, resulting from language (that "acts as a force
which alienates us from ourselves") and the universe of the poem, defines the self;
"the seeming absence of the author is the description of one of its manifestations,"
as the dialectic in the poem "Charles Simic," from *Return to a Place Lit by a Glass
of Milk* (1974), argues:

> Charles Simic is a sentence....
>
> What is the subject of the sentence?
> The subject is your beloved Charles Simic....

> What is the object of the sentence?
> The object, my little ones,
> Is not yet in sight.
>
> And who is writing this awkward sentence?
> A blackmailer, a girl in love,
> And an applicant for a job.

The structure, or ontological system, used in composing "Charles Simic" (the sentence) depends on the weather, the stars—that is, whichever whims the language dictates. Remember that Simic has said that "the vast possibilities of language introduces the author," who indeed is not "*one* 'I,'" but several: blackmailer, girl in love—the sense here is of an indefinite list because possibilities inherent in "the simple act of selectivity" are endless. The tone is slightly condescending: "The object, my little ones, / Is not yet in sight," resulting partially from the poem's catechismic design. The personal self has been effaced because the voice of "Charles Simic," the poem, finally, is an "anonymous presence," invisible, indeterminate, both posing and answering the questions which define the self described by its own poem.

The confusion of identity, which is one of Simic's methods to ensure a self-effacing voice, also relates to his concept of otherness, or bifurcated self which, as we have seen, is necessary in establishing a mythic vision from an historical consciousness. The subject of "Ax," from *Dismantling the Silence*, concerns the displacement of self from the body:

> The stench of blood and swamp water
> Will return to its old resting place.
> They'll spend their winters
> Sleeping like the bears.
> The skin on the breasts of their women
> Will grow coarse. He who cannot
> Grow teeth, will not survive.
> He who cannot howl
> Will not find his pack…
>
> These dark prophecies were gathered,
> Unknown to myself, by my body
> Which understands historical probabilities,
> Lacking itself, in its essence, a future.

The "dark prophecies" of the body indicate a return to a primitive self, one that is similar to Kinnell's notion of man's "bear-like" existence in his pre-civilized form. The atavistic imagery is suggested, too, in such lines as: "They'll spend their winters / Sleeping like the bears" in caves. In this poem, the otherness, that which uncovers the archetypal imagery for the speaker—the conscious self—is the physical body which here assumes the role of the collective unconscious, as the final stanza reveals.

In "Bestiary for the Fingers of My Right Hand," the speaker's confusion of identity suggests further that Simic's "I" is not one, but many actually. The poem betrays the speaker's disparate personality, each finger representing a separate facet:

> 1
> Thumb, loose tooth of a horse.
> Rooster to his hens.
> Horn of a devil. Fat worm
> They have attached to my flesh
> At the time of my birth....

> 4
> The fourth is mystery....
> He jumps by himself
> As though someone called his name....

> 5
> Something stirs in the fifth
> Something perpetually at the point
> Of birth. Weak and submissive,
> His touch is gentle.
> It weighs a tear.
> It takes the mote out of the eye.

That the fingers of his right hand comprise a bestiary—an allegory on the habits of imagined (or real) animals, a form common in medieval literature—again suggests the atavism revealed by the poem's speaker. And because each finger presents a differing side of the speaker as well as presenting the disparate natures of one another, "Bestiary for the Fingers of My Right Hand" demonstrates the division of the self from the body, just as "Ax" does. Like that poem also, "Bestiary" implies that contained within each self there is a vision of our primitive, animalistic origin, unknown to our present consciousness, but unveiled by means of an

otherness that is our collective unconscious. The conscious self is effaced in order
for that otherness to express this vision.

In "A Quiet Talk with Oneself," Simic shows more of his comic side. In the
"conversation" between the speaker and himself (whom the speaker calls "my
friend"), the speaker admonishes his self for not fulfilling his potential: "You too
were once full of promise, / Only to lapse, woefully, my friend," then gets involved
with his own rhetoric in choosing the appropriate images to illustrate his suggestion of the "lapse" in promise, and then says:

> But I digress. Just like that unfortunate Mr. Poe:
> Compulsive ratiocination on the subject of the self
> In the guise of a polar voyage without the means of retreat,
> While the poor ass keeps getting whipped and rained on.

The image of the ass is precisely that from which the speaker began his long di-
gression. To completely understand oneself, it is Simic's position, requires both
the historic and the mythic, the conscious self and the (often atavistic) collective
unconscious. Yet, like the speaker of "A Quiet Talk with Oneself," Simic is less serious than the confessional voice of the Lowell defining himself in relation to the
other mental patients in "Waking in the Blue," or the persona voice of Kinnell
suggesting that such self-definition only can be derived by returning to primitive
origins. In the following tacit admission of this comic aspect to Jackson, Simic
also betrays his skepticism of his own ontological theories, a skepticism that is
one subject of his poem "The Point," about which he remarked:

> Triangular stories start out and try to retrace their own steps but can't get
> back to their beginnings so they end up at some distance from the beginning
> before they return to it; by that time they've traced a strange figure. There's a
> comic aspect to all this. My favorite is "The Point," the story which takes one
> step and then immediately has a kind of regret. It's horrified at the whiteness
> of the page. (21)

Since the self-effacing mode of voice is intended to help uncover archetypal
imagery, express the mythic vision by returning to the collective unconscious—an
imaginary place in itself (the unconscious is not a physical place to which one can
return)—all of Simic's self-effacing poems "trace a strange figure"; even in the
world of a poem, Simic realizes, any voice may "end up at some distance from the
beginning" before returning to its intention. His theories of the unconscious-con-
scious, the separate selves, then, contain, perhaps, an aspect of comedy with

them. They may be slightly absurd even, which is a characteristic—evident from our discussion of Strand's work—of some poems using a self-effacing voice.

In the work of David Ignatow to follow, it will be shown that the poetic voice most often identifiable is also of this mode, even though he may have intended it as a persona "I" speaking as a representative of the community.

DAVID IGNATOW

DAVID IGNATOW SHARES WITH Mark Strand the concept that an exploration of a "darkness," an otherness of self, may lead to an understanding of one's self set in (and trying to survive) a chaotic contemporary world. Yet, as mentioned in the introduction to this chapter, Ignatow would like his poetry—that is, what he discovers in his poetry about the self, the individual's role in society—used to benefit the community, not himself exclusively. And, in common with Simic's use of the self-effacing mode, Ignatow's subjects, and many of his images, remain "rooted in the soil," although occasionally both subject and image may flare into the surreal or realm of the phantasmagoric. These characteristics tread into the boundaries of the confessional and persona modes; each may extend in practice to one or both. Ignatow's work is representative of such extension, but finally the voice that controls the poems to be discussed in the pages following is one that is neither personal—even though it may begin with a personal impulse—nor one that acts as the persona voice of the community, its representative speaker. Rather, Ignatow's voice more often fades, allowing the poem to become one of ideas, as Simic might refer to it, expressive of notions of self and community. He combines the personal with what he perceives to be the public concerns of the community, as he explained in an interview with Scott Chisholm:

> [M]y father is one element in the work, and guilt is a sense I derive from society itself. I think the whole society is laboring under a sense of predestined guilt. We're Puritan. No matter how you turn it or how you phrase it, we're guilty for cultural reasons—or lack of reasons which the culture withholds from us.
>
> I'd say, of course, that guilt is the one driving factor in my work. I am guilty, by all standards of ideal behavior and modes of existence, of falling far short of their demands. Of course I'm guilty—like everyone else. It's a guilt I live with, although in my daily life I try hard to act with some kindliness, ease, and love for my fellow man.... I'm American. It's all in the poems....
>
> Of course, I use myself personally. It's a technique that we Americans are using with Walt Whitman as a model. We've been following Walt Whitman in this path—except that we reinvent Whitman's ideals today and try to

point to their failure. As individuals, we still use ourselves now as the metaphors of failure of the American ideals. (23-4)

This passage helps explain the ostensible ambiguity in Ignatow's mode of voice,
and provides the necessary background in establishing that voice ultimately as
one of self-effacement. Contemporary poets of any mode are usually quick to
claim allegiance with Whitman, mostly because of aesthetic preference, as discussed in the introductory chapter. Lowell, and the poets of the confessional
voice, may point to Whitman's primary intention of celebrating the self, whereas
Berryman—as he was quoted—argued that Whitman's "I" is personal only in that
it stands as representative speaker of the community. Ignatow's patronage of
Whitman is for reasons apparently similar to Berryman's and those poets of the
persona voice. However, the vital distinction between Berryman and Ignatow, or
any poet of the self-effacing mode of voice, regarding the interpretation of Whitman's "I," can be found in Ignatow's final remarks of the above quoted passage:
"... we reinvent Whitman's ideals today and try to point to their failure. As individuals, we still use ourselves as the metaphors ... of failure of the American ideals." This remains consistent with the poet's intention of using the self-effacing
voice to speak for the community; the persona "I" may be said to speak *as* the
community voice. Further, the notion of failure alters, for the self-effacing poet,
the persona poet's adaptation of the Whitman "I": For Kinnell, the "everyman 'I'"
offers a hope for the future, but Ignatow's bespeaks the hopelessness of the
present, a result, he suggests, of our "predestined guilt," our hostility—American
"aggressive desire to dominate and direct ... to hurt others."

Ignatow, "by all standards of ideal behavior and modes of existence," fails to
satisfy the demands of society, a failure, he says, incurring because of "cultural
reasons—or lack of reasons which the culture withholds from us." In such a culture in which nothing is defined, in which only the certainty of societal guilt
looms upon its members, it becomes necessary to define oneself, to gain some
sense, at least, of one's certainty of person, if only tentatively, even if that means
viewing oneself as a nothingness. A void in the culture helps explain why everything surrounding it does not seem to relate. For Mark Strand's speaker was confused, alienated in an absurd world, until realizing his role of absence, which not
merely provided him with a satisfying self-definition, but defined his function in
such a world as well: "When I walk / I part the air / and always / the air moves in /
to fill the spaces / where my body's been. // We all have reasons / for moving. / I
move / to keep things whole." Ignatow, like Strand's speaker who embarks on a
search for his purpose in life because existence, to him, without purpose is meaningless, finds contemporary life confusing. It is, Ignatow writes in his *Notebooks*,

"as if a game has taken place in which the point is to come back to the very start by a puzzling, different route, and he who succeeds first is left waiting for the others to find their way out of the puzzle, and you are lonely waiting and would like to go back into the middle of the puzzle for the company at least you would find there" (361-62).

Whereas Strand's answer to this puzzlement was found in self-definition, Ignatow feels the puzzle is such a large burden that it cannot be solved with a "self-enclosed" conception of existence, but one embodying a self whose relationship to others is clearly marked and one clearly contributory to one's self-composition, as he recorded in his *Notebooks*:

> I can't reconcile myself to the thought that the world has to be...each person a self-enclosed existence with little or no connection among us; and yet we resemble each other physically. We communicate with each other for food, love, protection, money, status, and a kind of community.... I suppose the answer I am looking for is the abandonment of the principle of the individual life in order to give ourselves a larger, stronger basis in community. It certainly can't be done as individuals. Dante's answer of individual salvation does not apply to us today.... I disagree with the concept that each must find his or her salvation through personal trial and error.... It is Darwin who shattered any theoretical possibility of the eventual cohesiveness of the world, collaboration and cooperation among species, societies and individuals. (360)

The self, consequently, becomes effaced to allow for an integration with the community and with other selves of the community within the universe recreated in Ignatow's poetry. To accomplish "the abandonment of the principle of the individual life," Ignatow must employ the self-effacing mode of voice, not as the Whitmanesque "I" who celebrates his personal life, or the "I" who can be regarded as a persona, a spokesperson, but as an answer, an abandonment (not representation of the self that the persona "I" yields) of the concept of the individual life "in order to give ourselves a larger, stronger basis in community."

That Ignatow regards himself alienated from the present world, and therefore—like Strand's speaker—in need of fulfilling an important societal function in order to fuse with the community (and, consequently, the poetry then offers itself as a manifestation of Ignatow's having given himself "a larger, stronger basis in community") is evident in his following thoughts from *Notebooks*:

> It seems I begin every morning with a sense of my apartness from the world, with an underlying bitterness. I awake to feel it at once as perhaps existing already in my awakening sleep, the very process of awakening constituting this

sense of apartness and its bitterness. The world looks chaotic and hopeless, living feels useless, if not futile, by comparison with what I have left behind, and most of all my poems try to heal the gap.... I am he who, having fully awakened, would like to reform the past in the present, getting the present to resemble the past in the sense of wholeness in which the past of sleep was lived, a sleep, a kind of death.... Whitman was another who could not give up the sense of loss at awakening from sleep and put all of his gigantic energies into reforming the world in the image of sleep's condition ... Stevens ... may be right in throwing himself back upon his own sense of self to make that the center, the beginning and end of his whole world, instead of the actual world. I am not ready to acknowledge that, not while the need for wholeness is universal. (363-64)

Ignatow's philosophy, as expressed in this meditation, at first seems to confirm Strand's idea of a divided self, as suggested in part by the epigraph of *Reasons for Moving* from Jorge Luis Borges: "[W]hile we sleep here, we are awake elsewhere and that in this way every man is two men." But Strand's speaker, afraid of the other, dark, self—the one of sleep—would rather suffer insomnia than confront that otherness—that is, until he learns to submit to it, that darkness, which allows him to retreat from "the world of chaos outside," making his own sense of self (having recognized the otherness as an aspect of self) "the center, the beginning and end of his whole world, instead of the actual world," as Ignatow says of Wallace Stevens. And Ignatow, following what he interprets to be the example of Whitman, considers himself the poet "who, having fully awakened, would like to reform the past in the present, getting the present to resemble the past in the sense of wholeness in which the past of sleep was lived," he says, "a sleep, a kind of death, a kind of apotheosis, a catharsis, a sleep within a living, turbulent, formative world."

In shunning a retreat from "the actual world" through a complete self-turning inward, regarding one's self as the "center" of the world in favor of a more cathartic experience attained by having fused these two sides of self (defined by Ignatow as the self "awakening from sleep," one neither wholly awake nor asleep), Ignatow, it could be argued, shares Simic's goal for a representation of an historical consciousness, for keeping the conception of self (though it is an abstract idea) "rooted in the soil." This idea of self, "a kind of death," is similar to Kinnell's notion for returning to our primordial state of being, yet for Ignatow, this "death," or apotheosis, is an exemplary state which he desires "the present to resemble."

His poems, if they capture this essence by representing "the past in the sense of wholeness in which the past of sleep was lived,"—that is, the state of awakening—

have then moved towards solving the puzzlement of life, and subsequently they have helped the community in two ways. The one member of society, the poet (or speaker of the poem), is better self-defined, and so relates better to his society (as opposed to extreme introspection, and the division of self from "the world of chaos outside"), and the community benefits because, through the poem, the one member of society is extended "into the world, to be in contact physically, emotionally," etc., as Ignatow says, "with my contemporaries." If this occurs, the community need not be regarded as an alien, confusing, world.

And although Ignatow is referring to himself in these remarks, saying that his poems extend himself to the community, he is careful still to "abandon the principle of the individual life in order to give ourselves a larger, stronger basis in community." Consequently, when one member of that community defines himself in terms of two states of consciousness (the self awakening from sleep), he has in a sense given the individual life over for something larger, that which can relate to the many. In keeping with this concept, Ignatow must represent this idea of self in his poetry, and the only means through which he can is the self-effacing mode of voice. It is particularly important, in viewing Ignatow's poetry as work of this mode, to note that the previously cited selections from his *Notebooks* are helpful in distinguishing Ignatow from his poetic speaker. In these passages he meditates upon issues most bothersome to himself—that is, when he writes: "I begin every morning with a sense of my apartness from the world," we can be certain he intends that "I" to mean himself, given that these are entries in personal diaries ("...the *Notebooks*," writes Mills in the introduction, "were not begun or continued with publication in view but are instead a poet's working journals..."). But in the ensuing poetry, a distinction must be made, as always, between the first person speaker of a poem and the poet who composed it, who, as Hugo told us in the introductory chapter, rejected himself in order to compose it.

In *Tread the Dark* (1978), a title at once suggestive of a comparison with Strand's *Darker*, a volume which has been shown to largely concern the exploration of the "dark" regions of consciousness, or otherness—as so appropriately termed by Harold Bloom—Ignatow begins with several short poems with subjects by now familiar to us: absence, the divided self. Yet the presentation of these subjects is new in that the self-effacing speaker neither fears a confrontation with his otherness, his unconscious self, as Strand's does, nor seeks to modulate with that otherness in order to gain mythic insight of archetypal imagery as does Simic's. Instead, Ignatow's speaker attempts to shield himself from the central focus of discovery in these poems so that what he learns about the nature of self, about the individual's relationship and responsibility to the community, may be shared. The opening poem, "Brightness as a Poignant Light," illustrates several characteristics of his self-effacing poem:

> I tread the dark and my steps are silent.
> I am alone and feel a ghostly joy—wildly
> free and yet I do not live absolutely
> and forever, but my ghostly joy
> is that I am come to light...

> As I tread the dark,
> led by the light of my pulsating mind,
> I am faithful to myself: my child....

> I take comfort that I am
> my father, speaking as a child
> against my fatherhood....

There is a spiritual ambience conjured by the speaker's returning to the darkness; he becomes childlike because he finds that he has been renewed by his excursion into the dark. He is "light" and is able to tread the dark only "by the light," he says, "of my pulsating mind"; that is, the speaker has trodden into the darkest recessions of himself. That he is light—a "brightness"—places him in contrast with the other, the dark and dominant part of his self. The darkness represents his immediate origin, his father, and to continue inward eventually leads to an exploration of the self. He learns that which is true of any self-origin—that he is part of that from which he came: "I take comfort that I am / my father...." The "father" darkness and "child" brightness are inseparable, two aspects of a single self, for the heart beats to perpetuate the life of the darkness, and in doing so continues the life of the speaker. The speaker thinks it is for the darkness that the heart beats, because darkness is the domain of silence, of power, but by entering its realm, by treading the dark, the speaker has reached this very source of power, which is the inward self, the silent darkness of the unconsciousness previously unknown to the "light of the pulsating mind." Ignatow, then, divides the self (as do Strand and Simic) into a self that is known, a conscious self, and one that resides in the shadowy region of the invisible, the unconscious self, or what Simic termed the "anonymous self." Unlike either of them, however, Ignatow's speaker achieves for the conscious self a strengthening, a renewal of spirit, by contacting the unconscious, which is the source of power, the fatherhood.

   This conscious self, represented as the light, considers that the sole purpose in meeting his other was in preparation for death, which is nature's method of replenishment (one dies in order to make a place for another). The following un-titled selection, from *Tread the Dark*, continues this notion of death and renewal, and makes natural elements analogous with people:

> The seasons doubt themselves and give way
> to one another. The day is doubtful of itself,
> as is the night; they come, look around, slowly depart....
> People give birth to people, flourish
> and then die
> and the sun is a flame of doubt...

Ignatow here keeps returning to the human concern: The seasons "doubt them-selves" the way people do; that the sun is a "flame of doubt" which our bodies welcome suggests that we are happy to have life soon end and we are receptive to darkness (which is death) replacing it. The darkness, or death, becomes another means of birth, renewal, life. What began as an introspective self-investigation of the speaker in "Brightness as a Poignant Light" now has more universal applica-tion. The darkness on which the speaker treads (and which he found to be a strengthening source) is equated to nature's seasonal regeneration, and further, to humankind's generative life, which consequently opens the thought outward to include the community in a notion begun as self-inquiry. That this other—even if it is a death, albeit one that leads to a renewal of life—should not be feared is the imperative of the next poem, "With the Sun's Fire":

> Are you a horror to yourself?
> Do you have eyes peering at you
> from within at the back of your skull
> as you manage to stay calm, knowing
> you are being watched by a stranger?
>
> Be well, I am seated beside you,
> planning a day's work. We are contending
> with the stuff of stones and stars...

One self serves to calm the other; both function to "work" on the burden of self-definition, using, like Simic's speaker, cosmological means such as "the stuff of stones and stars." If one finds himself a horror, it is because the "day's work" of such investigation is yet to begin. It does, though, as the ensuing poem "Examine me, I am continuous" indicates, with the speaker addressing the self reflected in the mirror:

> Examine me, I am continuous
> from my first memory and have no memory
> of birth....
>
> Face in the mirror
> or star hidden by the sun's rays,
> you are always there but which am I
> and who is the mirror or the hidden star?
> Explain me as you are that I may live
> in time and die...

The face in the mirror is that of a "star hidden by the sun's rays," or death sphere (compare his earlier line: "the sun is a flame of doubt"—that is, the speaker's desiring death), in that its presence is hidden. It is an anonymous self, one that becomes visible only in darkness, which we know to mean an otherness, that which dominates, the speaker believes, since it holds the answers to the conscious self's questions regarding existence. The speaker arrives at some tentative conclusions, however, in the next poem, "The Two Selves," in which he expresses his desire to "withdraw into a stone," making him the embodiment of Kinnell's ultimate state of being, and aligning him with Simic's theory of fusing the conscious self with the unconscious by means of an object of the physical world:

> I existed before my mind realized me...
>
> So you began for me
> and I will whisper to your self
> to give in, to surrender, to close
> in remembrance, and I will give you up
> and withdraw into a stone, forever
> known to you.

The stone is "forever known" to the otherness because it is an altered state of existence, that darkness reached by the conscious self (the poem's speaker) in having transcended the ego—as Simic's does in order to penetrate the mythic vision of the unconscious—and being transformed to something that is a physical manifestation of the unconscious self, a stone. Therefore, the conscious self's withdrawing into a stone is known to the unconscious self because that "light" has before trodden into the dark region of the unconscious, and the darkness of the stone, the altered state of the conscious self, is the very realm of the unconscious.

Yet, as Ignatow says, "to look for the self in oneself" does not much advance any relationship with others of the community. To become a stone, as the speaker does in "The Two Selves," is not enough to satisfactorily explain the puzzlements presented by the universe, as he remarked in "A Dialogue at Compas":

> ...to understand is to love, and since we don't understand what it's about, we're confused, and confusions really don't allow for too much love. When we're desperate, we fall back upon those old assertions that Whitman made, that a man is part of the universe and must become identified with the universe.... And I can sympathize with it because where do we go from our total despair? We go back into ourselves. And when you go into yourself actually you lose touch with yourself. That's the paradox. Once you go too far into yourself you lose touch because your self is only found through interaction with others. I know my poetry is filled with this sort of material, and I've worked through it, but the school of irrelevance wants to say that the self doesn't exist any longer as we used to know it. To look for the self in oneself is to lose oneself in oneself.... We live tentative lives, and the love that you are thinking of, the love for life, is a love which is surrounded and modified, deeply modified, by caution. (65-6)

The ideal, then, is to "go back into ourselves," or define ourselves by means of the darkness within, perhaps, without "actually losing touch with yourself"; this is accomplished by keeping the focus of one's self in its "interaction with others," with its relationship to the community.

We have discussed Ignatow's poems in which the personal speaker has been effaced because of his self-transcendence to the region—and subsequent state of "existence" (the stone)—of the otherness, the life-giving aspect of the self, anonymous to one's conscious self. Yet these were poems largely of self-definition, of the speaker's losing himself, in essence, *in* his self, poems which do nothing—as Ignatow suggests—for the condition of the community in a time marked by bewildering irrelevancies and absurdities. One reaction a poet can have is to ignore the puzzlements and the self in relation to them, and so contribute more irrelevancies by working in what Ignatow terms "the school of irrelevance," which cares not to define the self because that school believes that "the self doesn't exist any longer as we used to know it." Ignatow also said in "A Dialogue at Compas": "...there is a French school of poetry, not exactly surrealistic but deriving from surrealism, with no intention of dealing with life as life, but dealing instead with the imagination as an autonomous experience.... [T]hat leads poetry into all sorts of strange byways, one of them being Ashbery's concentration on the mind and its values, observations, comments, and associations as merely stuff for processing, to what end we don't know" (64).

But Ignatow does not object to humor, such as Strand's, which is used to an end of self-realization; nor does he object to surrealism in poetry that is used to illustrate how modern life can be justifiably perceived. Both humor and surrealism can relate to the condition of the contemporary self, but they should not be employed as poetic elements to disregard the self. The poetry of the "school of irrelevance" is contrary to Ignatow's purpose, and the intentions of his self-effacing speaker. He says (in "A Dialogue") of Kenneth Koch, of the "New York school," that Koch's poetry is one "of irrelevance, intentionally so, to distinguish it from Ashbery's, which does not appear to be intentionally irrelevant. With Koch, I feel it's a conscious contrivance as a metaphor for disengagement from social commitment" (65). A poet, in order to write of the community, as did Whitman, Ignatow continued, must concern his work with the material of daily life and "the life which you carry around within you every day":

> I'm not saying that poetry has to be written as social commitment—hardly. But poets are living the way all of us live, eating and drinking and making love, and having families and working, so that for most poets the daily life must become the material. Not only the daily life but the life which you carry around within you every day. So it's both the internal and the external that must find themselves on the page. And this is the Whitman tradition. But that isn't the tradition which has gained prominence in the last ten years and been put forward as representative of American poetry at its best. (65)

That Ignatow's concern is related to the universe becomes the subject of the short poem "The Song" from *Figures of the Human* (1964). In this poem, the speaker writes of his daily life as it infuses the "internal" perception of the universe:

> The song is to emptiness.
> One may come and go
> without a ripple. You see it...
>   in a plane
> overhead, gone; man
> bowling or collecting coins,
> writing about it.

The celebration, or song of oneself, is to emptiness because the individual "may come and go / without a ripple," even, indicating his presence in the universe. The emptiness is of self, emptiness "among fish in the sea," or in any aspect of the physical world, including the emptiness in man's inclination to write poems about it. In this, the speaker of "The Song" is like Strand's, who is most alive when "emptied" ("I empty myself of my life and my life remains"). Yet, as Ralph

Mills posits in his article "Earth Hard," this poem "emphasizes more directly and definitely the absence of transcendental meanings for existence. The 'emptiness' to which the song is surrendered in the opening line Ignatow refers to elsewhere as 'the emptiness of consolation'.... As the poem implies, in the appearance and disappearance of creatures and things in the universe, in the activities of men, whether recreations, hobbies, or the writing of poetry, there is no further significance" (377). Whitman's idea of self-celebration is not enough. "How do we console ourselves in a world that can no longer be motivated by the ideals of the nineteenth century?" Ignatow wonders. "We haven't any ideals to speak of now and the spirituality is the sense of defeat. For us it's a defeat that forces us into a kind of humbleness," the humbleness of knowing that the puzzlement of contemporary society will not be solved by a better understanding of one's self, for the center of life in our time is not the self, but the community. The need for self-effacement, then, becomes more apparent: to allow a shift in focus from the self to the community. Ignatow admits in his *Notebooks* that he writes not to celebrate, but to escape himself:

> It is when I feel dread coming over me, dread of my existence, dread of myself in particular, when I become too much for myself, when a hole begins to form in me that is inviting me to fall in or a thickness gathers in me in which I fear I will suffocate as it spreads through me. I write to escape myself in this condition. I write to be distracted from myself that I begin to see is a nothing of huge proportions. (Qtd. in *New Naked Poetry* 112-13)

That his impetus to write poems derives from his self-view as "a nothing of huge proportions" informs his poetic voice, which, most appropriately, is of the self-effacing mode. Ignatow, or his poems' speaker, will continue suffering the dread of personal existence, it is my contention, until relieved by the act of writing a poem that is concerned with the community. In this way, Ignatow has escaped (or effaced himself) from the suffocating condition of the times when, as he says, "I become too much for myself," and he transforms from "a nothing of huge proportions" (that is, he effaces that state, or conception of that state, of selfhood) into a self of more worth. For Ignatow, that worth is earned not by poetry of irrelevance as practiced by the New York school ("It is an anomaly," he says, "since most of the poets who came to be representative of that 'school' were from out of town: Wisconsin, Minnesota, Oklahoma, Ohio..."), but by one of and for the community, and one's relationship to it.

Remarking on his poem "The Two Selves" (which we discussed in terms of the one self confronting the other, dark self—only to learn that there is nothing to be feared, that the darkness illuminates the conscious self), Ignatow, in an interview with Richard Jackson, speaks of the poet's relationship to the community:

> We have to serve society through ourselves. This is what the poet should do, however limited that service is in our present society. We define ourselves through others. So I don't personally have a sense of loss of identity. If I do question my identity, it is to question myself as a human being in relation to a tree, or the sea—it's to know myself as a human being, as a being in life, and to communicate that to others. In "The Two Selves," I meant the question in a physical sense—what was I before and after I was born? Did I ever know myself at the time of my birth? The poem... brings these things to the surface, to communicate them to others, to share our identity with others, to have a sense of community. (176)

One obvious way that Ignatow has "shared his identity with others"—besides through his poetry—was the publication of his journals (*Notebooks*). About thoughts expressed in them, he said in an interview with Alan Ziegler: "They're not so private. People tell me these are thoughts that they live with every day of their lives" (52). So in bringing "these things to the surface," and insofar as many in the community share these thoughts, perhaps Ignatow has succeeded in developing a sense of community. Important to any individual's conception of self-worth is the knowledge that he is not "a nothing of huge proportions," but equal to anyone else, and the sense that he belongs to the community, if only one limited to other poets or students of literature.

In "The Dream," from *Say Pardon* (1961), Ignatow's speaker—his personal self effaced from the poem—relates a horror of the city. In so doing, the speaker articulates a general fear of the community:

> Someone approaches to say his life is ruined
> and to fall down at your feet
> and pound his head upon the sidewalk.
> Blood spreads in a puddle.
> And you, in a weak voice, plead
> with those nearby for help;
> your life takes on his desperation.
> He keeps pounding his head....
> It is then you are awakened,
> the body gone, the blood washed from the ground,
> the stores lit up with their goods.

The speaker removes himself from the story of his own dream by addressing it in the second person "you," as if to suggest that his dream is common to anyone: "you" are in it, the speaker implies, not "I." That "someone," who in desperation pounds his head on the sidewalk, modulates with the "you" and further suggests the intention of commonality, which is more particularly emphasized by the shared experience of helplessness: No one nearby stops to help, and the "you" does not know how to render any aid. It is this shared despair—that the "you" understands the "someone's" desperation and that the "you" is the only passerby with enough sensitivity to want to help, but cannot—which warrants his life actually taking on the "someone's" desperation. The "you" of the poem bonds with the man pounding his head in the dream, and any person of a city can relate to the insecurity in the belief that no one would be willing to offer help—even to a man insanely bent on self-destruction in the grotesque manner depicted in "The Dream"—as well as relate to the dread of knowing that the morning after such an incident (as if it were a dream), the stores will light up once more, and the blood will have been washed from the ground. This evocation of horror of city life, ironically, makes "The Dream" a poem of the community. The use of the second person "you" invites the reader to relate to the dreamer in the poem (whereas an "I" can be regarded as a personal depiction of the poet, or the poem's speaker, the "you" opens the poem outward). "You," then, is a way of including the community in a poem about the way in which members of a community can (and often do) exclude one another by ignoring someone in desperate need of help.

It has been Ignatow's stated intention to efface himself, his personal voice, from his work in order to better serve the community with a poetry of everyone, for everyone. The result of such poetry, if successful, can be just as self-illuminating as Strand's or Simic's, however, in that the self would in effect be celebrated in the sense of its having realized its position in the community and its relationship to it. But, like Simic, Ignatow is not certain his theory is a viable one. In one of his more recently published poems (#63 from *Leaving the Door Open* [1984]—an inviting title, and one, possibly, suggestive of his skepticism)—his speaker states:

> I've wanted to write my way into paradise,
> leaving the door open for others too
> to walk in. Instead, I am scribbling
> beneath its walls, with the door shut....
>
> Friends, strangers and relatives look to me
> patiently or with sneers and amused tolerance,
> crowding around, waiting for the door to open

at my words, but all I can offer are these
questions, and they see me uneasy, seated
with my back against the wall,
my eyes closed to rest, to sleep,
to dream of paradise
we were to enter at my words.

Characteristic of the self-effacing poet, Ignatow leaves us "with the door open," with his speaker's ambivalence towards Ignatow's own poetic theories, an ambivalence more doubtful than hopeful: "to dream of paradise / we were to enter at my words." Just as Strand, who attained the ultimate self-effacement by composing poems "by somebody else," and Simic, who modified the seriousness of his rationale behind the theory of the mythic-unconscious self and the historic-conscious one (by comparing his speaker to "that unfortunate Mr. Poe: / Compulsive ratiocination on the subject of the self"), Ignatow seems to imply that any pretense of self-effacement for the advancement of the community (everyone "crowding around, waiting for the door to open / at my words") is absurd, that any voice must, finally, be personal ("my eyes closed to rest, to sleep, / to dream of paradise"), and that any subject must be, ultimately, the subject of self: "I am scribbling / beneath its walls, with the door shut."

For Ignatow, even though most definitely not intending any declaration of the unlikelihood of self-knowledge through the use of the self-effacing voice, this absurdity (that of leading us to believe he has been writing for us, "leaving the door open" for us to follow, when in fact, he has been "scribbling with the door shut") assures, if for none of the other reasons posited in the previous discussion of his theories and his work, that his poetry concerning the creation of a "paradise"—through which the community is served and consequently the self is defined by its place and relationship to it—will be read as personal poetry of the self-effacing mode.

IN HIS EARLIEST POETRY, before he adopted the persona mode of voice, John Berryman relied on the self-effacing mode to express his rather insecure notions regarding his love life (about which the journal entries—we read in chapter 2—reveal his despair over a "crumbling sex life"). Berryman's self-effacing speaker takes this form of voice because of his self-perception, one that could be the perspective of Ignatow's readers—if, of course, Ignatow's poetry is indeed celebratory of the community. That is to say, Berryman's speaker in "The Dispossessed" (the title poem from his *The Dispossessed* [1948]) has no self-conception other than that defined by whom he regards as his counterpart in an Italian opera he is watching. The poem's first four stanzas, quoted below, are all that is required to illustrate Berryman's self-effacing voice in this regard:

'and something that...that is theirs—no longer ours'
stammered to me the Italian page. A wood
seeded & towered suddenly. I understood.—

The Leading Man's especially, and the Juvenile Lead's,
and the Leading Lady's thigh that switches & warms,
and their grimaces, and their flying arms:

our arms, our story. Every seat was sold.
A crone met in a clearing sprouts a beard
and has a tirade. Not a word we heard.

Movement of stone within a woman's heart,
abrupt & dominant. They gesture how
things really are. Rarely a child sings now.

"The Leading Man's" self as portrayed for the audience, a self which has been prescribed by the composer (apparently unregarded by the self-effacing speaker) is demonstrative of the speaker's self, for the speaker actually has none of his own—he is dispossessed of knowledge of himself, in one sense of the title's meaning—and consequently adopts "The Leading Man's" as his own. In this way, he is Ignatow's ideal audience, or member of the community for which Ignatow intends his poems, in that Berryman's speaker has relied on art—has been waiting for it, apparently—to define not only himself, but his role in his relationship with the lady, just as Ignatow's "friends, strangers, relatives," he says, "look to me / patiently or with sneers / crowding around, waiting for the door to open / at my words." But they, like the voice which speaks for them, in having no other direction, no concept of their individual selves, are as self-effaced as the dispossessed speaker (who is dispossessed of self-conception) of Berryman's poem.

Robert Lowell, too, used the self-effacing voice to express a concern over his love life. He felt, apparently, that the confessional (or persona) mode would too nakedly reveal himself, his private self, in such an intimate experience as follows in his poems about sleeping with his wife. He first uses the confessional voice in "Man and Wife" and then uses the self-effacing in "'To Speak of Woe That Is in Marriage'" which were placed together in *Life Studies*. In the first, the confessional voice begins in the present, thinks back to an early date with his wife, then ends the poem again in the present:

Tamed by *Miltown,* we lie on Mother's bed...
At last the trees are green on Marlborough Street,
blossoms on our magnolia...
All night I've held your hand,
as if you had
a fourth time faced the kingdom of the mad...
you were in your twenties, and I...
outdrank the Rahvs in the heat
Of Greenwich Village, fainting at your feet—
too boiled and shy
and poker-faced to make a pass...

Now twelve years later, you turn your back.
Sleepless, you hold
your pillow to your hollows like a child;
your old-fashioned tirade—
loving, rapid, merciless—
breaks like the Atlantic Ocean on my head.

Lowell's biography can document some of the poem's details, and the narrative structure and sentence syntax ("All night I've held your hand")—common in the confessional "Memories of West Street and Lepke," for example—make a case for this poem being in the confessional mode. *Miltown* was the brand name of the tranquilizer prescribed to Lowell after one of his breakdowns through which his wife (then, Jean Stafford) patiently "nursed" him; she "faced the kingdom of the mad" only to turn her back on him in bed. The confessional voice relates how the speaker once, "heart in mouth," desired the woman whom he addresses in the poem but was too shy to make a pass, and now, "twelve years later," his desire for her again goes unsatisfied.

Here is Lowell on the same subject—the "old-fashioned tirade"—recast in the third person in "'To Speak of Woe That Is in Marriage'":

"The hot night makes us keep our bedroom windows open.
Our magnolia blossoms. Life begins to happen.
My hopped up husband drops his home disputes,
and hits the streets to cruise for prostitutes...
Oh the monotonous meanness of his lust...
It's the injustice...he is so unjust—
whiskey-blind, swaggering home at five.
My only thought is how to keep alive.
What makes him tick? Each night now I tie

ten dollars and his car key to my thigh....
Gored by the climacteric of his want,
he stalls above me like an elephant."

The speaker of this poem is the wife, who is offended because her husband "stalls"
and cannot satisfy her. He is "gored by the climacteric of his want"; he is unable to
perform sexually with his wife. (The physiological use of the term "climacteric" is
the period in one's life which marks a decrease in reproductive activity.) Therefore, the roles of the husband and wife in this poem have been reversed from their
roles in "Man and Wife"; the wife is now the one who wants some intimacy, even
if only an accidental caress of her thigh as her husband takes the money and car
key from her so that he can "hit the streets to cruise for prostitutes."

The entire poem is set in quotation marks as the monologue of the sole
speaker, the wife. In this way, in "'To Speak of Woe That Is in Marriage'" Lowell
has used the same subject and theme as he did in "Man and Wife" but he has effaced his own voice from it. The wife now observes the magnolia tree; the confessional voice of "Man and Wife" observed the blossoming of his tree on
Marlborough Street. She sees her husband as a "screwball" that "might kill his
wife, then take the pledge," but in "Man and Wife" the confessional voice thought
she lovingly "faced the kingdom of the mad" husband. The confessional voice of
"Man and Wife" has transformed into a self-effacing one because, in "'To Speak of
Woe That Is in Marriage,'" it expresses the confessional voice's thoughts, but not
from its own point of view; the personal voice is removed from "Woe," and the
wife-character, who is the narrator and voice of the poem, alone speaks. She is not
a persona for the first person speaker of "Man and Wife" because the husband
(the "Lowell" of the poem, since we have already accepted him as the confessional
voice of "Man and Wife") is her counterpart; they are two characters. Yet, having
read "Man and Wife," the speaker of "Woe" states the same theme as the confessional voice did in the former poem but in the absence of that voice—the personal voice has been effaced from "Woe."

And it is this mode, this use of the self-effacing voice, that is most common
in current practice, perhaps because—like Lowell who used it in "'To Speak of
Woe That Is in Marriage'" to cover the intimacy of the poem's subject—many poets in the 1990s prefer not to reveal their most private experiences in the more
personal confessional and persona modes, as will be discussed in the final chapter.

Five

 ∾

Personal Poetry in the 1990s

𝐼N CHAPTER 1, when reviewing the many plausible factors and influences relating to the appearance of personal poetry from 1959 to 1969, I indicated the apparent parallel between open form and the concern for self as the predominant subject of verse. It seemed poets increasingly wrote of the self as they relied less on traditional forms. Robert Bly has suggested that the political consciousness of the 1960s caused poets—in fact, most people—to become more self-involved, and so many thought they must enact some heroism in order to change society. Some poets accomplished this either by focusing the dramatic situation of the poem on the confessional speaker—so that, in this regard, poetry became more Romantic again—or by using that speaker as a voice of direction, one urging specific courses of action. Bly's own poetry of the time reflected both. He remarked: "It is as if in the sixties we kept looking at the dark side of the U.S. which pulled people into heroism and narcissism but in the seventies I looked at my own dark side" (qtd. in Baker 68). We can read this, perhaps, as a fair assessment of reasons for the "narcissistic" poetry of the 1960s and the resulting preponderance of the confessional voice. An "I" speaker in a poem which defines the poet's self would represent best that self as hero. As Bly turned from his 1960s heroic—or what he called "shamanistic"—role in "looking at the dark side of the U.S." to the more introspective examination of his "own dark side," his poetry contained more personal subjects such as his family and his biography, so that this self, as depicted in these poems of the confessional mode, became the (personal) hero of his verse.

Even though Bly has used the confessional voice more in his recent work such as the few newer pieces found in his 1992 collection of prose poems, *What Have I Ever Lost by Dying?* most of the poets of "the generation of 2000"—that is, those who will be between the ages of forty-five and sixty at this century's end, who, mostly therefore, would have had to establish themselves as poets in the 1970s, 1980s and early 1990s—have used it less, even sparingly, because they write primarily of subjects other than seemingly autobiographical experiences, although, of course, their subject matter may still derive in part from those experiences. Some of the poets of this generation have not merely abandoned their public "heroism"—as did Bly—in order to explore their individual "dark side," a more private heroism possibly. Rather, they have shunned personal poetry altogether, as though a narcissistic preoccupation and the heroic perception of the self can no longer provide a relevant basis for their present work. Whereas Bly regarded the investigation of his dark side as less narcissistic, perhaps some of the poets of the generation of 2000 feel that any subject devoted to the self—whether or not concerned with "heroism and narcissism"—must be now supplanted with topics more germane to the needs of their time, for the self as poetic subject is hardly the principal one it was a decade or so earlier.

The poets whom I distinguished in chapter 1 from those working with personal poetry, such poets as W. S. Merwin, John Ashbery, and James Merrill whose work is more imagistic and less informed by apparent autobiography or quotidian experience—although their poems sometimes use people, incidents, etc., from their personal history—are often intent on creating a lyrical expression, one more concerned, perhaps, with sound than with self. One result of such poetry is usually an indeterminate voice in the sense that it cannot be identified as that of a single person, or speaker, engaged in matters of self-identity or definition but rather as a separate entity (not as a means of personal inquiry in the way the self-effacing poets can use a "separate" voice). This is somewhat similar to the "omniscient" voice of prose fiction, a medium necessary for the act of conveying the images, the thematic messages—the *poem*—to the reader. Yet voice here is not regarded as a means of creating another self in verse. In such poetry, sound, metrical or metrically variable rhythms and cadence prevail over narrative accounts, for example, or most other characteristics we have seen common to personal poetry (in whichever mode). These poets are popular—especially among certain critical theorists, as I noted in the first chapter—and influential on some younger student-poets, who in graduate seminars might be taught by these critics. The influence of practicing an indeterminate voice also may be due in part to the wide distribution and easy availability of the method's practitioners' books. All of Ashbery's books are in print, for instance, but works of Weldon Kees and James Wright even are hard to find.

It is difficult to assess the extent of these influences on those still writing personal poetry currently, yet ever more within the last decade or so, many younger poets have become occupied once again with meter, sound, internal and end-line rhymes, assonance, and traditional prosodic forms. And most literary magazines today include several highly controlled free verse poems of regular stanzaic pattern—say, three stanzas of equal line-length to a poem (but usually not much more since these magazines seem hesitant to publish longish poems). However, just as the movement away from the New Critical objectivity and traditional forms towards the subjective self did not wholly exclude some use of the elements of prosody (meter, rhyme, classical allusions, etc., which we saw, for example, in Lowell's and Wright's personal poetry), the penchant now for more traditionally formal elements of meter, sound, and rhyme does not imply necessarily the complete abandonment of self as a matter of poetic discourse or subject, although it seems that the trend is towards the less personal.

Referring to many poets who were active in 1969, Mark Strand told us in chapter 1 that they "have made...a lifetime's work of the self, a self defined usually by circumstances that would tend to set it apart." In an interview with Cristina Bacchilega in 1981, Strand indicated that he believed those remarks were still applicable to many poets currently writing:

> I don't know where American poetry is going. I think it's impossible for anyone to say with any assurance where it's going. The things that I pointed out in 1969 probably still apply. That is, much American poetry is still self-involved, so to speak. Also, translation is a factor in many poets' work; they are influenced as much by foreign poets as they are by those who write in English.
>
> I think that there is, perhaps, a greater concern for forms and measures—at least, I notice this with my students. Perhaps we will have a period with a lot of rhymed and measured verse: the fifties revisited, that is the academic side of the fifties' poetry. This is not to say that in our age we'll see an Alexander Pope or a John Dryden; but, we have James Merrill. We may have little James Merrills. I don't know. (51)

Yet the self can continue to be represented in personal poetry even if written in imitation of Merrill's forms, of course, as Merrill himself has proven. And, as Strand said, although we cannot be certain of this poetry's future, personal poets remain active at the present, regardless of their use of more formal sound elements and their continuing arguments over the extensive use of self as subject. Personal poetry is, in fact, a viable and even favorite aesthetic choice of poets just starting out.

In chapter 1, we learned that a few years after personal poetry's wide acceptance over the—what Strand called—"terrific resurgence of formalist poetry in the fifties," poets began disagreeing over what best constituted subjects of self, or whether the self should be the primary focus of poetry at all. In 1973, Louis Simpson remarked of personal poetry that:

> ... [A] lot of it is confessional. A lot of it is just referential. Confession implies some emotional outpouring, but in many poems today there is only conversation. The man sits down and writes a poem that says, "You know, there's a war, I feel terrible, other people feel terrible, I'm calling up my friend and we're going to meet and have a little conversation." That's not a confessional poem; it's just a poem about daily, ordinary life, what he does every day. To me, this is kind of a pointless poetry. There's been a lot of it and it's not getting anywhere. (36)

Because the "ordinary life" of so many poets today is teaching, writing poems, and traveling the country reading them, the subjects of their personal poems reflect just that. "Out on the Circuit," one poem of many about the poet's life in academia in *The Collected Poems of George Garrett* (1984), provides us with a typical example:

> ... I was here, wherever I am,
> to read poems and to talk about poetry with students
> and my head is a booming buzzing ache of words,
> words, words, my own and other people's, said and unsaid.
> We wear the order of the laminated cliché like a convention badge....
> Willing to flash the latest clichés like expensive cuff links.
> Rich now in my coat of many colors, the reassuring check fitting
>   comfortable and heavy like a gun in a holster,
> I raise my glass to share a toast with the stranger in the mirror,
> to rejoice together in the inexhaustible resources
>   of self-deception....

In spite of all that the speaker of Garrett's poem dislikes, however, he remains a part of the "circuit," and collects his check—at the expense of hypocrisy, "self-deception," as the poem's last lines tell us. If the poet does not stay on the circuit, maybe he will lose the principal basis of his subject matter, as Simpson might argue.

BRUCE WEIGL

THE DISAGREEMENTS OVER THE nature and extent of self as subject, which were reflected in part by Simpson's 1973 remarks, have continued to the present, including the following polemical stance taken by Bruce Weigl in his 1984 review of Jonathan Holden's *Leverage*, a book of personal poetry:

> For a poet, relying too heavily upon autobiographical detail, structure, content, or strategy can be a dangerous thing. Such dependence can lull the writer into focusing too much attention on being true to actuality and not enough attention on the poem itself: on the language and on the possibilities of surprise that should always accompany the act of writing poems. Of course, this is especially deadly when the life being literally rendered doesn't happen to be particularly interesting. (113)

Weigl here reiterates Lowell's philosophy of (confessional) poetic composition—and betrays, presumably, his own. Lowell often emphasized that his personal experiences had to be worked into art, but that an essential nexus remained between the elements of his craft and his autobiography, as he told A. Alvarez in 1963: "...the thing was the joy of composition, to get some music and imagination and form into [my personal 'outpourings'] and to know just when to stop and what sort of language to put in..." (190). So too does Weigl primarily base his personal poetry on the seemingly autobiographical experiences of his boyhood and in the Vietnam war, neither of which is uninteresting, as seen in poems from his latest books, *The Monkey Wars* (1985), *Song of Napalm* (1988), and *What Saves Us* (1992).

Ultimately—as we have seen that poems of the confessional mode must do—the tone of Weigl's speaker combined with the veracity of the experience depicted in these poems will determine their confessionalism. The confessional speaker of the following poem, "Girl at the Chu Lai Laundry," records a moment in the Vietnam war when "the world stops / turning":

> All this time I had forgotten.
> My miserable platoon was moving out
> One day in the war and I had my clothes in the laundry.
> I ran the two dirt miles,
> Convoy already forming behind me. I hit
> The block of small hooches and saw her
> Twist out the black rope of her hair in the sun.

> She did not look up at me,
> Not even when I called to her for my clothes.
> She said I couldn't have them,
> They were wet...
> Who would've thought the world stops
> Turning in the war, the tropical heat like hate
> And your platoon moves out without you,
> Your wet clothes piled
> At the feet of the girl at the laundry,
> Beautiful with her facts.

The speaker evokes the Eliotic allusion (from "The Waste Land") of the woman holding out her black hair as if a rope, yet unlike Eliot—who saw the woman's hair stretched into a violin—Weigl's speaker, just like the girl at the laundry, relates simply the facts, and uses a strong narrative line and confessional voice to do so. He is surprised that his world can stop "turning in the war" the moment he is refused his still wet clothes from the laundry—while his platoon moves out leaving him behind, the laundry girl "beautiful with her facts." This poem (and others in *Song of Napalm*) also suggests Auden's great sentiment expressed in "Musée des Beaux Arts": that suffering "takes place / While someone else is eating or opening a window or just walking dully along." Children eat and talk, the laundry obliges its rules, even as war continues.

Weigl uses the confessional mode throughout much of his work, sometimes in poems that are proselike reminiscences of the speaker's boyhood, such as "1955" from *The Monkey Wars*, the first stanza of which follows:

> After mass father rinsed the chalice with wine
> Again and again.
> Drunk before noon
> He'd sleep it off in the sacristy
> While the other altar boys and I
> Rummaged through the sacred things, feeling up
> The blessed linen and silk vestments,
> Swinging the censer above us so it whistled.
> We put our hands on everything we could reach
> Then woke the father for mass.

The poem then ends with the speaker, who as an adult, recalls a spiritual experience: "I don't know why my hands should shake, / I'm only remembering something."

And the poem "Song of Napalm," bearing the inscription "for my wife," blends the confessional speaker's remembering a napalm attack in Vietnam with a domestic scene, set in the present, of the speaker at home with his wife:

> After the storm, after the rain stopped pounding,
> We stood in the doorway watching horses
> Walk off lazily across the pasture's hill.
> We stared through the black screen...
> Trees scraped their voices into the wind, branches
> Criss-crossed the sky like barbed wire
> But you said they were only branches....
>
> Still I close my eyes and see the girl
> Running from her village, napalm
> Stuck to her dress like jelly...
>
>   the girl runs only as far
> As the napalm allows
> Until her burning tendons and crackling
> Muscles draw her up
> Into that final position
> Burning bodies so perfectly assume. Nothing
> Can change that; she is burned behind my eyes...

Weigl's poems should suggest to us that many of the elements of the confessional mode of voice as practiced by his older contemporaries (Lowell and the later work of James Wright and Bly)—preceding him by a generation—are continuing through the mid-1990s. These elements include: simple, rather than decorative, diction (what Wright referred to as "the pure, clear word"), a reliance on narrative and complete, prosaic sentences—although a poem may break its lines at points not comprising a complete sentence—and, of course, the semblance of autobiography, all of which Weigl combines (as Lowell remarked of his *Life Studies* poems) to "get some music and imagination and form" into his personal "outpourings."

GARRETT HONGO

Other younger poets who continue to employ the confessional mode of voice, however, do not necessarily write such proselike lines as Weigl does. These poets are, as suggested earlier, more concerned with sound and rhythms. Garrett Hongo, for example, has used in his two books—*Yellow Light* (1982) and *The River of Heaven* (1987)—the confessional voice in many poems that are less narrative and more reliant on images than are Weigl's poems. Perhaps, too, they are more given to sound. The principal concerns of *Yellow Light*, a book of carefully ordered poems, are: the discovery of the history of the Issei (the first generation of Japanese immigrants to America), the forging of myths regarding the Issei and succeeding families, and the ethnicity peculiar to the poet's ancestral beginning. Structured in five movements, the poems' central speaker travels through his home neighborhoods, Japan, and America's western region. Engaged in searches that lead to the creation of myths and the recreation of ancient ones, these poems ultimately record the process by which the speaker learns to understand the importance of the immediate.

"Yellow Light," the opening poem, takes us to inner-city Los Angeles, the setting for the book's first movement, where a woman with groceries passes "gangs of schoolboys playing war" on her way home to cook dinner. This is what she sees:

> From the Miracle Mile, whole freeways away,
> a brilliant fluorescence breaks out
> and makes war with the dim squares
> of yellow kitchen light winking on
> in all the side streets of the Barrio....
> The moon then, cruising from behind
> a screen of eucalyptus across the street,
> covers everything, everything in sight,
> in a heavy light like yellow onions.

The combination of lyrical description with the narrative is representative of Hongo's technique. The plain language and unsheathed images contain, within the control of the voice, the emotions this scene evokes for the speaker remembering his mother's daily routine. Given the book's purpose of scheme, it is appropriate that the poems of this first movement address the speaker's early life and condition of home.

The subject of the nine-section poem "Cruising 99," marking the second movement of the book, is a pilgrimage toward the uncovering of the possibility for mythmaking. The voice, now detached from the personal memories of home and family, is relaxed, sometimes playful (as in "A Samba for Inada"), and is, finally, a voice seemingly of wonder, one caught in discovery. The poem begins with a "porphyry of elements," an "aggregate of experiences" of the speaker and two friends joy riding down the two-lane Highway 99. This porphyry (literally, a rock containing the minerals of two generations) comes to signify the primary theme of a collection of poems that, in subject and craft, embodies differing elements of the old and present-day Orient.

In the section "On the Road to Paradise," the fourth part of "Cruising 99," the speaker suggests that he will be wishing continually for "paradise" because his conception of it must somehow include "landscapes / in brocades, mist, wine, and moonlight," like a poem by Tu Fu, all conjuring mystery and all missing from Highway 99 *en route* through the desert:

> I wish this road would turn or bend,
> intersect with a spy movie, some Spanish galleon,
> or maybe a Chinese poem with landscapes
> in brocade, mist, wine, and moonlight.
> The California moon is yellow most of the time,
> like it was stained with nicotine,
> or sealed in amber like an insect.
> Why is it always better somewhere else?
> Why do I always wish I were Tu Fu?

Like the soft moonlight, paradise is elusive. By chance, the travellers meet an old hermit who tells them that his "desire to escape" is overwhelming. Dressed as the scarecrow in a *kimono* which the speaker and his companions encountered earlier, the hermit longs to:

> shout in unison with thunder
> roar with the assurance of Santana wind,
> leap out of these bonds of copper and steel,
> slough off this skin of cement,
> and walk south or north or even west
> into the weather and the sea.

His desire to transcend the restrictions of place and past can be read metaphorically as the speaker's yearning to create poetic landscapes, mystery, and myth from the barrenness of the desert.

Although the actual journey leads nowhere, a commitment to the creation of myth is born. The book's third movement, then, takes the speaker to Japan, the origin of his personal history, to begin his search to recover, expiate, create, mythify, and learn why the past acts as a "skin of cement." As the conclusion of "Postcards for Bert Meyers," a prayer is proposed for the restoration of a heritage, as it was at an earlier time, uncorrupted by history and migration:

Tomorrow to Ise,
to the shrines where my family
has not made pilgrimage
for more than a hundred years.
I'll toss a copper *yen*-piece,
clap twice and bow,
call on the land's most terrible god
to give us back our name.

Yet in the next poem, another part of the speaker's culture is treated less seriously. A Japanese dinner is described with savor and it holds a peculiar importance for him that cannot be shared:

Can your foreigner's nose smell mullets
roasting in a glaze of brown bean paste
and sprinkled with novas of sea salt?...

Who among you knows the essence
of garlic and black lotus root,
of red and green peppers sizzling
among squads of oysters in the skillet,
of crushed ginger, fresh green onions,
and pale-blue rice wine simmering
in the stomach of a big red fish?

Coming in a sequence of poems about the significance of the speaker's experience in Japan, these lines suddenly change the tone of the book's middle movement. At a point where Hongo easily can begin to sentimentalize (as Lowell's confessional verse is often accused of doing) the older world's culture, or to state a bitterness towards an America for failing to embrace this culture in order to enrich its own, or to lament the loss of the past, he evaluates the beauty of a sensual pleasure with grace and with an aggressive, yet tonally light, voice.

Japan has given the speaker, now back in America, a base from which he can confront the meaning of his life in relation to his cultural origin, one of the subjects of the fourth movement of the book. In the poem "Roots," the resolution of self and past is equated to a spiritual enlightenment:

One day soon, the old man and I
will go off together toward the Sierra,
squat on the brow of a sculptured hill,
tip the cup of sky to our lips,
drink a *sake* of cactus juice,

and wait for the moon to rise
over the salt flats near Manzanar....

When I pace the seven steps of the shrine in my soul,
the old man of my dreams will be me,
leaning into the wind blowing off the Mojave,
over Sierra passes and stands of sequoia,
circling around L.A. to spin out past Catalina
across the Pacific all the way to Asia,
and heritage will be an ancient flute
throbbing from its place in my heart
where his heart has found its roots.

Far from the discolored moon "stained with nicotine" that repulses the speaker of "Cruising 99," the desert moon, rising "over the salt flats near Manzanar," is now seen with a beauty befitting a Chinese landscape in a Tu Fu poem. The porphyry, the blending of the old man with the speaker, emerges, and the poem ends in a comforting peace, somewhat closer to "paradise."

Myths for the present, arising from the past, must be written, as called for in the long poem "Stepchild." Interspersed with passages by Carlos Bulosan and others regarding the history of Japanese immigrants, the speaker asks:

Where are the myths, the tales?...

They are with the poets,
the scholar transcribing
talks with survivors,
the masters of the stage,
the novelists collecting cosmologies...

The task defined, the speaker meets his responsibility in the last movement by creating stories about his childhood, the memories being summoned by looking at a photograph ("The Hongo Store 29 Miles Volcano Hilo, Hawaii"), about a failed labor strike attempt, written in haiku ("C&H Sugar Strike Kahuku, 1923"), about old men and friends ("Kubota" and "And Your Soul Shall Dance"), and, finally, about coming to peace with the history of personal experience and circumstance ("Something Whispered in the *Shakuhachi*"), a poem in which the speaker, a gardener of the past, states that he can, "when it's bad now,"

sustain the one thicket
of memory that calls for me
to come and sit

among the tall canes
and shape full-throated songs
out of wind, out of bamboo,
out of a voice
that only whispers.

Hongo utilizes the confessional voice as a means of personal discovery, much as Lowell did in *Life Studies*. The blending of the old man and the younger speaker (this "porphyry") is part of such a discovery.

Jim Barnes

THE POET JIM BARNES recently has extended the confessional mode to formulate something of a communal voice, one that retains its basis in the personal self while speaking from a generational viewpoint as well. Barnes has composed in his newest book of poetry, *The Sawdust War* (1992), a spiritual chronicle of his generation: the generation which lived through World War II but was much too young to understand fully that war's magnitude and terror. Neither combatants nor noncombatants, they stayed at home and played at fighting the world war which was far away in foreign countries across the oceans. Newsreels at the movie houses and nightly radio reports were as close as most children got. Their theater of war was the sandbox; theirs was "The Sawdust War," the highly glamorized news of the real war acting as the melodramatic prototype for their games. Barnes's book, then, divided into four sections, takes this childhood field of play as the provenance of his generation's collective conscience and explores its development through subsequent arenas, physical and metaphysical. This conscience, centering on loss, pervaded all that was to follow for The Sawdust War Generation: economic successes, social privileges, and political freedoms of the Cold War America they inherited. They were to accept this endowment with the belief that it was not really deserved, and they were to doubt their self-worth.

The title poem which opens the book is a remembrance of the confessional speaker's enacting the war in a large sawdust pile: "Digging down the dust, I began to reshape the world / I hardly knew: the crumbly terrain became / theaters of the war. I was barely ten." This sawdust war theater begins to smolder, which drama brings a disturbing authenticity to the child's play and concludes it with a near epiphany:

I could not see the fire: it climbed from deep
within. No matter how I dug or shifted dust,
I could not find the source. My captured ground

nightly sank into itself. The gray smoke
hovered like owls under the slow stillness
of stars, until one night I woke to see,
at the center, a circle of smoldering sparks
turning to flame, ash spreading outward and down.
All night the pile glowed red, and I grew ashamed
for some fierce reason I could not then name.

Although the ten-year-old boy could not then articulate his shame—which feeling resulted from his glimmering sense of the real war's purpose, its destructive permanence—he understands something about loss, something about guilt for his desiring the gaining of "good ground against the Axis," the fire now illuminating, perhaps, the foreign "enemy" as human beings. The sawdust pile burning from within can be read on a figurative level as the boy's social conscience having been ignited, if not inflamed, rendering his war play no longer pristine.

"The Cabin on Nanny Ridge," a poem about the war's constant presence in the minds of the children, is another remembrance, the adult speaker reflecting back on his helping to build a playhouse cabin:

Time
backed for us: we sang Cherokee
and Choctaw hymns, thatched the roof more

with words than with limbs and needles from
the pines. We were innocent of all
that we surveyed. The world at war
was far enough away no bombs
that they told us fell could fall....

Forty years have grayed the glyphs,
and of the cabin nothing remains
but worms and a slow memory
of days we thought would never end—
before other wars changed our lives.

The "world at war" in the veiled background of those youths "innocent of all [they] surveyed" suggests both the war's immediacy and timelessness, its effects indirect, influential, and indelible—if not always causally linked to the war. That the children sang Cherokee and Choctaw hymns as they worked reminds the speaker how ephemeral *and* continuous one's heritage can be, a heritage inclusive of the great Native American tradition, of "slow memory," and of living out childhood in a country engaged in a foreign war. There is a tension betrayed in the

final line; they were to experience forty years of other cultural, personal, and political "wars" which not only naturally curtailed these innocent days at Nanny
Ridge, but subdued even the memory of them.

The fearful uncertainty engendered by the war—by the horrors of Hitler in
particular—is reflected by the doubtful, worrisome tone in "On Hearing the
News That Hitler Was Dead," which leaves the speaker with an ominous "starless
night" to direct the future:

> The commentator's words on Hitler's death left
> us puzzled about the course of the war. A gift
>
> of light was what we children waited for.
> In the falling night we heard the far-off yowl
> of wild cats in the woods, or thought we did.
> The news leapt into the dark, wondering how
> the master race so-called could master now
>
> with Der Führer dead and the Russians drunk
> on German schnapps. But what if he were not
> the ashes they said were his? someone asked.
> Silence and sound grew thick. Outside, lamplight
> stumbled and fell into a starless night.

The intentional irregularity of the iambic pentameter lines and the subtle
deflection of end-rhymes in each stanza render a calming mood while betraying a
rage just barely held in control. The unsteady accentual rises and the rhymes,
both exact and slanted, cannot mask the panic and dread of the future in the
minds of both children and adults. The children wanted to hear their parents' as-
surance that Hitler was dead, the terror over. Their initial joy—what might have
been the long-awaited "gift of light"—at once yielded to the frightening possibility of Hitler's survival. Like the black panther which earlier in the evening was
trapped momentarily under the porch and which survived a shotgun blast before
fleeing into the dark woods ("In the falling night we heard the far-off yowl / of
wild cats in the woods, or thought we did"), Hitler—so it was feared—might be
alive still, leaving the children especially without certitude, without the light they
had been waiting for, the light signalling that the monster was dead, that they all
were safe. Instead, there is a darkness to appall, to carry with them into adulthood
and to temper their relationship to the land they inhabit and their understanding
of their place in history—as explored in the second section of this well-planned
book.

Entitled "After the Great Plains," this section reveals themes of nullity, absence, and loss as The Sawdust War Generation enters mature adulthood. Experience can teach an appreciation of an ambivalent beauty arising from such desolation as reflected by the landscape of the Great Plains. "Nothing remains the same in this long land," begins the poem "After the Great Plains," a line suggestive of Heraclitus's perception of the river: that of a continual flux while appearing to be constant, a simple truth applicable to life as well as land. The poem concludes with a stanza remarkable for its restraint, the speaker here understanding the importance of his awareness:

> After the Great Plains you are not the same.
> No matter which way you cross something stays
> firmly with you, a sense hard to name, like
> a pebble in the toe of your boot you can't shake
> out in this life.

Encounters with this land change the speaker, each experience with it remaining part of his life, persistent and unpleasant. The poem is a declaration, too, of his knowing—perhaps for the first time—that wisdom and age are earned responsibilities, that the past which makes one wise is an irritating, if not debilitating, burden. The land may endure, may be a constancy in his lifetime and provide solace, but it changes as the speaker's perception of it enlarges, and it thereby changes the speaker in turn.

This duality inherent to maturity, that with experience often comes the recognition of an undeniable and unforgettable pain, is the subject of the tension in "Soliloquy in My Forty-seventh Year," the central poem of the book's third section, called "Elegies for John Berryman and Others," a group of poems elegiac of the mutable land, of the loss of the innocent self, and of the present age. The speaker's soliloquy occurs in early morning at the time of year when winter just gives way to spring. It is a time for an inventory of his life, of life itself, leading to a resolution stated in the poem's last stanza:

> I shall not walk softly to atone,
> nor in anger move my own, but shall kneel
> now on this bare side of hill
> and kiss the dust
> and touch the stone
> leavings of dropped stars, turds, the spiel
> spider and grass, and sing clear and swill
> the late life come dumb into my trust.

The speaker is neither repentant nor angry, but firm in his decision to embrace this "late life come dumb into [his] trust." He chooses regeneration, chooses to be like the vernal world he inhabits and defines, over living the rest of his life in regret and lamentation for what he has done or failed to do. Here is a declaration of love for his age and circumstance, and a seizure of power of voice: to "sing clear and swill / the late life come dumb into my trust." In many ways, this line bespeaks the principal role of the poet, who is entrusted with speaking for the "dumb."

This view of life and purpose contrasts dramatically with that of the speaker's older contemporaries, John Berryman and others of "The Tragic Age" of American poets treated or mentioned throughout this study—poets such as Robert Lowell, Delmore Schwartz, Randall Jarrell, and Theodore Roethke among others. The poet-speaker of "Soliloquy in My Forty-seventh Year" would have found it easy to regard Berryman as something of a role model since both were raised in the same Oklahoma county. But, as the speaker "tells" Berryman in the elegy to him (from "Elegies to John Berryman"):

> Never knew you till you died.
> Shame on me. Pittsburgh County
> coal kept me black
> & pure.
>
> Didn't know a poet could be born
> in such a dirty town
> noted only for cheap coal
> & Italians who cooked
> cats in their spaghetti.
>
> Till you died. Never knew you
> cursed my native ground....
>
> They still dig coal in McAlester...
>
> They all knew your old man
> but thought you died in battle
> a long time ago.

The two men took startlingly divergent approaches to their poetry, their past and future. Berryman rejected his origins and tried to suppress them as he created another self in his poetry, much of it confessional outpouring in an attempt to reconcile the authentic self with the skilfully crafted persona of that self, as we saw in chapter 3. Berryman ended his life, as did his father, by suicide.

The speaker of *The Sawdust War*, however, cannot forget the past, and he makes it useful by drawing from it sustaining and emotionally moving memories from which to create his poems. He understands well his personal history and how he has yielded to the natural flow of time while retaining something of his unique centeredness, thereby altering, however slightly, the course of this inevitable flow of historical progression. In this, the speaker is an heir to the young Eliot of "Tradition and the Individual Talent." Yet he accepts the personal element of poetry—not the "impersonal theory" extolled by Eliot—without allowing it to become exclusive or private communiqués, keeping one eye on the public to gauge reaction as did Berryman. Instead, the poet-speaker's individual experience includes that of his generation; his personal voice becomes a trusted communal one. The conflation of the private and the public, transforming the expression of the "I" to mean "we," is reminiscent of the Robert Lowell of *For the Union Dead*, whose heir Barnes's speaker more rightfully is.

The final section of the book is set in Italy, where the speaker has travelled on a fellowship. A decade after his "Soliloquy," he finds himself pretty well satisfied, in "paradisal Bellagio" enjoying his earned stature as a poet, this fellowship a reward for the poems rent from a lifelong struggle with his heritage. The long poem at the heart of this section, "In Another Country: A Suite for the Villa Serbelloni," probes the speaker's relationship with his newly beloved Italy, one of the feared Axis countries he "warred" against in youth. The poem begins with a tour guide speaking: "Villa Carlotta where Mussolini died," but then says nothing more about it. The poem's speaker, though, tells us a more complete history of Mussolini's death:

> *Il Duce* lied
> to them in Rome and ran for the villa
> and fascist friends, ran to merchants in silk,
> lords who promised him Switzerland. You fight
>
> the urge to strangle the guide and make him get
> facts right.

It is significant that the speaker sees himself in the second person "you," for he is distanced from the immediate self, that self who is the personal speaker and often the subject of his poems—which brought him to Italy. This personal self knows the facts, and he has been trying to make sense of them in poetry. He comes to doubt even this, his own art, while surrounded by "the ghosts" of the great Italian artists:

How hard it is to write, even though you might
enjoy a fellowship, with the ghosts of bored

artists hovering about this pavilion.
We would like to reach the absolute in art,
the meaning behind the flowers and the stones,

a labyrinth that nearly takes our own
concept of paradise away with the riot
of rhododendrons and Dante's face grown

soft with love. Here in the Melzi Gardens
we look for the light that will let our words go on.
                                ("In the Melzi Gardens")

    The speaker has the artistic integrity to assess honestly his—and his con-temporaries'—capacity for "reaching the absolute in art," as Dante did, discover-ing and portraying the natural, the human pulses which make art everlasting and which help us to endure. "Here in the Melzi Gardens / we look for the light that will let our words go on." The collective voice, the "we," is now used openly, com-plementing the entire book's movement from the temporal and personal to the universal and communal. The "light" of certainty sought when a child on the night Hitler was reported dead now becomes the "light" of artistic truth sought when a mature poet.

    The Sawdust War does not present the speaker consciously questing for en-lightenment, yet the book does move steadily from uncertainty to a satisfying, if momentary, fulfillment, from a midwest America offering the speaker counter-vailing sources of pride, doubt, and shame to "another country," an Italy which has learned to incorporate the past—including World War II specifically which is still, a half century later, brought up daily in conversation—in order to strengthen the present and help look optimistically towards the future.

    Despite Barnes's deft use of allusions to John Berryman to place his speaker's perspective in a generational context, his use of voice does not of course constitute one of the persona mode, which has been used only occasionally in the 1980s and 1990s to date. While the occurrence through the early 1990s of the use of the confessional mode is evident, neither the persona nor the self-effacing mode has been much used of late. Some poets may prefer to think that their personal "I" is persona enough. That is, they often will disclaim any direct relationship be-tween their "I"s and authentic selves, and few would now remark, as Lowell did, that the "I" stands for the poet or the poet's self as defined by the poem. George

Garrett probably would insist that the first person speaker of "Out on the Circuit"—despite that poem's being in the confessional mode—is a persona, not to be associated necessarily with himself. But this is not the persona voice, in any of its uses, as practiced by Berryman, Kees, and Kinnell that we discussed in chapter 3.

FRANK GRAZIANO

ALTHOUGH THE SELF-EFFACING VOICE has not been used extensively by younger poets, Strand, Simic, and Ignatow, because they are still writing sometimes in this mode, ensure that it continues today. One book published within the last decade, *In Memory of Michael Morgan* (1986) by Frank Graziano, does not concern itself so much with the alien self's relationship to contemporary society as does the work of this mode we examined in the previous chapter, but it does take from Strand some elements, such as employing other writers' works as its own, relying on these selections—not so much for content—as its basis. In this regard, *In Memory of Michael Morgan* is of the self-effacing mode, in the manner that Strand's "Leopardi" is, because the quasi-narrative is that of an actual crime committed in South Carolina, and the allusions and images accompanying that narrative are taken from other works. (Strand took Leopardi's narrative, but set it in his contemporary circumstance, and interjected his wife's name into the poem, etc.) Graziano's is an interesting book to use as a representation of the current form of the self-effacing mode because it combines several of the sound techniques common to younger poets (which should be apparent in some of the selections I will quote) with the personal—but only peripherally—subject matter.

The structure of this book-length poem is informed by the modernist pastiche. Yet whereas Eliot, Pound, Joyce (and the many others) had serious intentions for incorporating what Eliot called, in "Tradition and the Individual Talent," the "whole of the literature of Europe from Homer" into their own verse and prose fiction, making some of that literature a part of their own, and desiring such pastiche to result in, as Eliot said, a "traditional" work (that is, one created by an author who is "aware that the mind of Europe—the mind of his own country, a mind which he learns in time to be much more important than his own private mind—is a mind which changes, and that this change is a development which abandons nothing *en route*, which does not superannuate either Shakespeare, or Homer..."), Graziano, rather, here gives us a pastiche closer to that of its more comic, or tragicomic, uses as practiced by a French school of painters who were consciously imitating—usually in order to mock—the paintings of other, older artists. To such imitative work the term "pastiche" was applied. That *In Memory of Michael Morgan* alludes to, paraphrases passages and employs lines—syntactically altered or verbatim—from a few acknowledged modern "classics"—thus comprising an extension of Eliot's diffuse list: European literature "and within it the whole of the literature of [an author's] own country..."— including Eliot's own "Ash Wednesday," the poetry of Robert Penn Warren (as the dust cover informs us) and others, such as lines from Yeats, images and themes from "The Waste Land" (although Graziano does not openly admit that these are also part of his poem, he furtively interlaces them with the other elements of his pastiche, losing these allusions, almost, in the horror evoked by the narrative, which includes an arbitrary act of murder), the poem is a modernist pastiche, one using works of literature—mostly modern, but the Old Testament is used as well—to help explain the frightening, perhaps pathological, behavior of Michael Morgan, a murderer and subsequent suicide.

Graziano, however—and in this he differs from the modernists, the followers of Eliot's "mythic method"—implies that these contemporary classics are only minimally relevant to Morgan's life, his confused consciousness, and that any "method" suggesting parallels between the myths contained in this literature and Morgan (who is a contemporary man) results in the comically absurd, which is, Graziano seems to suggest, an appropriate response to our time, to our culture (including literature, religion) and society that can do nothing to prevent or explain Morgan's crimes. Literature reflects Morgan's behavior; he actually can do little that has not been written about already, so literature is prescient in this regard. That is, the primary work Graziano uses in his pastiche is *I, Pierre Rivière*, a memoir written by Rivière, who in nineteenth-century France murdered his mother—who was then six months pregnant—his sister, and brother in order to relieve his father of what Rivière saw as the burdening pressures, the financial hardship, of raising a family. At one point in Graziano's poem, Morgan, barely conscious while choking from the blanket used as a rope in a failed suicide attempt, thinks of Pierre Rivière, but quickly adds: "[T]hat was odd; who was Pierre?" (9). This is our first indication of "authorial intrusion" in the sense that Morgan is capable of such an allusion to Rivière—to Eliot *et alii* in the ensuing pages—only insofar as Graziano, or more appropriately, the voice of the poem allows. This voice, not Morgan, makes the parallels between history and myth, between fantasy and fact, between the incidents described in *In Memory of Michael Morgan* and selected works of the "whole of the literature." Because *I, Pierre Rivière*, written in jail at the judge's request, clarifies the narrative of *In Memory of Michael Morgan*, it will be useful to analyze that work as it relates to Graziano's poem.

Rivière had read widely in religion and philosophy, and told an interrogating officer that his reading of Deuteronomy and Numbers provided him the necessary justification for committing parricide: to serve his father, he felt so directed, because his mother, sister, and brother were, he said, "in league to persecute my father." He wrote in his memoir:

> I wholly forgot the principle which should have made me respect my mother and my sister and my brother, I regarded my father as being in the power of mad dogs or barbarians against whom I must take up arms, religion forbade such things, but I disregarded its rules, it even seemed to me that God had destined me for this and that I would be executing his justice. I knew the rules of ordered society, but I deemed myself wiser than they, I regarded them as ignoble and shameful. I had read in Roman history, and I had found that the Romans' laws gave the husband the right of life and death over his wife and his children.

Rivière, then, is well chosen in reflecting Morgan: Rivière's reading failed to instill in him any intended moral teachings; instead he selected certain passages and construed them to match his sense of justice and duty. Morgan, following the Christian principle of losing oneself (the old self dies; a new, spiritual self is born), understands the "death" of one's self to be literal: "When he pushed *I have to die* down into the black water of old hope it bobbed up *He has to die...*" (20), and he murders an old man, a complete stranger, believing this man to be, somehow, that other self which must die. Both Rivière and Morgan distort what they read, yet both regard the Bible as it was intended: a code of conduct one should obey. The two men extrapolate highly individualistic and bizarre codes from it, however, of which Morgan's will become more evident in the following analysis of *In Memory of Michael Morgan*.

The poem begins on Good Friday (the title for the book's first section), the day in Christian history when Jesus was crucified—in service to his father—and on which day is the poem's setting for Morgan's suicide attempt because "he did not turn / to hope, because he did not hope," lines in derision of Eliot's poem declaring his faith—his hope—manifest by his conversion to Anglo-Catholicism. ("Ash Wednesday" marks the beginning of lent, forty days of penance in spiritual preparation for Easter.) We are told that Morgan no longer turns to hope, and so turns to suicide, because of his past, which includes:

> having crushed a sparrow
> between broken stones...
> because he enceepharatinged seven toads... (4)

This, within the first ten lines of the poem, gives us more proof that *In Memory of Michael Morgan* is intended as a type of pastiche (besides the more obvious use of Eliot), for "enceepharating" is the word used by Rivière in his memoir to describe a peculiar kind of crucifixion: "I crucified frogs and birds," he wrote of his child-hood. "I had also invented another torture to put them to death. It was to attach them to a tree with three sharp nails through the belly. I called that enceepharat-ing them...." This word is not in use in English; it was Rivière's—and now Mor-gan's, who, on this Good Friday, recalls his having crucified, "enceepharatinged," seven toads. Graziano calls our attention to this word by his—what I am certain is intentional—misuse of the past participle form; if it were a word found in our dictionaries, its past participle would be "enceepharated."

Morgan, who in his suicide attempt spins from his blanket-rope, hopes to stop spinning, stop "turning":

> And because he did not hope
> to turn again he grabbed
> the blanket which he used for a rope
> and—fist
> above fist, dizzy with his mouse-face
> blue like a vein—
> moled nose-against-wood toward the dirty bulb,
>
> choked up for a breath... (8)

Eliot's line is used more directly here. Whereas earlier, the syntax was inverted—changing its meaning from Eliot's "because I do not hope to turn" (turn, that is, to another religion, if any, or philosophy after committing himself to Anglo-Ca-tholicism) to Morgan's abandonment of hope, his loss of faith: "Because he did not turn / to hope, because he did not hope"—Graziano now inverts his own line, making it closer to Eliot's phrase: Morgan, "because he did not hope / to turn again," grabs the blanket to stop its spinning. This, of course, is an instance of the pastiche's comic effect, but it is also a tragicomic one in that Morgan, unlike Eliot who does not "hope to turn again" in order to preserve his newly acquired spiri-tual life, does not hope to turn, literally, again so that he might breathe, so to pre-serve his physical life, which he does.

Thus alive, yet in an altered state of consciousness, Morgan thinks of Ri-vière, as I previously noted, and of Jonah: "And the Lord spake unto the fish, and it vomited out Jonah upon the dry land" (10). Jonah, one will recall, because he was disobedient to the Lord's command, was thrown overboard by his own sailors into the sea where he was swallowed by a large fish—whale in the New Testament account. After three days, the Lord, satisfied that Jonah had been punished long enough, ordered the fish to expel him; thereupon, Jonah was a "new man," one, presumably, never to disobey the Lord again. This reference to Jonah suggests that Morgan, believing to have disobeyed the Lord by "enceepharating" toads, among other sinful acts, thinks he, too, can become a "new man" after being properly punished. From Morgan's perverted perspective, this punishment must take the form of killing the old self, the self that committed those acts. To Morgan, this is reasonable: "What is actual is actual only one time" (12), he suggests, which is Eliot's line verbatim, but used here to illustrate, and define, Morgan's state of mind. That is, Morgan, now wavering between life and death, attempting to transcend himself, considers that anything is possible because his state of consciousness would suggest to him that which is most likely for the moment, that which is "actual is actual only one time." And the poem moves easily from verse to prose, from what is seemingly Morgan's reality to his dreams, remembrances, and to his consciousness which evokes Rivière, Jonah, and the rest. The verse to prose reflects this consciousness, one which comprises the book's second section, "Philautia Street: The Nature of Reflection."

It is during the course of Morgan's "reflection" on self-love that we learn of his rationale for killing ("*I have to die... He has to die*") that I mentioned earlier: in order to beget a new self, one spiritually cleansed. Morgan is religious, although his prayers' motives are twisted: "I bless the earth that opens for the lowering of coffins. I bless the rose that bleeds in the crime without motive, and the hollow of sheets, and bed-cold" (24), lines which foreshadow Morgan's own (as seen by those not understanding his intention) motiveless crime. Morgan believes that "to love yourself is a way to love God" (28)—a line, incidentally, of Robert Penn Warren—and he shows his love by destroying what he believes to be his other self, a "self" that is actually another person, an old man—a stranger to Morgan—and owner of the house Morgan has absentmindedly entered. Morgan looks about, sees a picture of the man's wife (long dead), Camilla, hanging above the mantel, then uses the toilet. When Morgan flushes, the old man, "being in the grog and ozone of a dream," awakens and thinks it is Camilla coming to bed:

> The man with the mole, Michael Morgan, left the bathroom dragging his baggy-socked feet, pulling up his zipper, and put his foot down on the first step upward, which creaked.
> And the sleeper, hearing the flush and creak, even a hint of the slipper-slosh, being in the grog and ozone of a dream the sleeper rasped, "Camilla, Camilla, is that you, dear?" and this in the tone of St. Thomas, the doubter—

as though addressing the dead—and this seemed peculiar to the man with the mole, his name wasn't Camilla. (31)

Morgan having already "pushed *I have to die* down into the black water of old hope" and it having "bobbed up *He has to die*," is now presented with the opportunity to make his rationalization manifest, and so murders the old man in his bed by smothering him with a pillow. Morgan disregards the man's muffled screaming and thinks back to someone from his past calling his name, to his enceepharating the toads:

> *Miiiichael*
> *Miiiichael*

> he hears her
> and giggles tee hee hee
> while with the left hand a nail
> is held to the skin,
> the hammer, choked, swings past the squint
> and nose
> and the nail, first with a squish-bounce
> then thump against tree bark,
> goes in. And then another, to the left... (34)

(Given the nature of Morgan's mind, it is possible that he murders the man by enceepharating him, but more likely, thinking now only of his boyhood acts, he is unaware of committing murder; either way, his remembering enceepharating the toads serves as a partial catalyst for his crime.) Afterward, as this middle section of the book closes, we return to Morgan trying to hang himself with the blanket, thinking, because he is tired of hanging, about undressing for sleep, which again diverts his attention back to the murder of the old man:

> So, nude, lies down beside the dead man where once a wife lay and, finding the sheet-chill not to warm quickly, cuddles. But this won't do. He must get up with his little fig-like penis and roll the dead man to the wife-side of the bed, roll all of him over, then tuck himself into the body-warmth. (38)

In murdering the man, Morgan has freed himself from his old self, and consequently feels as rejuvenated as did Jonah upon his release from the fish. Like Jonah, Morgan believes he has served his penance, has successfully met the trial of having to relinquish his old self ("*He has to die*"). Yet it is a penance that must be reenacted again and again until his (this time) achieved suicide by hanging while in prison for his crime, as the book's final section, "Ash Wednesday: The Epilogue," reveals.

Morgan has a skewed sense of prioritizing those sins in most need of expiation. After he kills the old man, for example (perhaps because he associates the act with his boyhood guilt), he thinks of his sin of masturbating, confessing to Father Mulligan, and the ensuing guilt: "the sin he had lugged like a black stone lodged between lungs...." Yet none of his sins matters any longer, for his penance ends, ironically, on "Ash Wednesday," the first day of lent, or period of personal sacrifice, a day which includes—as the poem closes—Morgan hanging in his cell block, presumably to death because, aside from the poem being in his "memory," that is precisely how Pierre Rivière died, one of the many people Morgan thinks of during his penance. Five years after Rivière was sentenced to life imprisonment—commuted from the original death penalty because his crime "bore every sign of insanity"—he hung himself in his cell. Morgan's seeming knowledge of Rivière is "in memory" as well—his literal memory, which includes the memory, and accompanying burden, of history. Morgan in this regard is representative of contemporary man, bearing the collective guilt of all transgressions that have preceded him in literature and history, and his destiny—his need for the expiation of his sins, for destroying his old self, etc.—is subsequently thus determined. His memory can end only with his death, which I argue is the most satisfying interpretation of the book's final lines since his suicide, which atones for his crimes (in that it stops both his reliving them, especially the murder, and his repeated, unsuccessful, suicide attempts), provides the truest closure to a poem which exists solely "in memory" of Morgan. The poem concludes when Morgan's memory ceases—at his death.

Because the poem does not suggest that Morgan's life (as represented in verse)—simply because it mirrors in part Rivière's, or undertakes a perverted type of Eliotic religious conversion—is a manifestation of Eliot's "mythic method" or Joyce's adaptation of Vico's cyclical theory of history, Graziano moves beyond the limited intentions of the modernist pastiche in that Morgan's crime remains essentially motiveless to us: Neither historical precedent, such as that provided by Rivière's memoir, nor religious precedent (Jonah, and in a sense, Eliot) can account for it. The poem does not present any reasons or clear motives; such answers, as were proffered in modernist literature, are no longer viable, as *In Memory of Michael Morgan* suggests to us by its using a literature—historical and religious—which can complement and illustrate a horrific case of murder in our day, but cannot explain it. This contributes to the (darkly) comedic aspect of the poem's pastiche quality. Just as the French pastiche painters usually mimicked works not otherwise worthy of notice, Graziano includes in his account of Michael Morgan passages and ideas from works of literature which cannot explain satisfactorily Morgan's complex personality and resulting behavior. And in tempering the morbidity of the poem's subject by using that literature humorously at times, Graziano has found a suitable role for it in "post-modern" poetry, a poetry, that is, of the self-effacing mode, couched in the older guise of the pastiche, here manifest by Graziano's complete submersion in allusion, in adapting—and using literally—selections of others' works in making his own poem. He has borrowed this technique from Strand; *In Memory of Michael Morgan* is as personal to Graziano—in that the other authors' works speak for him—as "Leopardi" is to Strand. (Leopardi's poem addressed Strand's emotional condition exactly as it was at that moment, the setting of "Strand's" poem, so Strand substituted his wife's name for Leopardi's "Oh, my woman," for example.) Graziano sees Morgan as emblematic of himself, not as a persona, but as reflective of his personal view of the value of literature. Just as Morgan does not understand the allusions to literature (because the poem's speaker puts them there), or why he thinks of such, Graziano cannot understand how literature helps to explain the reason for a senseless murder, or how it is that Morgan's situation so accurately parallels Rivière's of the previous century.

GIVEN, THEN, THAT PERSONAL POETRY remains in contemporary practice by younger poets—particularly in the confessional mode—let us now review the current work of the (still living) poets whose poems discussed in chapters 2 through 4 were used as archetypal of the three modes of voice. Bly will serve as representative of the confessional poets (all deceased). He has used the confessional voice increasingly as he moves farther from his exploration of the unconscious—a poetry, heroic in nature, intended to teach us something about our behavior—which, as noted in chapter 4, resulted in poems concentrated on the projection of the emotive image (rather than the objective one—the object itself, that is—as was Williams's and Pound's concern). Of Bly's recent work, Deborah Baker has suggested:

> Bly has recently begun to work with the power of narrative or "character." With narrative he is able to discover the people, relationships and human events in his life, as in his prose poems. He has just finished a series of poems on his father. Bly's redefinition of the powers of poetry, emphasizing two powers, sound and rhythm, which he had ignored or dismissed earlier in his career, reveal not only Bly's creative growth, but also a new awareness of the importance of personal relationships and communication. (73)

The following excerpted poem, narrative in its structure, "For My Son Noah, Ten Years Old" from his *The Man in the Black Coat Turns* (1981), attests to his "new awareness" of his family:

> ...the old tree goes on, the barn stands without help so many years;
> the advocate of darkness and night is not lost....
> And slowly the kind man comes closer, loses his rage, sits down at table.
>
> So I am proud only of those days that pass in undivided tenderness,
> when you sit drawing, or making books, stapled, with messages to the world,
> or coloring a man with fire coming out of his hair.
> Or we sit at a table, with small tea carefully poured.
> So we pass our time together, calm and delighted.

"The kind man" who "loses his rage" can be Bly who has come to an understanding of his relationship with his son. Since the poem is "for" his son, the first two stanzas relay some truths which Bly has learned in life and wishes to pass on. The last stanza addresses his son more directly—although he is still speaking to us—and expresses his love for Noah. The poem begins with general assertions, but continually focuses on specific details until arriving at a personal narrative scene which includes Bly and his son. Whereas a poem from *Silence in the Snowy Fields* starts with personal reflection and then moves outward, "For My Son Noah, Ten Years Old" begins with reflections on the world, and ends with personal circumstance. The confessional voice here is used to "discover the people...in his life," specifically, the nature and importance of being close to his son.

Some of the poems in the second section of *The Man in the Black Coat Turns* reveal more blatantly Bly's use of the seemingly quotidian, and autobiographical, for his subjects, as the opening of "Eleven O'Clock at Night" would suggest:

> I lie alone in my bed; cooking and stories are over at last, and some peace comes. And what did I do today? I wrote down some thoughts on sacrifice that other people had, but couldn't relate them to my own life. I brought my daughter to the bus—on the way to Minneapolis for a haircut—and I waited twenty minutes with her in the somnolent hotel lobby. I wanted the mail to bring some praise for my ego to eat, and was disappointed. I added up my bank balance, and found only $65, when I need over a thousand to pay the bills for this month alone. So this is how my life is passing before the grave?

As Baker has noted, "Bly's willingness to talk about his life, to be more candid in his presentation of himself as a poet, a writer with no foreign poet to promote or political cause to champion, has also had a corresponding influence on his latest poetry" (73).

Bly devoted his short book *Loving a Woman in Two Worlds* (1985) exclusively to exploring his love for an unnamed woman as that love has extended from the early passion he felt as a young man to the now mature love, sustained, yet changed, over several decades. He continues in the confessional mode, using the poem to speak directly to the woman. And as the following stanzas taken from "In Rainy September" will show, in this, by addressing the poem to the woman, he is much like the James Wright of the poems lamenting the loss of "Jenny" (in "The Idea of the Good," for example, discussed in chapter 2):

> We close the door. "I have no claim on you."
> Dusk comes. "The love I have had with you is enough."
> We know we could live apart from one another.
> The sheldrake floats apart from the flock.
> The oaktree puts out leaves alone on the lonely hillside.
>
> Men and women before us have accomplished this.
> I would see you, and you me, once a year.
> We would be two kernels, and not be planted.
> We stay in the room, door closed, lights out.
> I weep with you without shame and without honor.

The tone of this poem, until the final line, is one of rationalization. The confessional speaker at first considers his separation from the woman as something natural ("The sheldrake floats apart from the flock"), but ultimately concludes that he cannot live without her, seeing her but once a year, and therefore he openly displays his grief over the imminent separation from her, just as Wright (but from the outset of his poem) shows his emotional responses—labels them in the poem—after losing Jenny.

Some biographical information will help elucidate both "For My Son Noah, Ten Years Old" and "In Rainy September," and further show how Bly transformed certain experiences from his life—and the emotions accompanying them—into personal poetry using a confessional speaker:

> In June 1979 Carol and Robert Bly agreed to a separation and divorce and went into equal parenting. In August they both moved to Moose Lake in the North Woods of Minnesota. Though maintaining separate households the Blys live within the same school district so the children are able to spend time with both parents. In November 1980 Bly married Ruth Ray who had lived with the Blys in Madison from 1973 to 1977 with her two children, Wesley and

Sam. It is possible that the personal upheaval and divorce from his first wife made him face the responsibilities of a parent and accept the sorrows and grief that such a decision involved for both of them. (Baker 67)

Although Bly's work is now mostly concerned with his personal relationships, the "human events in his life," his personal poetry of the confessional mode which has the most affect on younger poets is the early meditative pieces from *Silence in the Snowy Fields*. William Heyen, for example, seemingly patterned his *Evening Dawning* (1979) after Bly's first book. (Since *Evening Dawning* was written before either *The Man in the Black Coat Turns* or *Loving a Woman in Two Worlds*, Heyen could not have been influenced in this regard by Bly's poems of personal relationships, yet it is of note that *Silence in the Snowy Fields*, a volume published in 1962, could be, nearly two decades later, influential on the current poems of the confessional mode.) Heyen writes in the preface to his book that:

> The poems took place on the acre of ground behind our house in Brockport, New York. The insects and plants, the myriad summer ground gave me those poems.
>
> In August, 1978, my father and my brother ... built a small writing cabin for me at the back of this property. Early the following January, planning to work on a long poem, I sat down at an oak table in front of the picture window in that cabin, looked out at the snow, and wrote down, instead, more tiny poems, this time set in winter. They begin as I, the I I am in these poems, walk over Lord Dragonfly's frozen field toward my cabin.

Heyen implies that the "I" of these poems ("the I I am in these poems") is different from the "I" he is outside his poetry, that is, something other than the "I" when not the voice of his personal poems of the confessional mode. Heyen thereby corroborates Hugo's theory, as stated in chapter 1, that voice arises from the urge "to reject the self and to create another self in its place," a self, as Heyen suggests, which acts as the confessional speaker in a group of poems based on his autobiographical experiences of one winter. Here are two short sections from the book-length poem *Evening Dawning*:

xv
Rabbit tracks,
rabbit pellets,
my own footsteps
drifting with snow.

XXIII
I am thirty-eight.
Evening is dawning.

Like many of Bly's poems in *Silence in the Snowy Fields*, Heyen's poems, as these represent, are similar to the Romantic ode which begins with the confessional speaker (the hero of the poem, as Edmund Wilson informed us in chapter 1) meditating upon a personal subject—just as the Heyen speaker does with his age—then turning that outward, using the personal as an agent to comment on the universal. That "evening is dawning" is meant for anyone of that age, not just the thirty-eight year old confessional speaker. This kind of gesture, the offering to everyone a personal conclusion about life, is extended to near prophecy in Galway Kinnell's poetry of the 1980s and into the early 1990s as found in his two most recent books, *The Past* (1985), *When One has Lived a Long Time Alone* (1990), and *Imperfect Thirst* (1994).

When Rosenthal judged the "Life Studies" sequence as confessional because it was concerned with Lowell's "literal self," he meant "literal" in the sense of being closely true to fact, of accurately relating autobiography. Yet in much of *The Past*, Kinnell presents us with a personal poetry of the confessional mode that is also engaged with the poet's "literal" self—that is, a self that is defined and represented by the poem. This self, we know, is not necessarily true to fact, although we also know from reading the Lowell biographies that personal poems of this mode can rely on fact, as indicated by many details from the "Life Studies" sequence. The subject matter of personal poems does not require substantiation by "fact," however, in order for these poems to be confessional, as we have seen (primarily from our discussion of Wright's and Sexton's work) in chapter 2.

Kinnell, whose poetry of the late 1960s and 1970s was mainly concerned with the persona mode of voice ("The Porcupine" and "The Bear" from *Body Rags*) and ideation and the ensuing quest for knowledge (in *The Book of Nightmares*), has recently written of his domestic affairs, seemingly, his personal relationships, the "human events in his life" (as was suggested of Robert Bly's current work, also largely confessional). In doing so Kinnell has abandoned the persona mode in favor of the confessional. The following selection taken from the poem "After Making Love We Hear Footsteps," from *Mortal Acts, Mortal Words* (1980), is typical of his current personal poetry:

> let there be that heavy breathing
> or a stifled come-cry anywhere in the house
> and [Fergus] will wrench himself awake

and make for it on the run—as now, we lie together,
after making love, quiet, touching along the length of our bodies,
familiar touch of the long-married,
and he appears—in his baseball pajamas, it happens,
the neck so small...
              which one day may make him wonder
about the mental capacity of baseball players—
and says, "Are you loving and snuggling? May I join?"
He flops down between us and hugs us and snuggles himself to
       sleep...

Poems comprising *The Past* include more domestic scenes like the one depicted in "After Making Love We Hear Footsteps." Kinnell begins and ends this book (the middle section contains few personal poems) with a confessional poetry that explores the memories the speaker has retained, so that these poems are essentially a record of the speaker's past life of which he is conscious. (His personal history, that is, is comprised of other experiences too: memories he has forgotten or that have been left out of the poem for other reasons.) These memories define the self, then, to the extent that the self is represented by the poem. The opening poem of the book, "The Road Between Here and There," chronicles the many experiences—at various stops along the road—the speaker remembers. The speaker is travelling the "road between here and there," one with which he is long familiar, and, as he does so, he cites the places where he has read, loafed, listened to nature, etc.:

Here I stopped the car and snoozed while two small children crawled
       all over me.
Here I reread *Moby Dick* (skimming big chunks, even though to me it
       is the greatest of all novels) in a single day, while Fergus
       fished....
Here I arrive there.
Here I must turn around and go back and on the way back look care-
       fully to left and to right.
For here, the moment all the spaces along the road between here and
       there—which the young know are infinite and all others know
       are not—get used up, that's it.

The final lines have at least two meanings. The speaker, each time he travels the road, has another opportunity to remember more experiences of his past, and, in doing so, to retain a conception of himself, of that which has brought him to the present. Also, the lines suggest that there are "spaces along the road" that the speaker has, as yet, no reason to remember. However, he has the rest of his life to garner new experiences from those new "spaces." Once they are "used up, that's it"—meaning either that the speaker's physical life is actually over, or that the self which is defined by the speaker's memories of the past will "cease" when there are no longer spaces from which these memories are engendered, that is, when the aging speaker loses the capacity, or the desire, to do so.

The landscapes, or other types of "spaces," often serve as the catalyst for poems about the speaker's past. The following excerpt from the poem "The Old Life" shows the speaker standing along the shoreline watching the waves, a scene which makes him remember a time when once there with his lover. But the poem transcends, somewhat, being entirely personal and introspective by attempting a prophecy—while still using a personal experience as the basis for such an attempt:

> We stood
> among shatterings, glitterings,
> the brilliance. For some reason
> to love does not seem ever
> to hurt any less. Now it happens
> another lifetime is up for us,
> another life is upon us.
> What's left is what is left
> of the whole absolutely love-time.

The confessional voice here remembers a time in life when the couple—then much younger—stood in the same place, watching, as the speaker does now, the ocean's waves. Yet though the waves seem unchanged since that time, the speaker and the woman whom he addresses in the poem, he tells us, are nearing the end of a lifetime together: "another lifetime is up for us, / another life is upon us," which could bespeak several intentions. Even though the couple's "old life" is now in the past, it marks the beginning of "what is left / of the whole absolutely love-time," which can be said of the love of any couple: They have the future before them in which to share their love. "The Old Life" is prophetic in this sense, then, but the first person speaker still does not quite attain the objectivity of a more representative voice—a persona such as the Whitman "I" we discussed in relation to Berryman's work in chapter 3—for his "prophecy" is only incidental to his personal reflection. Or the final lines may be less suggestive of an optimistic future and rather mournfully, instead, be indicative of the end of the couple's relationship, in which case the last two lines could mean either that "what's left" is merely the memory of their past love-life, or that the time left "of the whole absolutely love-time" is that which remains in order to pursue another love relationship, presumably with another person. The confessional mode of voice, though apparently prophetic, is too personal to speak in behalf of anyone other than the first person "I" alone. Therefore, the "prophecy" of (the one interpretation of) the final line suggests the future, the probable course of behavior, of only the speaker.

That Kinnell does not intend his speaker as a Whitmanesque "I" (one that is a representative voice, at once both the speaker and everyone) becomes more apparent in his poems written in commemoration of deceased friends; his confessional "I" reflects on personal memories of them. One illustration of this is "On the Oregon Coast," dedicated as "*In memoriam* Richard Hugo," of which a selection follows:

> The last time I was on this coast Richard Hugo and I had dinner
> together just north of here, in a restaurant overlooking the sea.
> The conversation came around to personification....
> Our talk turned to James Wright, how his kinship with salamanders,
> spiders and mosquitoes allowed him to drift back down
> through the evolutionary stages.
> When a group of people gets up from a table, the table doesn't know
> which way any of them will go.
> James Wright went back to the end. So did Richard Hugo.
> The waves coming in burst up through their crests and fly very brilliant
> back out to sea....

Much of which the Kinnell speaker (as represented by the "I" of the poem, the first person confessional speaker) remembers about Hugo in this instance is the conversation about James Wright, who had then just passed away. The memory, evoked by the speaker's standing on the coast looking at the ocean (and in this, the speaker is like the one of "The Old Life" who recalled a time earlier in his life when watching "the waves collapse into themselves"; his being at a certain place on the coast evoked the memory of when he was there before with his lover) is, then, of a memory of still another friend. In this way, Kinnell interlaces one of his notions of "the past"—which is the book's principal thematic concern—namely, that one's personal history is only that which can be retained in memory.

The Kinnell "I" makes his tribute to Wright exclusively in the next poem, "Last Holy Fragrance" (subtitled "*In memoriam* James Wright"), in which this speaker's reading of a Wright poem, one he watched Wright compose one morning when they were in France at the same time, evokes for the speaker the following memory:

When by first light I went out
from the last house on the chemin de Riou
to start up the cistern pump, there he sat,
mumbling into his notebook at an upstairs window
while the valley awakened...
The next winter in Mt. Sinai, voiceless,
tufted with the shavelessness that draggles
from chins on skid row in St. Paul,
Minnesota, he handed me the poem
of that Vence morning. Many times since,
I have read it and each time I have heard
his voice saying it under my voice...

"Last Holy Fragrance" is a poem about the memories another poem (by another poet) brings to the Kinnell "I" speaker, and in this the author Kinnell has extended the conception of "the past" as presented in "On the Oregon Coast." In that poem, the speaker's returning to a certain place conjured another time spent there with Richard Hugo, but "Last Holy Fragrance" describes how the Wright poem—the one that the speaker recalls seeing Wright working on—affects the speaker's memory in two ways. By reading his friend's work, the speaker "hears" Wright's voice, and that same poem evokes the image of one morning "on the chemin de Riou" where the speaker saw him writing it.

The Kinnell "I" speaker in the poem "The Past" carries "a chair under one arm, / a desktop under the other, / the same Smith-Corona / on my back," he says, "I even now batter / words into visibility with" to a certain place on the beach so that he might remember "the details" of the experiences he had there over the last thirty years, details including:

the dingy, sprouted potatoes,
the Portuguese bread, the Bokar coffee,
the dyed oranges far from home,
the water tasting of decayed aluminum,
the kerosene stench. The front
steps where I sat and heard
the excitement that comes into sand,
the elation into poverty grass,
when the wind rises. In a letter
which cast itself down in General
Delivery, Provincetown, my friend
and mentor warned, "Don't lose
all touch with humankind."

The speaker remembers these details through the imagination of his memory, not necessarily the landscape, for it has changed—the Quonset hut he once "broke into without breaking it" is there no longer. But the speaker's desire to recall what he had done there in the past is enough to "reach the past." The anticipation of writing a poem about the desire to remember the past is what, ultimately, precipitates his memory of the place before actually arriving there and setting up his writing table. The poet Kinnell, who is the speaker of the poem, who—as he narrates the poem—"batters words into visibility," in this way acts to define himself by this very depiction of the confessional speaker, the Kinnell "I," of the poem.

These poems, which are typical of the first and final sections of *The Past*, openly relate a subject matter that—at the least—has the semblance of autobiography. They utilize the confessional mode of voice to do so, one perhaps "intended without question," as Rosenthal said of the voice of the "Life Studies" sequence, "to point to the author himself." They do, we can be certain, use a speaker that is the representation of Kinnell in his verse in order to record the images, the memories, which serve as the basis for his subject matter.

Mark Strand, too, has used the confessional voice more in his poems of the 1980s. We discussed one, "Shooting Whales" from the "New Poems" section of his *Selected Poems*, a section which he dates as 1980, in comparison to the other poems of the confessional mode in chapter 2. However, he began turning from his subjects of the bifurcated self, the concern for the other presence within us (which subjects required the self-effacing voice) toward the confessional mode in *The Late Hour* (1978). In "Pot Roast" from that book, for example, the speaker uses the occasion of eating a meal to remember his mother:

> I spoon the juices
> of carrot and onion.
> And for once I do not regret
> the passage of time....
>
>
> and do not care that I see
> no living thing...
> These days when there is little
> to love or to praise
> one could do worse
> than yield
> to the power of food....

> I think
> of the first time
> I tasted a roast
> like this.
> It was years ago
> in Seabright,
> Nova Scotia;
> my mother leaned
> over my dish and filled it...
>
> And now
> I taste it again.
> The meat of memory....
> I raise my fork
> and I eat.

At first, the speaker does not "regret / the passage of time" while eating because he enjoys pot roast; it is at least something of worth to him in "these days when there is little / to love or to praise." But then his meal becomes more significant. Although the speaker does not see anything alive as he eats, the vision of the first time he ate pot roast "lives" at this moment in his memory, so he raises his fork as if in praise of this "meat of memory" since there is little to love or praise, since there is no living thing except memory.

"My Mother on an Evening in Late Summer," from "New Poems," is like "Pot Roast" in that the speaker remembers his mother. In this poem, the speaker recalls from his childhood how his mother at home in Nova Scotia used to watch the ocean from her porch while relaxing with a cigarette after a long day's work. Her son, now an adult (and speaker of the poem) remembering such an instance, explains what his mother's thoughts must have been in those moments of reflection, as this selection from the poem illustrates:

> ... my mother will stare into the starlanes,
> the endless tunnels of nothing,
> and as she gazes,
> under the hour's spell,
> she will think how we yield each night
> to the soundless storms of decay
> that tear at the folding flesh,
> and she will not know
> why she is here

or what she is prisoner of
if not the conditions of love that brought her to this.

Although Strand has published two volumes of poetry since his *Selected Poems*—*The Continuous Life* (1990) and the book-length poem *Dark Harbor* (1993)—he has not used the confessional voice much since his gathering in the "New Poems" section of *Selected Poems*. The newer books are primarily lyrical meditations; neither one contains many personal pieces in whichever mode of voice.

Yet some other poems that have appeared in magazines since *Selected Poems* still display the sense of wit Strand showed in his earlier work—which contrasts with the more somber tone of his poems of the confessional mode—even though these poems are only marginally concerned with self-effacement and the self-effacing voice, as this excerpt from "The Poem" from the September 1984 issue of *The Atlantic Monthly* illustrates:

1. *The Poet to the Reader*

Dear Reader, though I spend my days and nights in hiding, wanting your attention and fearing it will be no more than the sad interest success finds in failure... only in your genius do my poems have life.... That is why...I have wanted to speak in you....

2. *The Reader to the Poet*

Dear Poet...I'm not sure I'm all you think I am, but my wife says there's more to most of us than meets the eye.... Lately, I have been plagued by uncertainty over our son. We live in an unfinished house.... As a poet, you will understand.

The poet tells the reader that his poem, which we do not see, is "an attempt to present the self I have so long hidden," yet he apparently has already presented this self. He reveals his fears to the reader ("wanting your attention and fearing it will be no more than the sad interest success finds in failure"), his personal, eccentric habits—and here he reminds us of the paranoid insomniac of Strand's "Sleeping with One Eye Open"—("I spend my days and nights in hiding"), his obvious desire for sympathy, and his romantic, idealistic regard of both the reader and the usefulness of poetry: "only in your genius do my poems have life." Perhaps, too, this is mere flattery. But the poet seems sincere in his wanting "to speak in" the reader, making the reader part of the poem—probably the poet has something like Eliot's objective correlative theory in mind.

Yet the reader little resembles the poet's notion of him, and he relates his concerns to the poet as the poet did to the reader: we live in troubled times, he does not understand his son, he lives in an unfinished house. He thinks that the poet will understand his troubles because poets, the reader assumes, are sensitive to contemporary issues that affect mankind. In particular, he assumes that the poet should be sensitive to problems stemming from an unfinished house since poets generally must deal with a lifetime of unfinished projects in the form of uncompleted or abandoned poems.

Each, however, assumes too much and misunderstands the other. The reader, it is evident, does not have the genius to bring to poems as the poet thinks he does, and the poet, who spends his days and nights in hiding, could not know the nature of the reader's problems, as the reader thinks he does. But "The Poem" accomplishes, in revealing the self the poet has hidden, what "the enclosed poem"—the one we do not see—was intended to do. The poet, then, has been effaced from "The Poem": We just see his prose letter to the reader. "The Poem" therefore approaches a use of the self-effacing mode because it discusses the relationship between the poet and his work—in the absence of that work and without showing it to real readers of "The Poem." That is, he creates another self to be represented in his poetry and necessarily hides his personal self from the poem. The poet, after all, desires to speak in the reader, not in himself. All this, of course, contributes to the absurdity of the piece.

And Charles Simic's poems of the 1980s and into the 1990s often incorporate elements of the absurd as well. Reading through Simic's poetry since his *Selected Poems* (1985)—the books *Unending Blues* (1986), *Nine Poems: A Childhood Story* (1989), *The World Does Not End* (1989), and *The Book of Gods and Devils* (1990)—one finds the poems more fablelike, disposed toward historical fantasy (like strolling about in the nineteenth century for example) rather than being so much concerned with the "I's" relationship to myth or to history as a means of consciousness—poems which require the use of the self-effacing mode of voice—as was his earlier work we examined in the previous chapter.

"Madonnas Touched up with a Goatee" (from his 1982 book *Austerities*) illustrates a type of poem common to Simic's current practice:

> Most ancient Metaphysics, (poor Metaphysics!)
> All decked up in imitation jewelry.
> We went for a stroll, arm and arm, smooching in public...

It's still the 19th century, she whispered.
We were in a knife-fighting neighborhood
Among some rundown relics of the Industrial Revolution....

There were young hoods on street corners
With crosses and iron studs on their leather jackets.
They all looked like they'd read Darwin and that madman Pavlov...

The witty references to the intellectual and physical ("industrial revolution") development of the last century, and the first person speaker's admittedly nostalgic emotion toward metaphysics (out of fashion in this century)—which Simic personifies as a woman "decked up in imitation jewelry" and very much at ease, knowing her way around the nineteenth century—are characteristic of Strand's type of self-effacing poem. But this poem is really little more than an amusement, one using history cleverly yet not as a way to recover our mythic unconscious or to explore our historical consciousness. Consequently the voice is not of the self-effacing mode since it is not concerned with the personal self's role in either myth or history, even though the personal voice of Simic is—because of the fantasy situation—obviously effaced from the poem.

Neither does David Ignatow employ the use of the self-effacing voice as often now as he did in his earlier poetry, as shown by the newer poems in *Six Decades: Selected Poems* (1993)—although he never has been occupied with the absurd as have Strand and Simic. As we saw at the end of chapter 4, Ignatow's work from the 1984 *Leaving the Door Open* would seem to indicate a somewhat new direction for his verse. Perhaps he feels he has exhausted the artistic and thematic possibilities of the self-effacing voice intended to bind and strengthen the community, or maybe his concerns are more philosophical now and so any particular mode of voice is of secondary consideration to the messages—other than the self's relationship to society—he wishes to convey in his work. Regardless of his intentions, Ignatow seems to have (for now) abandoned the idea of self-effacement for the sake of the community. That idea, he revealed in poem #63 of *Leaving the Door Open* (discussed in the previous chapter), is no longer plausible, particularly because it does require some measure of self-divestment. The older Ignatow has now deepened his thinking, as the following excerpted poem, #36 from *Leaving the Door Open*, would indicate. The speaker of this poem apparently has grown more at peace with himself as he has matured over the years, now less inclined to desire being impersonal or effaced from the self speaking of community concerns:

Here he is, sitting quietly, enjoying
his own presence...
          an understanding
that he is the one
with whom to sit at peace silently
in friendship...

Generally, the poets who once practiced the persona and the self-effacing modes of voice have turned in the 1980s and 1990s to the more immediately personal—the confessional voice—so that which Louis Simpson, writing in 1978, informed us of in chapter 1 still seems viable: "If one considers the impersonality of the modern bureaucratic state it is likely that, more and more, poetry will be written to express the life of an individual." Personal poetry, as apparent by the selected work of the young poets represented in this chapter and by many others—some mentioned in chapter 1, some writing at this moment, not yet known to us—probably will noticeably remain through this decade in whatever forms (lyric, epic, metered, etc.) it may next choose to adopt as its media. Yet personal poetry, it seems, surfaced most strongly in this century as a distinctive phase, one beginning in 1959 and very likely now significantly waning, so that the craft of the poets who practiced the confessional, persona, and self-effacing modes is more historical than archetypal of future poetry. Regardless of its course, however, American poetry of the past several decades always will be distinguished by its individualistic and personal voices which flourished under the political currents and intellectual thoughts of its time.

Works Cited

Baker, Deborah. "Making a Farm: A Literary Biography." Jones and Daniels 33–77.

Barthes, Roland. "The Death of the Author." *Image, Music, Text.* Trans. Stephen Heath. New York: Hill and Wang, 1977. 142–48.

Bellamy, Joe David, ed. *American Poetry Observed: Poets on Their Work.* Urbana: U of Illinois P, 1984.

Berg, Stephen, and Robert Mezey. Foreword. *Naked Poetry: Recent American Poetry in Open Forms.* Eds. Stephen Berg and Robert Mezey. Indianapolis: Bobbs-Merrill, 1969. xi–xiii.

———. Foreword. *The New Naked Poetry: Recent American Poetry in Open Forms.* Eds. Stephen Berg and Robert Mezey. Indianapolis: Bobbs-Merrill, 1976. xvii–xix.

Berryman, John. "A Peine Ma Piste." Rev. of *T. S. Eliot: A Selected Critique,* ed. Leonard Unger. *Partisan Review* 15.7 (1948): 826–28.

———. "Conversation with Berryman." With Richard Kostelanetz. *Massachusetts Review* 11 (1970): 340–47.

———. "The Imaginary Jew." *Kenyon Review* 7 (1945): 529–39.

———. "John Berryman." Interview with Peter A. Stitt. *Writers at Work: The* Paris Review *Interviews.* Ed. George Plimpton. Fourth Series. 1967. New York: Viking, 1976. 293–322.

———. "One Answer to a Question: Changes." *The Freedom of the Poet.* New York: Farrar, Straus and Giroux, 1976. 323–31.

———. *Recovery.* 1973. New York: Farrar, Straus and Giroux, 1980.

———. "'Song of Myself': Intention and Substance." *The Freedom of the Poet.* 227–41.

Bloom, Harold. "Dark and Radiant Peripheries: Mark Strand and A. R. Ammons." *Southern Review* (New Series) 8.1 (1972): 133–49.

———. *A Map of Misreading.* New York: Oxford UP, 1975.

———. Wallace Stevens: *The Poems of Our Climate.* Ithaca, NY: Cornell UP, 1977.

Bly, Robert. "Five Decades of Modern American Poetry." *Fifties* 1 (1958): 36–9.

Breslin, James E. B. *From Modern to Contemporary: American Poetry, 1945–1965.* Chicago: U of Chicago P, 1984.

Breslin, Paul. "How to Read the New Contemporary Poem." *American Scholar* 47 (1978): 357–70.

Browne, Michael Dennis. "Henry Fermenting: Debts to *The Dream Songs.*" *Ohio Review* 15.2 (1974): 75–87.

Crenner, James. Rev. of *Darker,* by Mark Strand. *Seneca Review* 2.1 (1971): 84–9.

Dickey, James. "Dialogues with Themselves." Rev. of *All My Pretty Ones,* by Anne Sexton. *New York Times Book Review* 28 (Apr. 1963): 50.

———. "Five First Books." Rev. of *To Bedlam and Part Way Back,* by Anne Sexton. *Poetry* 97 (1961): 318–19.

Eliot, T. S. "Hamlet and His Problems." *The Sacred Wood: Essays on Poetry and Criticism.* Third ed. London: Methuen, 1932. 95–103.

———. "Tradition and the Individual Talent." *The Sacred Wood.* 47–59.

———. "Yeats." *The Norton Anthology of English Literature.* Ed. M. H. Abrams, et al. Rev. ed. 2 vols. New York: Norton, 1968. 2:1825–35.

Elliott, Robert C. *The Literary Persona.* Chicago: U of Chicago P, 1982.

George, Diana Hume. *Oedipus Anne: The Poetry of Anne Sexton.* Urbana: U of Illinois P, 1987.

Ginsberg, Allen. "Allen Ginsberg." Interview with Thomas Clark. *Writers at Work: The* Paris Review *Interviews.* Ed. George Plimpton. Third Series. 1967. New York: Penguin, 1977. 279–320.

Graziano, Frank. *In Memory of Michael Morgan.* Bryan, TX: Cedarshouse P, 1986.

Gregerson, Linda. "Negative Capability." *Parnassus: Poetry in Review* 9.2 (1981): 90–114.

Haffenden, John. Introduction. *Henry's Fate & Other Poems, 1967–1972.* By John Berryman. New York: Farrar, Straus and Giroux, 1977. ix–xviii.

———. *The Life of John Berryman.* Boston: Routledge and Kegan Paul, 1982.

Hamilton, Ian. *Robert Lowell: A Biography.* 1982. New York: Vintage, 1983.

Hass, Robert. "James Wright." *Twentieth Century Pleasures: Prose on Poetry.* New York: Ecco P, 1984. 26–55.

———. "Lowell's Graveyard." *Twentieth Century Pleasures.* 3–25.

Heyen, William, ed. *American Poets in 1976.* Indianapolis: Bobbs-Merrill, 1976.

Howard, Richard. "Mark Strand: 'The Mirror Was Nothing Without You.'" *Alone with America: Essays on the Art of Poetry in the United States Since 1950.* Enlarged ed. New York: Atheneum, 1980. 589–602.

Hudgins, Andrew. "'I Am Fleeing Double': Duality and Dialectic in *The Dream Songs.*" *Missouri Review* 4.2 (1980–81): 93–110.

Hugo, Richard. "Richard Hugo." Interview with David Dillon. Bellamy 101–13.

———. "Statements of Faith." *The Triggering Town: Lectures and Essays on Poetry Writing.* 1979. New York: Norton, 1982. 67–74.

———. "Stray Thoughts on Roethke and Teaching." *The Triggering Town.* 27–36.

Ignatow, David. "Answering the Dark." Interview with Richard Jackson. Jackson, *Acts of Mind* 172–77.

———. "A Dialogue at Compas." *Open Between Us.* Ed. Ralph J. Mills, Jr. Ann Arbor: U of Michigan P, 1980. 61–102.

———. "An Interview: With Alan Ziegler." *Open Between Us.* 45–60.

———. "An Interview: With Scott Chisholm." *Open Between Us.* 21–44.

———. *The Notebooks of David Ignatow.* Ed. Ralph J. Mills, Jr. Chicago: Swallow P, 1973.

Jackson, Richard. *Acts of Mind: Conversations with Contemporary Poets.* University, Alabama: U of Alabama P, 1983.

———. "Charles Simic and Mark Strand: The Presence of Absence." Rev. of *Charon's Cosmology*, by Charles Simic, *The Late Hour* and *The Monument*, by Mark Strand. *Contemporary Literature* 21.1 (1980): 136–45.

Jaidka, Manju. "Interior Events: The Poetry of Anne Sexton." *Indian Journal of American Studies* 15.1 (1985): 45–55.

Jones, Richard, and Kate Daniels, eds. *Of Solitude and Silence: Writings on Robert Bly.* Boston: Beacon P, 1981.

Justice, Donald. Preface. *The Collected Poems of Weldon Kees.* vii–xi.

Kees, Weldon. *The Collected Poems of Weldon Kees.* Rev. ed. Ed. Donald Justice. Lincoln: U of Nebraska P, 1975.

Kessler, Jascha. "The Caged Sybil." *Saturday Review* 14 December 1968: 34–6.

Kinnell, Galway. "An Interview with A. Poulin, Jr., and Stan Sanvel Rubin." *Walking Down the Stairs: Selections from Interviews.* Ann Arbor: U of Michigan P, 1978. 20–32.

———. "An Interview with Margaret Edwards." *Walking Down the Stairs.* 12–19.

———. "An Interview with Wayne Dodd and Stanley Plumly." *Walking Down the Stairs.* 41–57.

———. "An Interview with William Heyen and Gregory Fitz Gerald." *Walking Down the Stairs.* 1–6.

———. "The Poetics of the Physical World." *The New Naked Poetry.* 133–36.

———. Preface. *Walking Down the Stairs.* ix–xiv.

Kumin, Maxine. "How It Was: Maxine Kumin on Anne Sexton." Foreword. *The Complete Poems.* By Anne Sexton. Boston: Houghton Mifflin, 1981. xix–xxxiv.

Libera, Sharon Mayer. "The Disappearance of Weldon Kees." *Ploughshares* 5.1 (1979): 147–59.

Lowell, Robert. "After Enjoying Six or Seven Essays on Me." *Salmagundi* 37 (1977): 112–15.

———. "A Conversation with Robert Lowell." Interview with Ian Hamilton. *The Review* 26 (1971): 10–29.

———. "91 Revere Street." *Life Studies.* New York: Farrar, Straus and Cudahy, 1959. 11–46.

———. "On Freedom in Poetry." *Naked Poetry.* 124.

———. "The Poetry of John Berryman." *New York Review of Books* 28 May 1964: 3–4.

———. "Robert Lowell in Conversation with A. Alvarez." *The Modern Poet: Essays from The Review.* Ed. Ian Hamilton. London: MacDonald, 1968. 188–93.

———. "Robert Lowell." Interview with Frederick Seidel. *Writers at Work: The Paris Review Interviews.* Ed. George Plimpton. Second Series. 1963. New York: Penguin, 1977. 335–68.

Martin, Jay. "Robert Lowell." *Seven American Poets: From MacLeish to Nemerov; an Introduction.* Ed. Denis Donoghue. Minneapolis: U of Minnesota P, 1975. 209–49.

Martz, William. *University of Minnesota Pamphlets on American Writers, no. 85: John Berryman.* Minneapolis: U of Minnesota P, 1969.

Mills, Ralph J., Jr. *Cry of the Human: Essays on Contemporary American Poetry.* Urbana: U of Illinois P, 1975.

———. "Earth Hard: The Poetry of David Ignatow." *Boundary 2* 2 (1974): 373–429.

Molesworth, Charles. *The Fierce Embrace: A Study of Contemporary American Poetry.* Columbia: U of Missouri P, 1979.

Nathan, Leonard. "The Private 'I' In Contemporary Poetry." *Shenandoah* 22.4 (1971): 80–99.

Ostriker, Alicia. "That Story: Anne Sexton and Her Transformations." Rev. of *The Complete Poems,* by Anne Sexton. *American Poetry Review* 11.4 (1982): 11–16.

Phillips, Robert. *The Confessional Poets.* Carbondale: Southern Illinois UP, 1973.

Plumly, Stanley. "From the New Poetry Handbook." Rev. of *Darker,* by Mark Strand. *Ohio Review* 13.1 (1971): 74–80.

Porterfield, Jo R. "The Melding of a Man: Berryman, Henry, and the Ornery Mr. Bones." *Southwest Review* 58 (1973): 30–46.

Rexroth, Kenneth. "Poets, Old and New." *Assays.* New York: New Directions, 1961. 206–39.

Rich, Adrienne. "Talking with Adrienne Rich." Interview with Stanley Plumly, et al. *Ohio Review* 13.1 (1971): 28–46.

———. "When We Dead Awaken: Writing as Re-Vision." Heyen, *American Poets in 1976* 278–92.

Ricks, Christopher. "Recent American Poetry." *Massachusetts Review* 11 (1970): 313–39.

Rosenthal, M. L. *The New Poets: American and British Poetry since World War II.* New York: Oxford UP, 1967.

———. "Poetry as Confession." Rev. of *Life Studies*, by Robert Lowell. *Nation* 19 September 1959: 154–55.

Ross, William T. *Weldon Kees*. Boston: Twayne. 1985.

Serchuk, Peter. "On The Poet, James Wright." *Modern Poetry Studies* 10 (1981): 85–90.

Sexton, Anne. "The Art of Poetry XV: Anne Sexton." Interview with Barbara Kevles. *Paris Review* 52 (1971): 159–91.

———. "Craft Interview with Anne Sexton." Interview with William Packard. *Anne Sexton: The Artist and Her Critics*. Ed. J. D. McClatchy. Bloomington: Indiana UP, 1978. 43–47.

———. "From 1928 to Whenever: A Conversation with Anne Sexton." Interview with William Heyen and Al Poulin. *American Poets in 1976*. Ed. William Heyen. Indianapolis: Bobbs-Merrill, 1976. 306–28.

Sexton, Linda Gray, and Lois Ames, eds. *Anne Sexton: A Self-Portrait in Letters*. Boston: Houghton Mifflin, 1977.

Simic, Charles. "Charles Simic." Interview with Wayne Dodd and Stanley Plumly. Bellamy 207–18.

———. "The Domain of the Marvelous Prey." Interview with Richard Jackson. Jackson, *Acts of Mind* 19–26.

———, and Mark Strand. Introduction. *Another Republic: 17 European and South American Writers*. Eds. Charles Simic and Mark Strand. New York : Ecco P, 1976. 17–19 .

Simpson, Eileen. *Poets in Their Youth: A Memoir.* 1982. New York: Vintage, 1983.

Simpson, Louis. "Capturing the World as It Is: An Interview with Louis Simpson." *Ohio Review* 14.3 (1973): 35–51.

———. "A Garland for the Muse." Rev. of *To Bedlam and Part Way Back*, by Anne Sexton. *Hudson Review* 13 (1960): 284–93. Rpt. in *A Company of Poets*. Ann Arbor: U of Michigan P, 1981. 56–66.

———. *A Revolution in Taste.* 1978. New York: Macmillan, 1979.

———. "Rolling Up." Heyen, *American Poets in 1976:* 332–40.

Smith, Dave. Introduction. *The Pure Clear Word: Essays on the Poetry of James Wright.* Ed. Dave Smith. Urbana: U of Illinois P, 1982. xi–xxviii.

Snodgrass, W. D. "A Poem's Becoming." *In Radical Pursuit: Critical Essays and Lectures.* New York: Harper and Row, 1975. 33–62.

———. "W. D. Snodgrass." Interview with David Dillon. Bellamy 219–30.

Stitt, Peter. "James Wright: The Quest Motif in *The Branch Will Not Break*." Smith 65–77.

———. "Stages of Reality: The Mind/Body Problem in Contemporary Poetry." Rev. of *Selected Poems*, by Mark Strand. *Georgia Review* 37.1 (1983): 201–10 .

Strand, Mark. "A Conversation with Mark Strand." Interview with Richard Vine and Robert von Hallberg. *Chicago Review* 28.4 (1977): 130–40.

———. "A Conversation with Mark Strand." Interview with Wayne Dodd and Stanley Plumly. *Ohio Review* 13.2 (1972): 55–71.

———. "Donald Justice." *Contemporary Poets.* Third ed. Ed. James Vinson. New York: St. Martin's P, 1980. 816–18.

———. "An Interview with Mark Strand." With Cristina Bacchilega. *Missouri Review* 4.3 (1981): 51–64 .

———. "An Interview with Mark Strand." With Frank Graziano. *Strand: A Profile.* Ed. Frank Graziano. Iowa City: Grilled Flowers P, 1979. 29–48.

———. "Notes on the Craft of Poetry." *Antaeus* 30–31 (1978): 343–47.

———. Preface. *The Contemporary Poets: American Poetry since 1940.* Ed. Mark Strand. New York: World Publishing, 1969. xiii–xiv.

———. "A Statement about Writing." *The Generation of 2000: Contemporary American Poets.* Ed. William Heyen. Princeton: Ontario Review P, 1984. 317.

———. "Untelling the Hour." Interview with Richard Jackson. Jackson, *Acts of Mind* 13–18.

Trilling, Lionel. *Sincerity and Authenticity.* Cambridge: Harvard UP, 1972.

Vendler, Helen. *Part of Nature, Part of Us: Modern American Poets.* Cambridge: Harvard UP, 1980.

Warren, Robert Penn. *Democracy and Poetry: The 1974 Jefferson Lecture in the Humanities.* Cambridge: Harvard UP, 1975.

Weigl, Bruce. "The Imagination as Biographer." Rev. of *Leverage*, by Jonathan Holden. *Poet Lore* 79 (1984): 113–21.

Williamson, Alan. *Introspection and Contemporary Poetry.* Cambridge : Harvard UP, 1984 .

Wilson, Edmund. *Axel's Castle: A Study in the Imaginative Literature of 1870–1930.* New York: Scribner's, 1931.

Wright, Annie. "Joining Hands with Robert Bly." Jones and Daniels 78–83.

Wright, James. "The Art of Poetry XIX: James Wright." Interview with Peter Stitt. *Paris Review* 16.62 (1975): 34–61.

———. "From a Letter." *Naked Poetry.* 287.

———. "James Wright." Interview with Bruce Henrickson. Bellamy 296–309.

———. "James Wright: The Pure Clear Word, an Interview." With Dave Smith. Smith 3–42.

———. "Something to Be Said for The Light: A Conversation with James Wright." Interview with William Heyen and Jerome Mazzaro. *Southern Humanities Review* 6.2 (1972): 134–53.

Young, David. "Galway Kinnell." *The Longman Anthology of Contemporary American Poetry 1950–1980.* Eds. Stuart Friebert and David Young. New York: Longman, 1983. 241–44.

Index

∾

Absurdity, 183–184, 191–193, 220, 262–263
Adams, Henry, 49
Aesthetic(s), 208
    of Berryman, 102, 105
    of Kinnell, 139
    of Lowell, 30, 35–36, 41–42, 45–46, 54
    of Sexton, 75, 79, 82, 88
    of Strand, 16, 168, 171–172, 184
    of Wright, 71
Allusion, in poetry, 8, 35
Alvarez, A.
    comments by, on Berryman, 106
    interviewing Lowell, 229
American poetry, 8
    influence of foreign poets, 14–15
    poetic form, 13–14
Antaeus, 188
Archetypes, in poetry, 191, 193–194. See also Imagery
Ashbery, John, 26–27, 215–216, 226–227
The Atlantic Monthly, 261
Auden, W. H., 1, 6, 8, 10–11, 20

Auden, W. H. (continued)
    works: "Musée des Beaux Arts," 230
Authentic self. See Self; see also under Poetic voice
Autobiography, 3–6, 12, 163–164, 226. See also Experience
    in Berryman, 104
    in Bly, 251, 254
    in Kees, 126
    in Kinnell, 148, 259
    in Lowell, 29, 31, 33, 35–40, 42–43, 45–46, 48, 53–54, 172
    in Sexton, 73, 78–82, 85–86
    in Weigl, 231
    in Wright, 65–68

Bacchilega, Cristina, interviewing Strand, 227
Baker, Deborah, on Bly, 250–253
Barnes, Jim, 236, 241–242
    works
        "After the Great Plains," 239

Barnes, Jim (*continued*)
    works (*continued*)
        "In Another Country: A Suite for the
            Villa Serbelloni," 241
        "The Cabin on Nanny Ridge," 237
        "In the Melzi Gardens," 242
        "On Hearing the News That Hitler
            Was Dead," 238
        The Sawdust War, 236, 241–242
        "The Sawdust War," 236–237
        "Soliloquy in My Forty-seventh Year,"
            239–240
Barthes, Roland, "The Death of the Au-
    thor," 23
Bellow, Saul, 110–111, 116, 120
Bennett, Joseph, on Lowell, 48
Berg, Stephen, *Naked Poetry*, 13–14, 18
Berkeley, George, 131
Berryman, John, 2–3, 7, 25, 27, 94, 122,
    129–130, 138, 146–148, 160, 208,
    220–221, 240–243, 256
    aesthetic of, 102, 105
    biography of, by Haffenden, 93
    comments on
        by Alvarez, 106
        by Eberhart, 111, 114
        by Haffenden, 91, 101, 106, 108, 110–
            112, 114
        by Hudgins, 118
        by Justice, 121
        by Kessler, 104
        by Libera, 130
        by Lowell, 104–105
        by Martz, 99
        by Molesworth, 105
        by Munford, 120
        by Porterfield, 104
        by Ricks, 104
        by Simpson, 94–95, 97–99, 116
        by Stitt, 103, 121
        by Vendler, 110
        by Warren, 111–114
    and death, 110–115, 118, 120–121

Berryman, John (*continued*)
    interviews of, by Kostelanetz, 99, 102,
        105
    mental health of, 103
    and persona mode, 4
    on poetry, 120–121
    at Princeton, 107
    suicide
        of father, 110–112
        of self, 106, 240
    works
        "The Ball Poem," 89–92, 98, 100
        Delusions Etc., 106
        The Dispossessed, 90–91, 220
        "The Dispossessed," 220–221
        The Dream Songs, 12, 93–94, 101,
            103–106, 108–110, 113, 116, 118–
            121, 130, 178
        Dream Song *121*, 113, 119
        ——— *146*, 109–110, 115
        ——— *147*, 115, 117
        ——— *149*, 117
        ——— *151*, 119
        ——— *153*, 116
        ——— *157*, 108, 120
        ——— *235*, 112
        Henry's Fate & Other Poems, 101, 106
        His Toy, His Dream, His Rest, 104, 108
        Homage to Mistress Bradstreet, 12, 98–
            101, 103
        "The Imaginary Jew," 95–96
        Love & Fame, 106
        "One Answer to a Question: Changes,"
            100
        "A Peine Ma Piste," 122
        Recovery, 96–97, 106
        "'Song of Myself' Intention and Sub-
            stance," 100
Bible, 245
    Old Testament, 244
        Genesis, 192–193, 197
        Numbers, 245
        Deuteronomy, 245
    New Testament: Mark 9, 43, 188

Blackmur, R. P., 3, 15, 107, 116
  works: "The Language of Silence," 3
Bloom, Harold, 26, 178–179, 211
  comments by
    on Stevens, 166
    on Strand, 168, 173, 177–178
  works
    "Dark and Radiant Peripheries," 177–
      178
    A Map of Misreading, 23
Bly, Robert, 12, 14, 26, 54–55, 58, 64, 68,
  160, 201, 225–226, 231, 253–254
  comments on
    by P. Breslin, 200
    by Baker, 250–253
  works
    "Eleven O'Clock at Night," 251
    The Fifties, 13, 55
    "Five Decades of Modern American
      Poetry," 12–13
    "For My Son Noah, Ten Years Old,"
      251–252
    "In Rainy September," 252
    Loving a Woman in Two Worlds, 252–
      253
    The Man in the Black Coat Turns, 251,
      253
    Silence in the Snowy Fields, 13, 251,
      253–254
    "Turning Inward at Last," 200
    What Have I Ever Lost by Dying?, 226
Borges, Jorge Luis, 182, 210
  works: "Borges and I," 181
Bradstreet, Anne, 98–100
Breslin, James, 7–8
  works: From Modern to Contemporary, 7
Breslin, Paul
  comments by
    on Bly, 200
    on Simic, 200
  works: "How to Read the New Contem-
    porary Poem," 200
Brooks, Cleanth, 7
Browne, Michael Dennis, 106

Byron, George Gordon (baron), 22

Caligula, 161
Chisholm, Scott, interviewing Ignatow,
  207–208
Collective unconscious, 193, 196, 200–201,
  203, 205–206
Confessional mode. See under Poetic voice
Confessional poetry, 5, 21–22, 25–26, 72–
  73. See also under Poetic voice
Crane, Stephen, 97–98
Crenner, James, comments by on Strand,
  179, 181
Crime, in poetry, 56
Critical theory, 23, 26–27
Crusoe, Robinson, 129–130, 136

Death, in poetry, 119, 138–141, 143–145,
  147, 149, 154, 157, 160, 213
Deconstruction
  and personal poetry, 23
  and the self, 23
  in poetry, 199
Dialectic, in poetry, 199, 203
Dickens, Charles, Bleak House, 188
Dickey, James, on Sexton, 81–83
Dickinson, Emily
  works: "I Heard a Fly Buzz When I
    Died," 138–139, 145, 154
Dodd, Wayne, interviews
  of Kinnell, 139, 148–150
  of Simic, 193–194, 197, 200
  of Strand, 166
Doty, George, 55–58
Drummond de Andrade, Carlos, 185–186,
  191
Dulles, John Foster, 49

Eberhart, Richard, comments by
  on Berryman, 111, 114

Eberhart, Richard, comments by (*continued*)
  on Lowell, 39
Edwards, Margaret, interviewing Kinnell, 151
Eliot, T. S., 1, 6, 8, 10, 17, 33, 35, 127–128, 130, 243–244, 246, 249
  impersonal theory of poetry, 8–9, 32–33, 241
  impersonality in art, 122
  influence of, 122
  and New Criticism, 7
  works
    "Ash Wednesday," 244
    "The Love Song of J. Alfred Prufrock," 134
    "Tradition and the Individual Talent," 8, 241, 243
    "The Waste Land," 128, 230, 244
    "Yeats Lecture," 9
Elliott, Robert C., 3–4, 6
  works: *The Literary Persona*, 3
Emerson, Ralph Waldo, 26
Experience
  personal, 2, 5, 8
  in poetry, 2, 4–6, 10–11, 13, 15, 18, 24, 29, 42, 164, 179, 188. *See also* Autobiography

Faber and Faber, 39
The Fifties, 13
Fitzgerald, F. Scott, 101
Fitz Gerald, Gregory, interviewing Kinnell, 148
Fortunato, Mary Jane, on Kinnell, 146
Foucault, Michel, 199
Free verse. *See under* Poetic form
Frost, Robert, 41, 118
  death of, 111

Garrett, George, 243
  works
    The Collected Poems of George Garrett, 228
    "Out on the Circuit," 228, 243
George, Diana Hume, 5
  comments of, on Sexton, 81
  works: *Oedipus Anne*, 5
Ginsberg, Allen, 6, 35
  and autobiography in poetry, 12
  works: *Howl*, 6
Gonne, Maud, 125
Graziano, Frank, 243–244, 246, 249–250
  interviewing Strand, 169, 171, 188
  works: *In Memory of Michael Morgan*, 243–250
Gregerson, Linda
  comments by, on Strand, 172–173
Grief, in poetry, 113, 115, 119, 121
Guilt, in poetry, 207–208

Haffenden, John
  comments by, on Berryman, 91, 101, 106, 108, 110–112, 114
  works: *The Life of John Berryman*, 93
Hall, Donald, 6
Hallberg, Robert von, interviewing Strand, 174
Hamilton, Ian, 37, 41
  works: *Robert Lowell*, 29
Hass, Robert
  comments by,
    on Lowell, 36
    on Wright, 66–67
Hemingway, Ernest, suicide of, 112–113
Henricksen, Bruce, 68
Heraclitus, 239
Herbert, George, 174
Heyen, William, 54, 76, 78–79, 253
  interviewing Kinnell, 148–149
  works: *Evening Dawning*, 253–254
Historical consciousness, 199, 204, 206, 210
  in poetry, 202

History, in poetry, 191–193, 196, 197, 249
Holden, Jonathan, *Leverage*, 229
Hongo, Garrett, 231–232, 234, 236
works
"And Your Soul Shall Dance," 235
"C&H Sugar Strike Kahuku, 1923," 235
"Cruising 99," 232–233, 235
"The Hongo Store 29 Miles Volcano Hilo, Hawaii," 235
"Kubota," 235
"Postcards for Bert Meyers," 233–234
The River of Heaven, 231
"Roots," 234–235
"A Samba for Inada," 232
"Something Whispered in the *Shaku-hachi*," 235–236
"Stepchild," 235
Yellow Light, 231–232
"Yellow Light," 232
Howard, Richard
comments by, on Strand, 170–171, 173–174
works: *Alone With America*, 173–174
Hudgins, Andrew, 119
comments by, on Berryman, 118
Hudson Review, 48
Hugo, Richard, 1, 8, 211, 253, 257–258
works
"Statements of Faith," 164
"Stray Thoughts on Roethke and Teaching," 21
Humor, in poetry, 216

Ignatow, David, 16–17, 25–26, 165, 207, 220, 243, 263
comments by, on Koch, 216
comments on, by Mills 165, 211, 217
interviewed, by Jackson, 218
and self-effacing mode, 4
works
"Brightness as a Poignant Light," 212–213

Ignatow, David (*continued*)
works (*continued*)
"A Dialogue at Compas," 17, 215–216
"The Dream," 218–219
"Examine me, I am continuous," 213–214
Figures of the Human, 216
Leaving the Door Open, 219, 263–264
Notebooks, 25, 208–211, 217–218
Say Pardon, 218
Six Decades: Selected Poems, 263
"The Song," 216
"*Tread the Dark*, 211, 213
The Two Selves," 214–215, 217
"With the Sun's Fire," 213
Imagery, 191, 207
archetypal, 193–198, 200–201, 205–206, 211
in poetry, 2, 57, 193, 226, 232
of the self, 2
Impersonality, in poetry, 164, 166–167, 171, 174, 197. *See also under* Eliot, T. S.
Irony, in poetry, 8, 113–115, 119

Jackson, Richard
comments by, on Simic, 199
interviews
of Ignatow, 218
of Simic, 164, 195, 197–200, 203, 206
of Strand, 184
works: "The Presence of Absence," 199, 203
Jaidka, Manju, comments by, on Sexton, 83
James, William, 49
Jarrell, Randall, 114, 116, 240
death of, 111, 113–114
Jonah, 246–248
Joyce, James, 243, 249
Jung, Carl, 193, 200
Justice, Donald, 173, 185
comments by
on Berryman, 121
on Kees, 123–124, 126, 129–130
comments on, by Strand, 185

Kafka, Franz, 154

Keats, John, 1

Kees, Weldon, 25, 27, 94, 122, 138, 164, 227, 243

    comments on

        by Justice, 123–124, 126, 129–130

        by Libera, 130

        by Rexroth, 124, 129–131, 134

        by Ross, 126, 129–131

    and persona mode, 4, 129

    works

        "Aspects of Robinson," 129, 132–135

        The Fall of the Magicians, 129

        "For My Daughter," 122–126

        "How to Be Happy: Installment 1053," 125

        The Last Man, 122

        "The Lives," 122

        Poems 1947–1954, 122, 129

        "Relating to Robinson," 129–130, 136–137

        "Robinson," 129, 131–132, 134

        "Robinson at Home," 129, 134–137

        "The Speakers," 127–129

Kenyon Review, 35, 111

Kermode, Frank, comments by , on Lowell, 39

Kerouac, Jack, *On the Road,* 12

Kessler, Jascha, comments by, on Berryman, 104

Kinnell, Fergus, 139–140, 143

Kinnell, Galway, 7, 94, 138, 160, 162, 196, 205–206, 208, 210, 214, 243, 254–255, 257–258

    aesthetic of, 139

    comments on, by Young, 138

    interviewed, by Plumly, 139, 148–150

    and persona mode, 4

    works

        "After Making Love We Hear Footsteps," 254–255

        "The Bear," 149, 155–160, 254

        Body Rags, 146, 148–149, 160, 254

Kinnell, Galway (*continued*)

    works (*continued*)

        The Book of Nightmares, 139–143, 145–146, 150, 160, 196, 254

        "Freedom, New Hampshire," 138

        Imperfect Thirst, 254

        "Last Holy Fragrance," 257–258

        "Lastness," 143–145

        "Lost Loves," 147–150

        Mortal Acts, Mortal Words, 254

        "Night in the Forest," 149–150

        "The Old Life," 256–257

        "On the Oregon Coast," 257–258

        The Past, 254–255, 259

        "The Past," 258–259

        "Poetics," 138–139

        "The Poetics of the Physical World," 138

        "The Porcupine," 149–155, 254

        "The Road Between Here and There," 255–256

        "The Shoes of Wandering," 142

        "Under the Maud Moon," 140

        Walking Down the Stairs, 141

        What a Kingdom It Was, 138

        When One has Lived a Long Time Alone, 254

Kinnell, Maud, 139–140, 143

Koch, Kenneth, 26–27, 216

    comments on, by Ignatow, 216

Kostelanetz, Richard, interviewing Berryman, 99, 102, 105

Kumin, Maxine, 82

Kunitz, Stanley, 5

Larkin, Philip, comments by, on Lowell, 39

Leopardi, Giacomo, 188, 191

    works: "La Sera Del Di' Di Festa," 189–190

Libera, Sharon, comments by,

    on Berryman, 130

    on Kees, 130

Life, 100

Lowell, Robert, 3–7, 18, 23, 25, 27, 29, 57, 62, 65–66, 73, 79, 84, 118, 122, 125–126, 160, 162, 173, 208, 221–222, 229, 231, 234, 240, 242
  aesthetic of, 30, 35–36, 41–42, 45–46, 54
  and autobiography, 38
  comments by, on Berryman, 104–105
  and confessional mode, 4
  as conscientious objector, 47
  comments on
    by Eberhart, 39
    by Hass, 36
    by Kermode, 39
    by Larkin, 39
    by Martin, 36
    by Rosenthal, 39, 254, 259
  education
    Brimmer School, 48
    St. Mark's, 160–161
  institutionalization of
    McLean's Mental Hospital, 43–45
    Payne-Whitney Clinic, 48
    West Street Jail, 46–49
  and mental illness, 29, 36–37, 73
  and poetic form, 30, 36–38
  poetic style of, 30, 33–34, 39–40
  and prose, 36–37
  works
    "91 Revere Street," 37, 48
    "After Enjoying Six or Seven Essays on Me," 37, 42
    "Caligula," 160–161
    "Commander Lowell," 40, 42
    "Dunbarton," 33–35, 42, 45, 89
    For the Union Dead, 38, 42–43, 51–52, 160, 241
    For the Union Dead, 42–43
    History, 161
    "Home After Three Months Away," 48–49, 51
    Imitations, 186
    "July in Washington," 43, 51–53

Lowell, Robert (continued)
  works (continued)
    Life Studies, 4, 6, 10, 12, 23, 30–44, 48–50, 64–65, 79, 174, 221, 231, 236
    Lord Weary's Castle (1946), 31–35
    "Man and Wife," 221–223
    "Mary Winslow," 32
    "Memories of West Street and Lepke," 43, 46–51, 54, 172, 222
    "In Memory of Arthur Winslow," 32
    "Middle Age," 42–43
    "The Mouth of the Hudson," 43, 51–53, 59, 166
    Notebook, 37–38
    "The Nihilist as Hero," 161–162
    "The Old Flame," 42
    "Skunk Hour," 41–42, 51
    "'To Speak of Woe That Is in Marriage,'" 221–223
    "Waking in the Blue," 43–46, 48, 50–51, 54, 57, 73, 83–85, 206
    "Water," 42
    "Winter in Dunbarton," 32–35, 42

MacLeish, Archibald, 57
The Manchester Guardian Weekly, 39
Mariani, Paul, works
  Dream Song: The Life of John Berryman, 93
  Lost Puritan: A Life of Robert Lowell, 29
Martin, Jay, 30–32, 35
  comments by, on Lowell, 36
Martz, William, comments by, on Berryman, 99
Mazzaro, Jerome, 54
Memory, in poetry, 249, 257–260
Mental illness
  and Lowell, 29, 36–37, 73
  in poetry, 44–45, 78, 81–85, 87–88
Meredith, William, 111
Merrill, James, 25–27, 226–227
Merwin, W. S., 27, 226

Meter, 37–41, 86
  and open poetic form, 8, 13, 20, 39
  and subject matter, 37, 41
Meyers, Jeffrey, *Manic Power: Robert Lowell and his Circle*, 29
Mezey, Robert, *Naked Poetry*, 13–14, 18
Middlebrook, Diane Wood, *Anne Sexton: A Biography*, 71, 83
Mills, Ralph J., 7–8, 13
  comments by, on Ignatow, 165, 211, 217
  works
    Cry of the Human, 6–7, 12
    "Earth Hard," 217
Milton, John, *Paradise Lost*, 51
Modernism, 1, 6, 8, 11, 14, 243
Molesworth, Charles, comments by, on Berryman, 105
Munford, Howard, comments by, on Berryman, 120
Myth, 194, 196
  in poetry, 191–199, 202
Mythic vision, 206, 214

Naked Poetry, 38
Narrative, 231
  in poetry, 19, 24, 37–38, 44–45, 48–49, 51, 53, 65, 155, 231, 243–244, 251
Nathan, Leonard, 21
  comments by, on Wright, 65, 67–68
  works: "The Private 'I' in Contemporary Poetry," 65–66, 120
The Nation, 4, 39
Nature, in poetry, 60–63, 67, 138, 149–150, 159, 194
New Criticism, 6–7, 10, 12, 19, 32, 227
  influence of, 11
  and poetic form, 7–8, 13, 18, 20
New Naked Poetry, 217
New Republic, 125
New York Review of Books, 104
New York Times Book Review, 82
Nietzsche, Friedrich, 60
Nist, John, *In the Middle of the Road*, 186

Objectivity, 23
  in poetry, 8, 12, 19, 25, 61, 104, 164
Orne, Martin, 82, 85
Ostriker, Alicia, 78–79

Packard, William, 83
Paris Review, 12, 54, 58, 71–72, 79–80, 88, 103
Partisan Review, 122
Pastiche, 243, 249
  in poetry, 243–244, 246, 249–250
Paz, Octavio, 179
  comments by, on Strand, 175
Persona, 1–3, 6
  in Berryman, 100–104, 106, 110, 118, 121, 256. *See also under* Poetic voice
  in Garrett, 243
  in Graziano, 242
  in Ignatow, 208–209
  in Kees, 137
  in Kinnell, 146, 148, 160
  in Sexton, 77–78, 81–82
  in Strand, 166
  in Whitman, 101, 125, 256
Personal poetry, 1–3, 6, 8, 10, 12, 18, 23, 26–27, 43, 77, 226–228, 250, 264
  American, 4, 8
  and audience, 17–18, 24, 45, 74
  cultural influences on, 22–23
  and poetic form, 19–20, 39
  poetic voice of, 42
  and Romanticism, 21, 23, 120
  as self-expression, 20
  subject matter of, 19
Phillips, Robert, 5, 13, 19
Plath, Sylvia, 11, 79, 116
  suicide of, 112
  works: *Ariel*, 13
Plumly, Stanley, 15
  comments by, on Strand, 174
  interviews of
    Kinnell, 139, 148–150

Plumly, Stanley (*continued*)
  Simic, 193–194, 197, 200
  Strand, 178–179, 185
Poet
  separation from speaker, 4
  sincerity and authenticity of, 2
Poetic form, 6, 13–14, 32, 35–38, 41, 54, 71,
  83, 227
  dialectic, 118–119
  elegy, 106, 108–109, 113–115, 117–119,
  138, 240
  free verse, 16, 19, 32, 39, 71
  and line-breaks, 39
  lyric, 192
  meter, 8, 13, 20
  narrative, 19, 24, 37–38, 44–45, 48–49,
  51, 53, 65, 155, 231, 243–244, 251
  and New Criticism, 7–8, 13, 18, 20
  open, 32, 39–40, 42, 225
  and personal poetry, 19–20, 39
  and subject matter, 14, 16, 37–38, 41–42
  rhythm, 7, 19, 32, 38–41, 44–45
Poetic speaker, 3–6, 32, 34–35, 54, 59, 63,
  67–68, 81, 83, 105, 109, 119, 149, 166,
  171, 182–183, 211
  and audience, 75
  impersonal, 172–173, 175, 198, 202
  poet as, 64–66, 69
  sincere self as, 4
  sincerity of, 73, 79, 84, 90
  and tone, 175
Poetic voice, 1–3, 5–6, 35, 39, 42, 46, 51–52,
  60–61, 63, 65, 101–102, 109, 118–119,
  123, 125, 139, 148, 166, 208
  and audience, 50, 65, 67, 71
  authentic self, 2–3, 4, 5–6, 15, 30, 51, 64,
  73, 78, 80–81, 84, 86–87, 89
  impersonal, 174
  modes of, 4–5, 24–25, 27
   confessional, 4–6, 10, 24–26, 29–30,
   34–36, 40, 42–43, 45, 50–52, 54,
   56–59, 62–66, 68–71, 73–75, 77–
   87, 89–90, 92–93, 98, 105–106,

Poetic voice (*continued*)
  modes of (*continued*)
   confessional (*continued*),120–121,
   125–126, 147, 160–161, 163–166,
   172–174, 178, 181, 184, 190, 206–
   208, 221–223, 225–226, 229–231,
   236, 242–243, 250–254, 256, 259,
   261, 264
   persona, 4, 6, 15, 22, 24, 54, 59, 92–94,
   102, 104, 106, 108, 120, 122, 125,
   130, 132, 138, 146, 154–155, 160–
   165, 173, 181, 196, 206–207, 220,
   223, 242, 254, 264
   self-effacing, 4, 6, 24, 26, 105, 163–
   165, 175, 181, 183–185, 188, 190–
   191, 194, 197, 201, 203–204, 206–
   209, 211–212, 217, 220–221, 223,
   242–243, 250, 259, 261–264
  and persona, 106
  and poetic form, 45
  self, private, 3, 5, 80–81, 87–88
   public, 3, 5, 24–25, 35, 45, 51–52, 54,
   56, 59, 65, 71
   sincere, 2–4, 15, 24, 45
  sincerity of, 58, 62, 66, 68, 75–76, 78, 89
  tone of, 122–128, 138, 167, 172–175,
   184–185, 188, 191, 252, 261
  universal, 101–105, 129, 155, 160, 164–
   165, 257
Porterfield, Jo R., comments by, on Berryman, 104
Poulin, A., Jr., interviewing Kinnell, 145–
  146
Pound, Ezra, 2–3, 6, 243
  works
   Personae, 2
   "Vorticism" essay, 2
Prosody, 13, 16, 35

Ransom, John Crowe, 7, 32, 57
Rexroth, Kenneth, comments by, on Kees,
  124, 129–131, 134
Rich, Adrienne, 14–15, 18, 167

Rich, Adrienne (*continued*)
  works: "When We Dead Awaken
    Writing as Re-Vision," 14
Richards, I. A., 72, 175
Ricks, Christopher, comments by, on Ber-
  ryman, 104
Rilke, Rainer Maria, 139, 141
  works: "The Song of the Blind Man,"
    120
Rimbaud, Arthur, 79
Rivière, Pierre, 244–247, 249–250
  works: *I, Pierre Rivière*, 244
Robert Lowell: Interviews and Memoirs, 29
Robinson Crusoe, 129–130, 136
Roethke, Beatrice, 111
Roethke, Theodore, 116, 193, 240
  death of, 111, 119
  works
    The Lost Son, 12, 194
    Praise to the End!, 194
Romanticism, 22
  and personal poetry, 21, 23, 120
Rosenthal, M. L., 4, 6, 31
  comments by, on Lowell, 39, 254, 259
Ross, Ralph, 111, 120
Ross, William, comments by, on Kees, 126,
  129–131

Satire, in poetry, 127–128
Schwartz, Delmore, 94–95, 106–108, 115,
  117, 240
  death of, 109–110, 115–116, 119–120
  and mental illness, 108
Seidel, Frederick, 7
Self, 2, 23, 209, 217. *See also under* Poetic
  voice
  absence of, 168, 170–171, 173–175,
    177–179, 184, 191, 211
  alienation, 25
  and deconstruction, 23
  definition, 5–6, 15–17, 24, 31, 36, 43,
    50–51, 53, 57, 167–168, 174, 177, 179,

Self (*continued*)
  definition (*continued*),185, 197, 203,
    206, 208–209, 211, 213, 215
  examination, 5, 30, 32, 35, 64, 70, 167,
    170, 172
  identity, 13, 16, 18, 24, 32, 165, 184
  knowledge, 14–15, 170
  literary, 2–3
  obsession, 15
  and personal poetry, 20
  in poetry, 13–14, 16, 21–24, 84–85, 88,
    135–136, 141, 143, 146, 169, 174, 183–
    184, 204, 212, 214–215, 221, 227–229,
    262
  private, 3, 5, 80–81, 87–88
  public, 3, 5, 24–25, 35, 45, 51–52, 54, 56,
    59, 65, 71
  rejection, 1, 8
  sincere, 2–4, 15, 24, 30–31, 45
  as subject matter, 16, 24
Serchuk, Peter, comments by, on Wright, 57
Sexton, Anne, 5, 27, 30, 46, 71, 89, 167
  aesthetic of, 75, 79, 82, 88
  and confessional mode, 4
  comments on
    by George, 81
    by Jaidka, 83
    by Simpson, 79, 81–82
  and mental illness, 75, 78
  and psychotherapy, 71–73, 75, 78
  works
    All My Pretty Ones, 82
    Anne Sexton: A Self-Portrait in Letters,
      71, 73, 75
    To Bedlam and Part Way Back, 77, 81,
      83, 86
    Complete Poems, 82
    "The Double Image," 74–78, 80
    Live or Die, 82
    "Said the Poet to the Analyst," 86, 88
    Transformations, 79
    "Unknown Girl in the Maternity
      Ward," 76–78, 80
    "You, Doctor Martin," 82–86

Sexton, Linda Gray, 73
Shakespeare, William, 116, 122
  works: *Hamlet*, 51
Shapiro, Karl, *The Bourgeois Poet*, 12
Simic, Charles, 27, 164, 191, 206, 210–212,
  214, 219–220, 243, 262–263
  comments on
    by Breslin, 200
    by Jackson, 199
  interviews of
    by Jackson, 164, 195, 197–200, 203,
      206
    by Plumly, 178–179, 185
  and self-effacing mode, 4
  in Yugoslavia, 194
  works
    Another Republic, 186, 191–192
    Austerities, 192
    "Ax," 204–205
    "Bestiary for the Fingers of My Right
      Hand," 205
    The Book of Gods and Devils, 262
    "Charles Simic," 203–204
    Charon's Cosmology, 199, 201–202
    A Childhood Story, 262
    "Description," 202
    Dismantling the Silence, 195, 204
    "Eraser," 199
    "Fork," 196
    "History," 192–193, 197, 201
    "Knife," 196, 200
    "Madonnas Touched up with a Goa-
      tee," 262–263
    "My Shoes," 196
    Nine Poems
    "Poem," 195
    "The Point," 206
    "Position Without a Magnitude,"
      201–202
    "The Prisoner," 201–202
    "A Quiet Talk with Oneself," 206

Simic, Charles (*continued*)
  works (*continued*)
    Return to a Place Lit by a Glass of Milk,
      203
    Selected Poems, 262
    "Stone," 195–197
    "The Spoon," 196
    "Table," 196
    Unending Blues, 262
    The World Does Not End, 262
Simpson, Eileen, 95–96, 106–107, 115–116,
  120
  comments by, on Berryman, 94–95, 97–
    99, 116
Simpson, Louis, 8, 10, 15, 20, 25–26, 102,
  228–229, 264
  comments by, on Sexton, 79, 81–82
  on confessional poetic voice, 44
  works: *A Revolution in Taste*, 10–11, 20,
    49, 102
Smith, Dave, 23, 61, 68
  comments by, on Wright, 56
  works: *The Pure Clear Word*, 23
Snodgrass, W. D., 5, 10, 26, 74, 78
  works
    Heart's Needle, 10, 13
    "Heart's Needle," 74–76
    In Radical Pursuit, 10–11
Solipsism, 131–132, 194
Sontag, Susan, 21
The Spectator, 39
Stafford, Jean, 222
Stevens, Wallace, 170, 210
  comments on, by Bloom, 166
  works
    *The Collected Poems of Wallace
      Stevens*, 166
    "The Man with the Blue Guitar," 168–
      169, 172
    "Le Monocle de Mon Oncle," 166
    "The Paltry Nude Starts on a Spring
      Voyage," 166
    "Peter Quince at the Clavier," 166
    "The Snow Man," 184

Stitt, Peter, 60, 70, 96–97
    comments by, on Strand, 173
    interviewing Berryman, 103, 121
    works
        "James Wright: The Quest Motif in
            The Branch Will Not Break," 64
        "Stages of Reality," 173
Strand, Mark, 17, 19, 25, 27, 160, 163, 194,
    197, 207–209, 216, 219–220, 227–228,
    243, 250, 259, 261, 263
    aesthetic of, 16, 168, 171–172, 184
    comments by, on Justice, 185
    comments on,
        by Bloom, 168, 173, 177–178
        by Crenner, 179, 181
        by Gregerson, 172–173
        by Howard, 170–171, 173–174
        by Paz, 175
        by Plumly, 174
        by Stitt, 173
    interview of, by, Jackson, 184
    and self-effacing mode, 4
    works
        Another Republic, 186, 191–192
        "Black Maps," 180
        The Continuous Life, 261
        The Contemporary American Poets,
            14–15
        Contemporary Poets, 185
        Dark Harbor, 261
        Darker, 170, 172–174, 177, 179, 181,
            211
        "The Dirty Hand," 185–188
        "Eating Poetry," 162
        "Elegy for My Father," 171
        "Giving Myself Up," 170–173, 175
        "The Guardian," 175, 177–179
        "For Jessica, My Daughter," 190
        "Keeping Things Whole," 167–168,
            171, 175, 185
        The Late Hour, 190, 259
        "Leopardi," 189–190, 243, 250
        "The Man in the Mirror," 182–185
        "My Death," 181

Strand, Mark (continued)
    works (continued)
        The Monument, 168–172, 185
        "My Life," 180–181
        "My Life By Somebody Else," 180–
            183, 185
        "My Mother on an Evening in Late
            Summer," 260–261
        "Notes on the Craft of Poetry," 19
        "The One Song," 180
        "The Poem," 261–262
        "Poem after Leopardi," 189
        "Pot Roast," 259–260
        "A Reason for Moving," 167
        Reasons for Moving, 16, 162, 167, 173–
            174, 183, 185, 210
        "The Remains," 172, 175, 177, 179
        The Sargeantville Notebook, 165, 167
        Selected Poems, 89, 175, 189–190, 259,
            261
        "Seven Poems," 179
        "Shooting Whales," 89–90, 259
        Sleeping with One Eye Open, 168, 173,
            176, 178, 182, 184
        "Sleeping with One Eye Open," 175–
            176, 261
        "A Statement about Writing," 167
        The Story of Our Lives, 171
        "The Tunnel," 178–179, 182, 184
        "Violent Storm," 176
        "When the Vacation Is Over for
            Good," 176
        "The Whole Story," 182, 185
Structure. See Poetic form
Subject matter, 166, 174, 207
    and meter, 37
    and poetic form, 14, 16, 37–38, 41–42
    in poetry, 185, 243, 254
Suffering, and poetry, 120–121, 134
Suicide, in poetry, 112, 244–246, 248–249.
    See also Berryman, John
Surrealism, 181, 184, 191, 207, 216
Symbolism
    and personal experience, 17–18

Symbolism (*continued*)
  in poetry, 10, 35, 200

Tate, Allen, 7, 32
Thomas, Dylan, 85, 116
Trilling, Lionel, 2–5, 26, 30, 75, 89, 173
Unger, Leonard, *T. S. Eliot: A Selected Critique*, 122
Universality, 9, 213
  in poetry, 101–104, 126, 148, 152, 160, 165–166

Valéry, Paul, 1
Vendler, Helen, 23
  comments by, on Berryman, 110
  works: *Part of Nature, Part of Us*, 110
Vine, Richard, interviewing Strand, 174
Voice. *See* Poetic voice

Warren, Robert Penn, 7, 20, 244, 247
  comments by, on Berryman, 111–114
  works: *Democracy and Poetry*, 20–21
Washington, D.C., in poetry, 53
Weigl, Bruce, 16, 38–39, 229–231
  works
    "1955," 230
    "Girl at the Chu Lai Laundry," 229–230
    The Monkey Wars, 229–230
    Song of Napalm, 229–230
    "Song of Napalm," 231
    What Saves Us, 229
Whitman, Walt, 10, 17, 42, 58, 100, 146–147, 208, 210, 216–217, 256
  and persona, 101, 125
  and poetic voice, 103, 104
  works: "Song of Myself," 155
Wilbur, Richard, 108
Williams, William Carlos, 10, 32, 41
Williamson, Alan, 2, 22–23
Wilson, Edmund, 22–23, 254
  works: *Axel's Castle*, 22

Wordsworth, William, 21–22
  works: *The Prelude*, 49, 148
Wright, Annie, 68
Wright, James, 7, 23, 27, 30, 46, 54, 71, 227, 231, 257–258
  aesthetic of, 71
  comments on
    by Hass, 66–67
    by Nathan, 65, 67–68
    by Serchuk, 57
    by Smith, 56
  and confessional mode, 4
  works
    "At the Executed Murderer's Grave," 55–58, 63
    "Autumn Begins in Martins Ferry, Ohio," 59–61, 63
    "A Blessing," 62–63, 67, 90
    The Branch Will Not Break, 54, 59, 61–63
    Collected Poems, 68
    "Depressed by a Book of Bad Poetry, I Walk Toward an Unused Pasture and Invite the Insects to Join Me," 61–62
    "From A Letter," 58, 71
    "Gambling in Stateline, Nevada," 64–68
    The Green Wall, 54
    "Hook," 70–71
    "The Idea of the Good," 64, 68–71, 252
    "Lifting Illegal Nets by Flashlight," 64, 67–68, 71
    "Lying in a Hammock at William Duffy's Farm in Pine Island, Minnesota," 59–63, 71
    "Outside Fargo, North Dakota," 64, 66–68
    Saint Judas, 54–55, 58–59

Wright, James (*continued*)
  works (*continued*)
    Shall We Gather at the River, 54, 64, 68,
      70
    To a Blossoming Pear Tree, 70–71
    "To the Muse," 64, 68–69

Yeats, Anne Butler, 125
Yeats, William Butler, 1, 9–10, 244
  influence of, 124
  works
    Michael Robartes and the Dancer, 124
    "A Prayer for My Daughter," 124–125,
      190–191
    "The Second Coming," 124
    A Vision, 124

Young, David, comments by, on Kinnell,
  138

Zeitgeist, 101–102
Ziegler, Alan, interviewing Ignatow, 218

Colophon

෬

Cover, book design, and typography
by Timothy Rolands

Text is set in Minion,
designed by Robert Slimbach
and released by Adobe in 1989.
Display is set in ITC Galliard,
designed by Matthew Carter
and originally released by
Merganthaler Linotype in 1978.

Printed and bound by Edwards Brothers,
Ann Arbor, Michigan
Distributed by University Publishing Associates